Aristocrats and Traders

SEVILLIAN SOCIETY IN THE
SIXTEENTH CENTURY

Aristocrats and Traders

SEVILLIAN SOCIETY IN THE SIXTEENTH CENTURY

by RUTH PIKE

Cornell University Press | ITHACA AND LONDON

HN
590
S4
P54

First published 1972 by Cornell University Press.
Published in the United Kingdom by Cornell University Press Ltd., 2–4 Brook Street, London W1Y 1AA.

International Standard Book Number 0-8014-0699-4
Library of Congress Catalog Card Number 76-37756

PRINTED IN THE UNITED STATES OF AMERICA
BY VAIL-BALLOU PRESS, INC.

Librarians: Library of Congress cataloging information appears on the last page of the book.

73-3416

Contents

Tables

Preface

Spain in the sixteenth century lacked the racial and spiritual homogeneity that the Spanish monarchs beginning with Ferdinand and Isabella had sought to attain. That uniformity was the common aspiration of Spanish society during this period cannot be denied, but the ideal bore little relation to reality. No better example of the complexity of sixteenth-century society can be found than Seville, which, as a result of its monopoly of the Indies trade, became the most famous and important city in the country. Not a "city but a world"—as it was described by its native son Fernando de Herrera—Seville, because of its size, cosmopolitanism, and economic-boom atmosphere, naturally attracted all kinds of diverse elements. It provided a haven for the unassimilated and the social outcasts and a favorable environment for the enrichment and rise of *conversos* (Jewish converts and their descendants) and commoners.

This book represents an attempt to understand the colorful world of sixteenth-century Seville through a study of its social classes—their characteristics and functions—and to trace the impact on Sevillian society of the new ideas and values resulting from the opening of the New World. Special attention is given to the lower strata of society, with information drawn from both historical and literary sources, but the main focus is on the privileged classes. The principal theme challenges two of the most frequent assumptions about Spanish history in the sixteenth century: the Spaniards' lack of aptitude for trade and the total abandonment of commercial endeavors by ennobled merchants in favor of an aristocratic life based on land and rents. This study establishes the existence of a group of aristocratic trading families of *converso* and common descent who came to dominate the transatlantic trade as well as the political, religious, and cultural life of Seville during this period.

For a work such as this the available documentation is as ample as it is scattered and fragmentary. I have relied heavily on archival sources, primarily documents drawn from the Municipal and Protocols Archives of Seville. In addition I found a number of valuable sources (administrative correspondence and materials relating to the church and to the Moriscos) in the manuscript section of the Biblioteca Nacional, the Archivo Histórico Nacional, and the Real Academia de Historia in Madrid. I was also able to use the important collection of documents in the manuscript section of the British Museum, which to my knowledge have never been utilized in any study of Seville during this period.

I am grateful to the American Philosophical Society and the Research Foundation of the City University of New York for funds to complete research on this study. I also thank the archivists and librarians who gave so freely of their time both in Spain and England: in Seville, especially Señorita Hermencina Mejía, of the Municipal Archives, and Don Alberto Palao, of the Laboratorio de Arte of the University of Seville.

Parts of Chapter II which appeared in the *Business History Review*, XXXIX (1965), 439–465, and the *Kentucky Romance Quarterly*, XIV (1967), 349–365, are reprinted by permission. Parts of Chapter IV were published in the *International Journal of Middle East Studies*, II (1971), 368–377, and are reprinted by permission of Cambridge University Press; and in the *Hispanic American Historical Review*, XLVII (1967), 344–359, and are reprinted by permission of the publisher, copyright 1967, Duke University Press, Durham, North Carolina. Parts of Chapter III which appeared in *Hispania*, LI (December 1968), 877–882, are reprinted by permission.

R. P.

New York, New York

Abbreviations

Archives and Libraries

AGS: Archivo General de Simancas, Valladolid.
AHN: Archivo Histórico Nacional, Madrid.
AMS: Archivo Municipal, Seville.
APS: Archivo de Protocolos, Seville.
BM: British Museum, London.
BNM: Biblioteca Nacional, Madrid.
BRAH: Biblioteca de la Real Academia de Historia, Madrid.

Published Sources

CDI, 1st ser.: *Colección de documentos inéditos, relativos al descubrimiento, conquista y organización de las antiguas posesiones españolas de América y Oceanía.* Madrid, 1864–1884. 42 volumes.

CDI, 2d ser.: *Colección de documentos inéditos relativos al descubrimiento, conquista y organización de las antiguas posesiones españolas de ultramar.* Madrid, 1885–1932. 25 vols.

CPI: *Catálogo de pasajeros a Indias durante los siglos XVI, XVII y XVIII.* Seville, 1940–1946. 3 vols.

Gestoso: José Gestoso y Pérez, *Ensayo de un diccionario de artífices que florecieron en Sevilla desde el siglo XIII al XVIII inclusive.* Seville, 1899–1908. 3 vols.

RGS: *Registro General del Sello.* Valladolid, 1950——. 10 vols.

Notaries

Aguilar (VII): Gonzalo Alvarez de Aguilar, oficio VII.
Alcalá (V): Juan Alvarez de Alcalá, oficio V.
Almonacid (IX): Pedro Almonacid, oficio IX.
Barrera (I): Alonso de la Barrera, oficio I.
Becerra (IV): Cristóbal de la Becerra, oficio IV.
Castellanos (V): Francisco de Castellanos, oficio V.
Cazalla (XV): Alonso de Cazalla, oficio XV.
Cívico (VIII): Alonso de Cívico, oficio VIII.
J. Cuadra (I): Juan de la Cuadra, oficio I.
M. Cuadra (I): Mateo de la Cuadra, oficio I.
Díaz (XV): Francisco Díaz, oficio XV.
Fernández (IX): Pedro Fernández, oficio IX.
Franco (XV): Juan Franco, oficio XV.
García (IX): Luis García, oficio IX.
Godoy (III): Baltasar de Godoy, oficio III.
León (XIX): Gaspar de León, oficio XIX.
López (X): Diego López, oficio X.
Palma (XX): Diego de la Palma, oficio XX.
Pérez (II): Hernán Pérez, oficio II.
A. R. Porras (III): Antón Ruiz de Porras, oficio III.
F. R. Porras (III): Fernán Ruiz de Porras, oficio III.
L. Porras (XXIV): Luis de Porras, oficio XXIV.
Portes (X): Melchor de Portes, oficio X.
Quijada (I): Bartolomé Quijada, oficio I.
Ruiz (XII): Fernán Ruiz, oficio XII.
F. Segura (IV): Francisco Segura, oficio IV.
J. Segura (IV): Juan Segura, oficio IV.
M. Segura (IV): Manuel Segura, oficio IV.
Toledo (II): Gaspar de Toledo, oficio II.
Tristán (XVII): Pedro Tristán, oficio XVII.
Vallecillo (XV): Bernal González Vallecillo, oficio XV.

Note on Currency

Spanish coins of the sixteenth century were the following:

Ducat = 375 maravedís
Escudo = 350 maravedís; 400 (after 1566)
Real = 34 maravedís
Cuarto = 4 maravedís
Blanca = ½ maravedí

The maravedí was the smallest unit of account in the Castilian monetary system; its approximate value was one-sixth of a cent.

Aristocrats and Traders

SEVILLIAN SOCIETY IN THE
SIXTEENTH CENTURY

I

Population Trends:
The Demographic Revolution
of Seville

The discovery of America and the establishment of the
Casa de Contratación in Seville in 1503 converted this Andalusian port town into a thriving international metropolis.
"Was not Seville and all Andalusia the furthest point and
the end of all land, and now it is the middle to which come
the best and most esteemed of the Old World . . . to be
carried to the New." [1] The fabulous riches that arrived
from America attracted to its banks individuals from all
over Spain and the rest of Europe as well. Within a period
of roughly fifty years its population doubled and it became
the largest city in Spain. Seville's rapid demographic growth
captivated the attention of contemporaries. As early as the
1550's the prominent Sevillian physician Dr. Franco described the town as a "mare magnum." [2] By the end of the
century Lope de Vega and other Golden Age writers generally referred to the city as a "new Babylonia." In fact,

[1] Fray Tomás de Mercado, *Summa de tratos y contratos* (Seville,
1587), p. A2.
[2] M. de Cervantes Saavedra, *Rinconete y Cortadillo*, ed. R. Rodríguez Marín (Seville, 1905), p. 68.

this term "Babylonia" eventually found its way into thieves' jargon (*germanía*) of the period as a synonym for Seville.[3]

While contemporary observers were duly impressed with the numerical superiority of Seville as a sign of its new prosperity, most of them were either reluctant or unable to give any actual figures. None of Seville's sixteenth-century historians ventured any estimates of the total population of their town, although Alonso de Morgado, a long-time resident of the Triana quarter, felt well enough informed about that district to state that it contained around 4,000 householders in 1587. Seventeenth-century accounts present exaggerated numbers that fluctuate from source to source. An example is the figure of 230,000 inhabitants for Seville as claimed by Rodrigo Caro in 1634.[4]

Unlike the chroniclers, modern historians have long been intrigued by the rise of Sevillian population in the sixteenth century and have tried to measure and chart its course.[5] This has been a difficult and unrewarding task for the available sources are few and their reliability is dubious. Moreover, none of the existing documents contain figures for the total number of inhabitants, but rather for the *vecinos pecheros* (taxpaying householders). This problem is almost insurmountable since there is really no way to determine

[3] *Romancero de Germanía,* ed. J. Hesse (Madrid, 1967), p. 138; Lope de Vega Carpio, *La Dorotea,* ed. E. Morby (Berkeley, 1958), Act II, scene ii, p. 133; Luis Vélez de Guevara, *El diablo cojuelo,* ed. F. Rodríguez Marín (Madrid, 1951), p. 144.

[4] Alonso de Morgado, *Historia de Sevilla* [Seville, 1587], reprinted by the Sociedad del Archivo Hispalense (Seville, 1887), p. 333; Rodrigo Caro, *Antigüedades y principado de la Illustríssima ciudad de Sevilla* (Seville, 1634), p. 47v.

[5] See, for example, the writings of Antonio Domínguez Ortiz as cited in this chapter; also by the same author, "La población de

the exact numerical relationship between *vecinos* and inhabitants. Several multipliers have been used, but none of them can ever be completely satisfactory. Spanish historians have generally adopted the coefficient five, but many French scholars like Fernand Braudel feel that 4.5 is more realistic.[6]

Birth and mortality rates are among the most important factors in determining the multiplier. Although it is generally assumed that many children were born to the individual family in the sixteenth century, infant mortality took a heavy toll. Therefore the average family was really not larger than it is today, that is, it consisted of four members, but the total number of children at any given time must have been more than now.[7] Since Seville contained so many wealthy merchant families in addition to a sizable resident nobility, the number of individuals in each household was probably greater than in most Spanish cities. Servants and slaves were especially numerous in Seville, and slaves were widely distributed among all classes of the population, including artisans. All of this leads us to adopt five as the most convenient multiplier for Seville. This does not include, however, the large transient population—foreigners, seamen, beggars, and Moriscos—all of whom abounded in Seville, or the nobility and the clergy who were exempt from paying taxes. Collective units such as hospitals and

Sevilla en la Baja Edad Media y en los tiempos modernos," *Boletín de la Sociedad Geográfica Nacional*, LXXVII (1941), 595–608.

[6] Fernand Braudel, *La Méditerrannée et le monde méditerranéen à l'époque de Philippe II* (Paris, 1949), p. 348; A. Domínguez Ortiz, *La sociedad española en el siglo XVII*, I (Madrid, 1963), 60–61.

[7] Domínguez Ortiz, *La sociedad española*, I, 64.

jails are also omitted from this count.[8] Unfortunately, the exact numbers of these groups can never be determined, and all figures for them are largely guesswork.

While all of our sources estimate population in terms of *vecinos*, the ecclesiastical censuses also use the classification *personas de confesión y comunión*. The meaning of this term is debatable. Ruiz Almansa interprets it as including parishioners fifteen years or older, but Domínguez Ortiz claims that it was general practice in the sixteenth and seventeenth centuries to begin confession at from twelve to fourteen years of age and to take communion as early as age seven. In any event young children (who as stated before must have been more numerous than today) would have been excluded from this count. Domínguez Ortiz feels that the figures for *personas de confesión y comunión* should be increased from 20 to 25 per cent to include them.[9] Again much of the floating population would not be counted in any ecclesiastical census since they were not attached to any parish and many probably did not attend church regularly.

There are three ecclesiastical censuses for Seville in the sixteenth century, dated 1561, 1565, and 1588, respectively. Two of these *vecindarios*, those of 1561 and 1588, contain figures for the number of *vecinos* and *casas* (houses) in

[8] Until 1586 when Cardinal Rodrigo de Castro reformed their administration and reduced their number, there were one hundred hospitals in Seville. The two largest were the Hospital de la Sangre and the Hospital de San Hermenegildo (known popularly as the Hospital del Cardenal) with one hundred and eighty beds, respectively. See Morgado, *Historia*, pp. 356–370. For more about conditions in the Seville jail, see Chapter IV.

[9] Domínguez Ortiz, *La sociedad española*, I, 60; J. Ruiz Almansa, "La población de España en el siglo XVI," *Revista internacional de sociología*, I (1943), 136.

each Sevillian parish, while the census of 1588 also includes statistics for *personas de confesión*.[10] It is not clear whether or not the secular clergy were included in the census of 1588; an attempt was apparently made to list them in 1561, but it is not complete.[11] As for the census of 1565, although the parish lists are no longer in existence, the totals for the various categories still remain.[12] Other material relating to Sevillian demography in the sixteenth century includes figures drawn from the fiscal tallies of 1530 and 1591–1594 (totals only) that were published by Tomás González in his *Censo de población de las provincias y partidas de la Corona de Castilla* published in 1829. In addition to these sources there has now emerged from the Sevillian Archives another fiscal census compiled in 1534.[13] The importance

[10] AGS, Expedientes de hacienda, leg. 170, "Vecindario de Sevilla (año 1561)," folios 507–695 (microfilm copy, courtesy of Professor Richard L. Kagan). The census of 1588 has been published by Tomás González, *Censo de población de las provincias y partidas de la Corona de Castilla* (Madrid, 1829), p. 334.

[11] See Chapter II for a discussion of this point.

[12] The figures for 1565 were originally copied by the chronicler Argote de Molina and incorporated into his "Aparato de historia de Sevilla," BNM, MS. 18291. They were published in 1882 by J. Matute y Gaviria, *Noticias relativas a la historia de Sevilla que no constan en sus anales* (Seville, 1886), p. 51.

[13] AMS, Varios Antiguos, carpeta 125, "Padrón de los vecinos pecheros de Sevilla (año 1534)." I encountered this document which contains statistics for Seville and six neighboring towns belonging to her district in the Sevillian Municipal Archives in the summer of 1968. To my knowledge, it has never been used in any demographic study. The only printed reference to it that I have ever found is in José Gestoso y Pérez, *Ensayo de un diccionario de artífices que florecieron en Sevilla desde el siglo XIII al XVIII inclusive* (Seville, 1899–1908). It was apparently one of the sources that he used to compile his catalogue of Sevillian artisans, but after that it seems to have fallen into oblivion.

of this *padrón* cannot be measured. With its parish lists in-
tact, it provides the additional statistical information that
enables us to study Sevillian population before the great
rise in the second half of the sixteenth century.

Table 1. Sevillian population in 1534

Parish	*Vecinos*	Widows
Santa Ana (Triana)	636	181
Santa María	1,193	238
Barrio de la Mar	609	129
Barrio de Génova	85	14
Barrio de Francos	219	38
Barrio Nuevo	27	12
Barrio de Castellanos	253	45
Santa María Magdalena	345	255
San Vicente	341	196
San Lorenzo	316	131
San Miguel	78	18
San Andrés	121	37
San Martín	178	57
San Juan	179	105
Santa Catalina	257	107
Omnium Sanctorum	387	108
San Pedro	128	48
Santa Cruz	123	50
Santa María la Blanca	90	50
San Bartolomé el nuevo	26	6
San Bartolomé el viejo	87	17
San Nicolás	106	49
San Isidro	173	47

San Salvador	688	190
San Esteban	109	48
San Ildefonso	136	48
Santiago	104	52
San Román	130	40
Santa Lucía	110	46
San Julián	92	40
San Marcos	127	66
Santa Marina	129	63
San Gil	179	72
Total	6,568	2,365

Source: AMS, Varios Antiguos, carpeta 125.

The census of 1534 provides statistics for five categories of inhabitants: *vecinos*, widows, minors, paupers, and *exentos* (those exempt from taxes), divided into twenty-eight parishes including Santa Ana in Triana (an extramural quarter of Seville that lay across the Guadalquivir and was connected to the metropolis by a wooden pontoon bridge). There are individual lists for each parish and category of inhabitants (arranged according to barrios and streets) on which all names and occupations have been inscribed.[14] Every list contains separate tallies in addition to a final grand total for each parish. The only exception is the parish of San Gil which lacks the official totals; the figures given in Table 1 for San Gil therefore represent an approximate count only. Furthermore it would be unwise

[14] In contrast to 1534, separate lists for the various categories of inhabitants were not used in the census of 1561. All denizens of Seville—widows, paupers, and even Moriscos and Negroes—were included under the classification *vecino*. Futhermore occupations are not listed for all of the parishes in 1561.

to draw any conclusions from the statistics for minors, paupers, and *exentos* since they are incomplete. Eight parishes give numbers for minors; just five of them register the *exentos*. The real value of this census lies in the figures for *vecinos* and widows.

Although this census claims to represent all territory within the city limits, it covers in fact only areas within the city walls. The extramural districts of San Bernardo and La Calzada (later called San Roque), both of which belonged to the parish of Santa María, were apparently omitted. Nor is there any indication that the *huerta* region outside the Marcarena Gate in San Gil or the barrio of Los Humeros near the Royal Gate were included in the count. All of these outlying districts were sparsely populated at the time, but they were precisely the areas, especially San Bernardo and San Roque, that felt the demographic upsurge so sharply in the following decades.[15]

Even without San Bernardo and San Roque the parish of Santa María with its 1,193 *vecinos* emerges as the most populated Sevillian district in 1534. Nothing else could compare with it, and this is not difficult to understand since it had been for centuries the center of Sevillian business life. The best shops and the richest merchants were located here. Moreover, it was the spiritual center of the city, containing the Cathedral and the palace of the Archbishop. The municipal government also maintained its headquarters here, originally in rented space owned by the Cathedral chapter and then in a magnificent city hall (completed in 1564) on the Plaza de San Francisco.

[15] See Chapter IV for a description of these two parishes.

The parish of San Salvador (688 *vecinos*) adjoining Santa María occupies the second position. This district grew up around the large church of San Salvador that served as the city cathedral until the end of the fifteenth century. It was also a prestigious residential and business quarter. In third place stands the parish of Santa Ana in Triana with 636 *vecinos*. In the sixteenth century Triana was a manufacturing area, containing the famous soap and ceramic industries, and was the favorite quarter of the seafaring population.[16] Most of the inhabitants of Triana were in some way connected with the *carrera de Indias* and for that reason it tended to be a highly transient district and one that grew enormously in the second half of the century. Together the three parishes of Santa Ana, San Salvador, and Santa María accounted for 38 per cent of the city's householders.

Outside of these three central parishes the largest accumulations of *vecinos* could be found in Omnium Sanctorum (385 *vecinos*), Santa María Magdalena (345), San Vicente (341), and San Lorenzo (316). Omnium Sanctorum, San Vicente, and San Lorenzo were large peripheral parishes whose limits extended outward toward the northern walls of the city. They were poor districts populated by unskilled workers and impoverished artisans. Significantly, Omnium Sanctorum was the center of social protest and rebellion in both the sixteenth and seventeenth centuries.[17] Conditions in San Vicente were somewhat bet-

---

[16] The occupations listed in the census of 1534 for the *vecinos* of Triana reflect the district's maritime and manufacturing orientation.

[17] See Chapter III.

ter than in the other two parishes because of its numerous wealthy noblemen. Santa María Magdalena, on the other hand, had a more prosperous population of merchants and artisans.

None of the rest of the parishes included in the census of 1534, with the exception of Santa Catalina, had more than 200 *vecinos*. Among the smallest parishes were those that had formerly made up the ancient *judería* (Jewish quarter)—San Bartolomé el viejo (187 *vecinos*), San Bartolomé el nuevo (26), Santa María la Blanca (90), and Santa Cruz (123). In the sixteenth century a few families of *converso* origin (Jewish converts and their descendants) still lived in these districts, especially Santa Cruz, but a far greater number had moved to other areas of the city like the parishes of Santa María and San Salvador. Fear of the Inquisition forced the *conversos* to disguise their origin, and one of the best ways to accomplish this was to change their residence.

The census of 1534 gives a total of 6,568 *vecinos* and 2,365 widows. These figures approximate those published by González for the year 1530: 6,634 *vecinos* and 2,229 widows. Emigration to the New World and high mortality rates for those engaged in the *carrera de Indias* account for the small number of *vecinos* and the corresponding abundance of widows. Epidemic disease, which was especially virulent during the first two decades of the century, also took a heavy toll in lives. In the plague of 1507, for example, more than 1,500 persons were buried in the church of La Magdalena during the third week of May alone, and this sad spectacle was repeated in many parishes. The town was deserted; life came to a halt; and according to an eye-witness grass grew in the usually crowded and bustling plazas of San Francisco and San Salvador. In 1524 the city was struck by another pestilence that contemporaries believed was the most widespread contagion they had ever seen.[18]

Severe epidemics and emigration to the Indies, with the consequent loss of life involved in that enterprise, were decisive in keeping Sevillian population small in the first quarter of the sixteenth century. Nevertheless, González' figure of 45,000 inhabitants for Seville in 1530 is much too low, for it does not take account of the transient population, clergy, or collective entities. On the other hand, Domínguez Ortiz' estimate of 60,000 people for the same date without counting the transients seems too high.[19] My study of the census of 1534 leads me to conclude that in that year Seville must have had around 55,000 inhabitants, including the floating population, clergy, and collective units. This conclusion seems to be in accord with the existing historical factors.

The great rise in Sevillian population began in the 1540's and reached its height in the 1580's. These years of dramatic growth were followed by a decade of relative stability and preservation of previous gains in the 1590's until the plague of 1599–1601, after which there was a slow but regular

[18] In 1525 the Venetian traveler Andrea Navajero noted: "Por estar Sevilla en el sitio en que está, salen de ella tantas personas para las Indias, que la ciudad se halla poco poblada y casi en poder de las mujeres" (J. García Mercadal, ed., *Viajes de extranjeros por España y Portugal*, I [Madrid, 1952], 851). For more about the plague, see Matute y Gaviria, *Noticias*, p. 54.

[19] Domínguez Ortiz, *La sociedad española*, I, 140; González, *Censo de población*, p. 84.

decline.[20] It is possible to establish two cycles through which Sevillian population passed in the sixteenth century. The first takes up the initial four decades, an era of little growth and in fact loss of population in the 1520's and 1530's. The second cycle is characterized by a rapid and steady increase that culminates in the 1580's and then levels off in the 1590's. If we accept the figures given in the ecclesiastical censuses of 1561, 1565, and 1588, the fastest rate of growth occurred in the years from 1534 to 1565. In 1565 there were 21,803 *vecinos* (29 parishes), which means that the number of householders had more than doubled since 1534. By 1588 their numbers had increased to 25,986 (29 parishes), a substantial advance for a twenty-five-year period, but nothing to compare with the previous period (Table 2). The voluminous collection of *vecindades* (peti-

Table 2. Comparative figures for Sevillian population in the sixteenth century (in *vecinos*)

Parish	1534*	1561	1588
Santa Ana (Triana)	817	1,530	3,115
Santa María	1,489	2,705	3,183
Santa María Magdalena	604	1,552	1,360
San Vicente	539	1,314	2,770
San Lorenzo	447	1,047	1,215
San Miguel	96	244	278
San Andrés	158	337	366
San Martín	237	661	746
San Juan	288	518	633

[20] For the plague of 1599–1601 and population decline in the first half of the seventeenth century, see Antonio Domínguez Ortiz, *Orto y Ocaso de Sevilla* (Seville, 1946), p. 42.

Santa Catalina	370	706	843
Omnium Sanctorum	495	1,292	1,771
San Pedro	176	388	243
Santa Cruz	189	264	378
Santa María la Blanca	143	154	137
San Bartolomé	144	328	408
San Nicolás	156	237	280
San Isidro	220	353	468
San Salvador	878	1,577	1,866
San Esteban	157	293	282
San Ildefonso	187	315	251
Santiago	156	350	315
San Román	170	504	502
Santa Lucía	156	405	657
San Julián	132	342	471
San Marcos	193	503	497
Santa Marina	192	357	599
San Gil	251	636	1,030
San Roque	—	—	922
San Bernardo	—	—	400
San Telmo †	—	213	—
San Juan de Arce †	—	88	—
Total	9,040	19,213	25,986

* Figures for widows and paupers have been added to those for *vecinos*. In the censuses of 1561 and 1588 these two categories were included as *vecinos*.

† Ecclesiastical enclaves—San Juan de Arce belonged to the Military Order of San Juan; San Telmo to the Bishop of Morocco until 1566, then the Inquisition.

Sources: AMS, Varios Antiguos, carpeta 125; AGS, Expedientes de hacienda, leg. 170; Tomás González, *Censo de población de las provincias y partidas de la Corona de Castilla* (Madrid, 1829), p. 334.

tions for denizenship) for these years in the Municipal Archives of Seville attests to the reality of this phenomenon. The press of petitions was so great that the city finally decided to take steps to limit them. In 1597 the residence requirements were increased from seven to ten years and an examination was ordered of all grants that had been conceded over the previous ten years on the grounds that "many of them had been obtained fraudulently." [21]

The upward movement of Sevillian population in the sixteenth century appears even more striking when measured by parishes. Table 3 contains figures for twenty-seven

Table 3. Growth of Sevillian population, 1534–1588
(in *vecinos*)

	Increase		
Parish	1534–1561	1561–1588	1534–1588
Santa Ana (Triana)	704	1,585	2,411
Santa María	1,316	478	1,694
Santa María Magdalena	948	190*	756
San Vicente	775	456	2,231
San Lorenzo	600	168	768
San Miguel	148	34	182
San Andrés	179	29	208
San Martín	424	85	509
San Juan	230	115	345
Santa Catalina	336	135	473

[21] AMS, Actas capitulares, siglo XVI, cabildo 16 de julio de 1597, escribanía 1.

Omnium Sanctorum	797	480	1,276
San Pedro	212	145*	67
Santa Cruz	75	114	189
Santa María la Blanca	11	17*	6*
San Bartolomé	184	80	264
San Nicolás	81	43	124
San Isidro	133	115	248
San Salvador	699	289	988
San Esteban	136	11*	125
San Ildefonso	128	64*	64
Santiago	194	35*	159
San Román	334	2*	332
Santa Lucía	249	252	501
San Julián	210	129	339
San Marcos	310	6*	304
Santa Marina	165	242	407
San Gil	385	394	779

* Loss in population.

Sources: AMS, Varios Antiguos, carpeta 125; AGS, Expedientes de hacienda, leg. 170; González, *Censo de población*, p. 334.

Sevillian parishes with increases shown for three periods: 1534–1561; 1561–1588, and 1534–1588. All parishes registered large gains during the years 1534–1561, most notably Santa María, Santa María Magdalena, and Santa Ana (Triana) in that order. During the following period (1561–1588) increases were less substantial, and seven parishes seem to have suffered population reductions, but only in one case (Santa María la Blanca, the smallest parish) did these losses wipe out earlier advances. Santa María Magdalena, for example, gained 948 *vecinos* in the years 1534–

1561, lost 190 between 1561 and 1588, but in 1588 there were still 756 more *vecinos* in this parish than in 1534.

As for proportionate growth, the greatest increase occurred in the parish of San Vicente where the number of *vecinos* rose from 539 in 1534 to 2,770 in 1588 (Table 2). Size and location were the chief factors in promoting its fast growth. There was plenty of land for building and expansion in this district, and it was conveniently located near the river and not far from the business center of the city. The second fastest growing parish was Santa Lucía, followed by San Gil, Santa Ana in Triana, and in sixth place Omnium Sanctorum. Although these four parishes were located at opposite ends of the city (Santa Lucía, San Gil, and Omnium Sanctorum in the north and northeast, Triana in the west), they had similar populations—poor artisans and unskilled workers. In addition all of them had large numbers of such non-*vecino* inhabitants as transients, Moriscos, and slaves.[22]

Despite its relatively poor showing in proportionate growth, the parish of Santa María still had the largest number of *vecinos* (3,183) in 1588, followed by Santa Ana with 3,115. San Vicente had taken over the third place formerly held by Santa Ana, with San Salvador relegated to the fourth position. Omnium Sanctorum was fifth, followed in order by Santa María Magdalena, San Lorenzo, and San Gil. The small number of *vecinos* registered for San Bernardo and San Roque is not surprising since both of them were poor parishes full of transient and marginal people. The same is true for several other parishes such as

[22] For a discussion of slaves who lived outside their masters' homes, see Chapter IV.

San Ildefonso, San Román, and Santiago, all of which had fewer *vecinos*, but a larger floating population. It seems therefore that by 1588 there had been a shift of population away from the central parishes and toward the peripheral ones, so that a greater proportion of Sevillians lived in those outlying areas at the end of the century than in 1534. The masses or "restless *plebe*" of the chroniclers had become concentrated in the northern parts of the city, whereas the wealthier classes still resided in the traditional southern portion.

Although it is not difficult to grasp the reality of a Sevillian demographic revolution in the sixteenth century, the causes for it are elusive. The usual explanation has centered around the movement of Spaniards from the central and northern parts of the country and foreigners (especially Genoese, Germans, Flemings, and Portuguese) into the city in the hope of sharing in the New World enterprise.[23] For some Seville was the beginning of a greater adventure in the Indies; for others it was an *El Dorado* in its own right. Cervantes expressed it best when he said that Seville was "the asylum of the poor and the refuge of the outcasts." [24] There was also a continuous stream of landless peasants from the countryside into Seville, about whom the city authorities never ceased complaining. They made up the hordes of beggars and unemployed who roamed the streets

[23] Large numbers of Portuguese entered Seville after the union of Spain and Portugal in 1580. Most were artisans or merchants, and the majority were *conversos*. See Domínguez Ortiz, *Orto y Ocaso*, pp. 44–46; also R. Pike, *Enterprise and Adventure: The Genoese in Seville and the Opening of the New World* (Ithaca, 1966).

[24] M. de Cervantes Saavedra, *El coloquio de los perros* in *Novelas ejemplares*, ed. F. Rodríguez Marín, II (Madrid, 1957), 235.

in search of food and who were often undistinguishable
from the substantial criminal elements. To these groups
there must be added the Granadine Moriscos who began
to enter the city after the failure of the Alpujarras Rebellion, 1568–1570, and the sizable slave population.[25]

Urban concentration was itself a factor in population
growth. While overcrowding, filth, and food shortages
caused high mortality rates in normal times and were cata-
strophic during epidemics, fertility was apparently high
too.[26] The same crowded conditions of city living seemed
to encourage a higher marriage frequency and an increased
illegitimacy. This was especially true in a "boom town"
like Seville where fortunes were made and lost with amaz-
ing rapidity and society was constantly undergoing change.
The parish registers studied by Domínguez Ortiz show in
effect that the birth rate went up dramatically in Seville
during the second half of the sixteenth century. In the
parish of Santa María (El Sagrario) the number of recorded
births rose from 34 in 1534 to 540 in 1562. The highest
point is reached in 1594 with 685 births, after which there
is a tendency toward stabilization at 600 a year. The same
trend can be observed in San Vicente where there were
125 births in 1534 as contrasted to 240 in 1570. Domínguez
Ortiz calculated a "crude birth rate" of about 36 per thousand in El Sagrario and around 31 to 40 in San Vicente,
which is considered high by modern standards. In all,

[25] For a discussion of the Moriscos and slaves, see Chapter IV.
[26] K. Helleiner, "The Population of Europe from the Black
Death to the Eve of the Vital Revolution," *The Cambridge Economic History*, ed. E. E. Rich and C. H. Wilson, IV (Cambridge,
1967), 78.

Seville must have had more than 25,000 *vecinos* by the end of the century, which represents a leveling off from the peak of near 26,000 *vecinos* reached in the 1580's. The total population of the city at this time was probably more than 100,000.[27]

Whether the demographic growth of Seville in the second half of the sixteenth century was due primarily to immigration or whether it owed something to a rise in fertility is a question that is difficult to answer without more quantitative data. That these two factors worked together seems quite plausible and perhaps explains more satisfactorily the high plateaus of the 1590's in face of the many and prolonged epidemic outbreaks of the previous decade. The plagues of the 1580's caused heavy death tolls both in Seville and her surrounding countryside. During the pestilence of 1581 (which actually began in 1580 and lasted on and off until 1583) the city was forced to set aside quarters in four hospitals for plague victims, but these facilities were far from sufficient.[28] In 1587 the plague returned and continued for three more consecutive years. It does not

[27] Domínguez Ortiz, *Orto y Ocaso*, p. 42; *La sociedad española*, I, 64. Domínguez Ortiz believes that if the clergy, Moriscos, and floating population are added, Sevillian population reached 150,000 at this time (*La sociedad española* I, 140). His conclusions are based on the ecclesiastical census of 1588, which gives a figure of 120,517 for "personas de confesión" (Domínguez Ortiz' total is 121,990, an obvious error in calculation). I feel that these groups, although numerous, were smaller than he has assumed.

[28] Fernando de Torres y Portugal, Count of Villar, "Relación de sus servicios y méritos," BNM, MS. 9372-Cc-42. See also BM, MS. Add. 28.257, "Carta del Asistente Conde de Coruña al Presidente de Castilla dando cuenta de peste que sufría la ciudad," 12 April 1581.

seem that the demographic losses caused by these epidemics could have been made up by immigration alone, but it is reasonable to assume that these periods of pestilence were followed by a greater number of marriages and childbearing by survivors.[29] Therefore the demographic stability of the 1590's may have been the result of a fortuitous combination of a high birth rate and immigration. And it was not until the very end of the century that this trend was reversed. The turning point seems to have been the plague of 1599–1601, which heralded the advent of a new era in Sevillian demographic history—a period of stagnation and decline in the seventeenth century.

[29] See G. Utterström, "Climatic Fluctuations and Population Problems in Early Modern History," *Scandinavian Economic History Review*, III (1955), 36.

II

The Elite*

In the sixteenth century Sevillian society underwent a profound transformation. New social and economic values were created and old ones discarded as a result of the city's new position as chief port for the Indies. Traditional beliefs emphasizing virtue and valor as the basis for nobility fell into disuse. An acquisitive society was emerging, and a spirit of gain overwhelmed the city. Greed for money and dissatisfaction with social and economic status became the common affliction of all Sevillians. The riches from the New World seemed to cast a spell over the whole town, especially at the arrival of the fleet when they were "carried in ox carts through the streets from the Guadalquivir to the Casa de Contratación." [1] To the famous *pícaro* Guzmán de Alfarache Seville was the city where "silver ran as freely as did copper in other parts." [2]

---

* Parts of this chapter appeared in the *Business History Review*, XXXIX (1965), 439–465, and the *Kentucky Romance Quarterly*, XIV (1967), 349–365, and are reprinted by permission of the publishers.

[1] Morgado, *Historia*, p. 166.

[2] Mateo Alemán, *Guzmán de Alfarache*, in Angel Valbuena Prat, *La novela picaresca española* (Madrid, 1956), p. 551.

NOBLES

If Sevillian life was characterized by materialism and
covetousness, no group reflected this more than the local
nobility. Like their counterparts in the rest of Spain, they
had made warfare, politics, religion, and traditional farming
their principal activities for centuries. Since trade, was associated with social stigma, it was left to outsiders and
foreigners. In the sixteenth century the opening of the New
World and the conversion of their city into a thriving business center forced the Sevillian nobility to revise their ideas
and patterns of life. Padre Tomás de Mercado, scrupulous
observer of Sevillian life, carefully noted these changes. He
wrote that "the discovery of the Indies had presented such
wonderful opportunities to acquire great wealth that the
nobility of Seville had been lured into trade when they saw
what great profits could be made." [3]

The conversion of the nobility to commerce further increased the incursions of merchants into its ranks. The
Sevillian nobility had never been a closed caste; there had always been movement between the upper ranks of the merchant class and the lower echelons of the nobility through
marriage and ennoblement. It was not unusual, especially
in the fifteenth century, for wealthy mercantile families,
many of *converso* origin, to intermarry with families of
noble lineage, even with those of the high nobility. In the
sixteenth century marriages between the scions of the oldest
noble families and the daughters of merchants became a
normal occurrence. Even the nobility who did not invest

[3] Mercado, *Tratos y contratos*, p. A2.

in trade were often forced by necessity or greed, "to marry into merchant families," and "the power of gold made nobles out of commoners." [4]

The penury of the royal treasury also contributed to the ennoblement of rich merchants in Seville as elsewhere in Spain during this period. The sale of rights of *hidalguía* was a profitable source of income at a time when royal financial demands were great. Throughout the century the Seville city council complained to the king about this practice, but seemingly to no avail. Finally, in 1582, a timely subsidy of 50,000 ducats secured a royal promise not to sell any more *hidalguías* in Seville or its district.[5]

Like the *hidalguías* municipal posts formerly reserved to the nobility were also offered on the market to the highest bidder. The positions of *veinticuatro* (alderman) and *jurado* (common councilman) were freely bought and sold, and by the last quarter of the century the average price for an aldermanship was 7,000 ducats. Merchants solicited city posts not only for their inherent social prestige, but also for their obvious economic advantages. At least this was the opinion of a majority of the city council in 1598 when they claimed that most of those who tried to purchase municipal positions were merchants who wanted to use them to further their business interests.[6] The Seville city council may have had the reputation of being one of the most aristocratic in Spain because of the requirement of nobility for

[4] *Ibid.*, p. A2.

[5] Santiago Montoto de Sedas, *Sevilla en el imperio, siglo XVI* (Seville, 1938), p. 60.

[6] AMS, Actas capitulares, siglo XVI, cabildo de 8 de april de 1598.

councilmen as well as aldermen, but the fact remains that most of the men who served on it were ennobled merchants, many of whom were of *converso* origin.

Once a merchant purchased a title of nobility and a seat on the municipal council he was considered the legal equal of the traditional nobility. The title of "Don" was placed before his name and the qualification of "merchant" eliminated after it. The ennobled merchants, or new nobility, then took their places beside the old nobility, and through intermarriage and bonds of interest both groups merged to form, by the end of the century, a compact social class— the city's new ruling elite. Yet the fusion of the old and new nobility did not destroy the existent current of social prejudice toward the new *hidalgos*. The literature of the period expresses unequivocally discriminatory feelings in this regard. The old nobility made only one organized attempt to discriminate against the parvenus. In 1573 a few members of the first families of the city petitioned the king to allow them to form a religious confraternity restricted to nobles. When the city council learned of this action, it immediately sent a statement to the monarch opposing it. The reason for this intervention is clear. The council members believed that "the objective of such a confraternity is not good will, nor religious or pious acts, but rather to give the said brothers the power to make and break *hidalgos* . . . as it would cause disgrace among those who would not be accepted as members, and only those who would be received would be considered truly noble while those who would not want to join would be suspect."[7] Needless to

[7] Marqués de Tablante, *Anales de la Plaza de Toros de Sevilla*, as quoted in Montoto de Sedas, *Sevilla*, pp. 187–190.

say, the Sevillian nobility never succeeded in establishing a confraternity.

Undoubtedly, conditions in Seville greatly stimulated the steady ennoblement of wealthy merchants, but this also occurred in other parts of western Europe during the sixteenth and seventeenth centuries. More significant is that in Seville nobles traded and that despite the prevailing Castilian idea that trade and nobility were incompatible, it does not appear that the Sevillians felt that their mercantile activities dishonored them in any way.[8] Domínguez Ortiz has argued that Sevillians were influenced in this regard by the flexible attitude of the many foreigners, especially Genoese and Flemings, resident in Seville during the sixteenth century.[9] While it is undoubtedly true that the Sevillians had the example of these foreigners before their eyes, the mercantile background of many noble families must have also helped to shape their mentality. In the fifteenth century some Sevillian *hidalgo* families of commercial origin were heavily involved in the administration of rents and the farming of taxes and a few also continued to invest in trade of one kind or another. Neither of these practices was regarded as detrimental to their *hidalguía*. In the sixteenth century even the great magnates did not feel that investment in trade as long as it was wholesale and on a large-scale basis compromised their status in any way.[10] And the attitudes of these noble entrepreneurs were defi-

[8] Cristóbal Suárez de Figueroa, *El pasagero*, ed. F. Rodríguez Marín (Madrid, 1913), p. 201.

[9] Domínguez Ortiz, *Orto y Ocaso*, p. 51.

[10] Joseph de Veitia Linaje, *Norte de la Contratación de las Indias occidentales* (Seville: I. F. de Blas, 1672), pp. 115–116.

nitely capitalistic, and became even more so as their ranks
were increasingly infiltrated by ennobled merchants.[11]

While aristocratic prejudice did not prevent the old nobility from acting like "real capitalists," the ennobled traders in turn were not entirely converted to the aristocratic
way of life. Certainly these parvenus invested in land and
juros, established *mayorazgos* for their heirs, and tried to
follow the traditional aristocratic patterns, but the special
position of their city—the opportunities for quick wealth
through trade—influenced them to continue to trade and
to encourage their sons to do so. It was not unusual for the
younger sons of the new nobility to go to America as
agents for their fathers. In 1557, for example, Bartolomé de
Jerez, son of the Councilman Alonso Hernández de Jerez,
traveled to Tierra Firme to serve as his father's factor there.
A year later, Pedro Vélez left for the Indies with merchandise belonging to his father, Councilman García de Con-
treras. Moreover, the new nobility often permitted their
daughters to marry wealthy merchants and cooperated in
commercial ventures with their plebeian sons-in-law. Councilman Francisco Ruiz married his daughter to merchant
Fernando Pérez, his associate in several ventures. Don Francisco himself married into the old nobility so that the Ruiz
family represented a true fusion of the old and new
groups.[12]

Even before the widespread entrance of merchants into
its ranks, the nobility was not a homogeneous class. At the
top were the grandees and the *títulos* who monopolized all

[11] Pike, *Enterprise and Adventure*, p. 7.
[12] CPI, III, nos. 3348 (Vélez); 1844 (Jerez); APS, Cazalla (XV),
27 July 1551, Libro II, fol. 897; *ibid.*, 10 June, Libro I, fol. 655v.

titles such as duke, marquis, and count. Below these were
the *caballeros* and *hidalgos*, who were members of the secondary or lower nobility. The terms *hidalgos* and *caballeros*, used in a generic sense to denote noble lineage, were
employed indiscriminately during this period. Although this
latter category covered most of the first families of Seville,
the great lords were also well represented. At the end of
the sixteenth century, according to Argote de Molina, there
were fifteen titled noblemen in the city, foremost among
whom were the Dukes of Medina Sidonia, Arcos, and Alcalá.[13] These aristocrats were distinguished basically by
their possession of vast landed estates and their extensive
wealth. The chronicler Lucio Marineo Sículo gives the following figures for the annual revenues of the magnates of
Seville during the early years of the reign of Charles V: [14]

Title	Annual income (ducats)
Duke of Medina Sidonia	55,000
Duke of Béjar	40,000
Duke of Arcos	25,000
Marquis of Ayamonte	30,000
Marquis of Tarifa	30,000
Marquis del Valle	60,000
Count of Gelves	10,000

Although their revenues were derived principally from
their rural holdings, the great lords spent little time on their
estates, whose management they left to paid administrators

[13] Argote de Molina, "Aparato de historia," p. 166.
[14] Lucio Marineo Sículo, *Obra de las cosas memorables de
España* (Alcalá de Henares, 1539), fol. 24–25v.

and overseers. Country homes served mainly as temporary
refuges from the heat of summer or from the ravages of a
plague. During most of the year they resided in the city
where they passed their time cultivating an elaborate way
of life symbolic of their class. This involved spending huge
sums on costly dress, ornate home decoration, lavish food,
and maintaining large entourages of servants. Liberality
was above all the mark of the great nobleman.

In the late fifteenth and first decades of the sixteenth centuries much of the wealth of the magnates went into the
construction of magnificent palaces, every one of which, in
the opinion of the chronicler Luis de Peraza, could have
housed royalty. One of the most unusual of these ducal resi-
dences was the Casa de Pilatos, begun in the last years of
the fifteenth century and completed in 1533 by Fadrique
Enríquez de Ribera, Duke of Alcalá and first Marquis of
Tarifa. Inspired by his recent pilgrimage to the Holy Land,
he styled it after what was claimed to be the house of Pon-
tius Pilate in Jerusalem. It was a masterpiece of *azulejos* and
fine stucco work and was filled with *objets d'art* that the
first duke of Alcalá, don Perafín de Ribera, had sent from
Rome.[15]

The life of the great lords also included active patronage
of the arts. The titled families vied with each other for the
patronage and friendship of distinguished talented persons.
From 1559 until 1581 the palace of don Alvaro Colón y
Portugal, Count of Gelves and great-grandson of Chris-
topher Columbus, was the favorite meeting place for the
Sevillian school of poetry led by Fernando de Herrera,

---

[15] Luis de Peraza, "Historia de la imperial ciudad de Sevilla,"
quoted in Montoto de Sedas, *Sevilla*, pp. 225, 227.

called "el divino." It was here that Herrera fell in love with Doña Leonor de Milán, Countess of Gelves, to whom most of his amorous poems are directed. Not only were these aristocrats patrons of *literati* and painters, but some of them were writers, painters, and connoisseurs of books in their own right. The first Marquis of Tarifa was a humanist and collector of antiquities; the Duke of Alcalá (1584–1637) devoted his spare time to collecting books, painting, and studying Latin works.[16]

Besides engaging in intellectual endeavors and patronizing culture, the Sevillian magnates were deeply involved in municipal politics. They, in effect, controlled the city government through monopolization of some of the most important municipal offices, such as the positions of chief constable, chief magistrate (there were four of these officials), chief clerk of the city council, standard bearer, and governor of the royal Alcázar. The Duke of Alcalá, for example, controlled six municipal posts, in addition to the office of chief constable, worth some 375,000 maravedís.[17] But the predominance of the great lords had unfortunate results for the Sevillian government, for the aristocrats, divided among themselves and jealous of each other's power, drew the municipality into their factional struggles. In the fifteenth

[16] For information about the Duke of Alcalá, see J. González Moreno, *Fernando Enríquez de Ribera, Duque de Alcalá* (Seville, 1968). The relations between Herrera and the Counts of Gelves are described in F. Rodríguez Marín, "El divino Herrera y la Condesa de Gelves," in *Miscelánea de Andalucía* (Madrid, 1927), pp. 155–202.

[17] BNM, MS. 18225, "Relación de los mrs. que el duque de Alcalá mi señor tiene de renta este año de 1618 en esta ciudad de Sevilla y su arzobispado." The Alcázar of Seville was built by Pedro I of Castile (1350–1369) as a royal residence.

century Seville had been torn by feuds among the great
houses, especially between the two principal factions, the
Ponces and Guzmanes. By the opening years of the sixteenth century, the Guzmanes (House of Medina Sidonia)
had seemingly triumphed over their rivals, the Ponces.
(House of Arcos), and their victory enabled them to tighten
their control over the city government. During these years
the Guzmanes with the support of King Ferdinand the
Catholic (to whom they were related through marriage)
and later Charles V were the real masters of Seville.[18]

Regardless of their wealth, power, and pre-eminence in
society, very little is known about the great noble houses
in the sixteenth century. Aside from an abundant collection
of eulogistic genealogical accounts, detailed studies of the
Sevillian noble houses are practically nonexistent. The main
reason is that most of the material for such a study is still
in private homes and family archives. Some utilization has
been made of documents available in national and municipal
archives, but this information—mainly scattered financial
records, correspondence with the government, and evidence
given in lawsuits—can only supplement the rich deposits to
be found in the family archives.[19] Fortunately, one aspect
of the life of the Sevillian magnates is amply revealed in
the Sevillian Protocols—their participation in the transatlantic trade, an activity that clearly set them apart from
their Castilian counterparts.

[18] King Ferdinand's natural granddaughter, Ana of Aragon, was
married to the Duke of Medina Sidonia. For a modern interpreta-
tion of these struggles, see M. Giménez Fernández, *Bartolomé de
las Casas*, II (Madrid, 1960), 942–946.

[19] For comments on the lamentable state of research on the great
noble houses, see Domínguez Ortiz, *La sociedad española*, p. 161.

As a rule the principal investment of the magnates in the New World trade was the ownership of vessels engaged in the *carrera de Indias*. As lords of other Andalusian ports like Cadiz and San Lucar de Barrameda, they had been shipowners in their own right for centuries. In the fourteenth and fifteenth centuries great lords like the Duke of Medina Sidonia had provided ships for expeditions which aimed at both trade and privateering against Moorish shipping and the coastal towns of Granada and North Africa.[20] Given this tradition it is not difficult to understand their involvement in the sixteenth century in the *carrera de Indias*, but other factors also favored their participation. Actually, the cost of outfitting and maintaining these ships was so large that it would have been difficult for any individual, unless he was a member of the upper nobility, to undertake it alone. Vessels were either owned outright by a great lord or the ownership was shared by several persons of lesser status and wealth. A typical division would be among three individuals: two capitalists, either members of the lower nobility or merchants, and a shipmaster.

It appears that the magnates would have liked to monopolize Sevillian shipping through their control over the vessels engaged in the transatlantic trade. At least this is what was attempted by Don Alvaro de Bazán, who was the first to use his own large galleons for the transport of merchandise and treasure to the New World. He invented a new type of galleon and copied from the Genoese and Venetians the galleas or galeaza, for which he obtained an ex-

[20] Richard Konetzke, "Entrepreneurial Activities of Spanish and Portuguese Noblemen in Medieval Times," *Explorations in Entrepreneurial History*, VI (1953–1954), 116, 117.

clusive building concession in February 1550. These new vessels were given the monopoly of carrying the king's treasure from the Indies, might load whatever articles private merchants chose to entrust to them, and were subject to the ordinary rules governing the American trade. In addition, Bazán was named captain general of the Indies trade for fifteen years.

There was much opposition to these terms from the Seville Merchant's Guild or Consulado and also in the Council of the Indies, but the contract was confirmed, and Bazán's patent as captain general was issued on August 1, 1550. One year later, however, a group of Sevillian shippers petitioned the Consulado to sue Don Alvaro on their behalf, claiming that he "was attempting to have his own ships of heavy tonnage chartered for the *carrera de Indias* to the detriment of the other lighter vessels." Eventually, the Consulado appealed to the crown to "restore free navigation with the Indies for all ships although of lesser tonnage than those owned by the said Alvaro de Bazán." [21]

Besides their control over the vessels in the *carrera de Indias* the great lords also invested in the wholesale trade of both merchandise and slaves. One of the best examples of entrepreneurship among the members of the upper nobility is the Ponce family. Luis Ponce de León, Lord of Villagarcía and Rota and a cousin of the discoverer of Florida, sent goods to the Indies and maintained factors there from

[21] C. Fernández Duro, *Armada española desde la unión de los reinos de Castilla y León* (Madrid, 1895), I, 327, 440; APS, Cazalla (XV), 1 June 1551, Libro I, fol. 506; *ibid.*, 9 June, fol. 649; C. Haring, *Trade and Navigation between Spain and the Indies in the Time of the Hapsburgs* (Cambridge, Mass., 1918), p. 264.

the first decade of the century. One of his agents on the island of Hispaniola was Juan Armero, who in 1518 admitted that he had fraudulently withheld from Luis Ponce de León 7,000 pesos that he had brought to Seville in two trips from the Indies where he was serving along with Fernando de la Torre as a factor of that nobleman. And there was even a rare example of female enterprise for Luis Ponce's wife, Doña Francisca Ponce de León, operated the vessels *San Telmo* and *San Cristóbal* in her own name.[22] Another family member, the Duke of Arcos, Rodrigo Ponce de León, owned several vessels plying the seas between Seville and the New World, while at mid-century his relative Fernando Ponce de León invested in the slave trade and sent large quantities of merchandise to America.[23]

Like the magnates, the lower nobility was also deeply involved in the trade between Seville and America, but their investment was more varied. Whereas the participation of the titled noblemen was carefully confined to the wholesale trade and ship ownership, the lower nobility were engaged in the same transactions as the nonnoble merchants, and only their names distinguish them from the latter. They invested in sea loans, gave sales credit, owned ships, participated in the Afro-American slave trade, went to America to sell their goods, maintained overseas factors, and invested in such New World enterprises as cattle raising, sugar pro-

[22] About the *San Telmo,* see APS, García (IX), 28 Feb. 1508, Libro I, fol. Principio del legajo; about the *San Cristóbal,* H. and P. Chaunu, *Seville et l'Atlantique, 1504 a 1650,* I (Paris, 1955), for the year 1508. About Juan Armero, see APS, López (X), 22 Oct. 1518, fol. Registro de Indias, núm. 19.

[23] APS, Portes (X), 28 Oct. 1550, Libro III, fol. Primer tercio del legajo; *ibid.,* Castellanos (V), 8 Oct. 1525, Libro III, fol. 592.

duction, and pearl fishing. Their preoccupation with mercantile activities is not surprising considering the background of most of these *hidalgo* families. It is a well-known
fact that very few of the ancient aristocratic families still
existed in Seville in the sixteenth century. The majority of
the families that claimed *hidalgo* status in this period were
of commercial and, in many instances, *converso* descent.
The stigma of their origin was carefully hidden under clev-
erly constructed genealogical tables that could prove the
existence of aristocratic ancestors for the most unlikely families. One of the best examples of a leading *hidalgo* family
with a forged ancestral tree was the Alcázar, who produced
several generations of traders, churchmen, government officials, and writers, including the famous poet Baltasar del
Alcázar, called the "Sevillian Martial." [24] The story of the
Alcázars is not just the case history of one successful family, but rather of a whole group of families of commercial
and *converso* descent who were closely allied through marriage and mercantile interests. That all of these elite families shared the same background is most revealing of the
character of Sevillian society during this period.

The Alcázars placed their forebears among the original
first families of Seville. They claimed to have descended
from a certain Pedro Martínez del Alcázar, nephew of the
Master of Uclés, who received land in the *repartimiento*
of Seville made by Alfonso X of Castile. Pedro del Alcázar,
the leading member of the family at the opening of the sixteenth century and the grandfather of the poet Baltasar del

[24] Baltasar del Alcázar (1530–1606) was the author of epigram-
matic and materialistic verse in the style of the classical writers
Anacreon and Martial.

Alcázar, was then a lineal descendant of that noble knight
Pedro Martínez del Alcázar. At least this was the ancestry
that a family member, the chronicler Diego Ortiz de Zúñiga, fabricated for them in his *Discurso genealógico de
los Ortizes de Sevilla* (Cadiz, 1670). Ortiz de Zúñiga's work
was apparently a response to certain charges that had been
made against the family in the seventeenth century. On two
occasions—in 1627 and 1639—when members of the family
tried to qualify for entrance into the Order of Calatrava,
testimony in both inquiries branded the Alcázars as commoners and *conversos*.[25]

That these accusations against the Alcázars had a firm
basis in reality can be seen from the career of Pedro del
Alcázar, the first member of the family to gain prominence.
Alcázar served as alderman (*veinticuatro*) on the city council and farmed both the custom duties (*almojarifazgo*) and
the ecclesiastical revenues of Seville for many years.[26] He
owed his positions to his money and his connections with
the House of Medina Sidonia. In the fifteenth century, as
has been noted, wealth was the door to advancement for
families of commercial and *converso* origin. It brought them
the favor of the high nobility, who became dependent on
them for loans and who in some cases intermarried with
them. In Seville the House of Medina Sidonia especially
solicited and received the support of the New Christians
in their struggles with the Ponces and ultimately became

[25] The accusations of 1627 have been published by J. Jordán de
Urríes y Azara, *Bibliografía y estudio crítico de Jáuregui* (Madrid,
1899); for those of 1639 see AHN, Ordenes militares, Pruebas de
Calatrava, no. 71. Excerpts from this inquiry are in Baltasar del
Alcázar, *Poesías*, ed. F. Rodríguez Marín (Madrid, 1910).

[26] Alcázar, *Poesías*, p. xi.

their chief protectors. In 1465, for example, when the Sevillian masses rose up against the *conversos* and tried to kill
them and seize their property, the Duke of Medina Sidonia
and his followers armed themselves and drove off the at-
tackers. By the opening years of the sixteenth century the
alliance between the New Christians and the House of
Medina Sidonia had worked to their mutual advantage. The
Guzmanes controlled the city, and *conversos* like Pedro del
Alcázar occupied important positions in the municipal government.[27] As for Alcázar's role as a tax farmer, this profession was as traditional among the *conversos* as it had
been among their ancestors, the Jews.[28] Significantly, it also
was a favored occupation in the Alcázar family; several of
Pedro's descendants farmed the municipal taxes during the
sixteenth century.

This same Pedro del Alcázar participated in the Sevillian
compositions—those complicated financial transactions between King Ferdinand and the New Christians during the
first decade of the sixteenth century. In return for large
contributions to the royal treasury the king made over to
those penanced and condemned by the Inquisition, or their
heirs, all confiscated property that had been seized from

[27] The role of the *conversos* in the Sevillian city government and
their alliance with the House of Medina Sidonia is discussed in
F. Márquez Villanueva, "Conversos y cargos concejiles en el siglo
XVI," *Revista de Archivos, Bibliotecas y Museos*, LXIII (1957),
503–540. The episode of 1465 is described in Juan de Mata Carriazo,
Los anales de Garci-Sánchez, jurado de Sevilla, in *Anales de la
Universidad Hispalense*, XV (1953), 52.

[28] For a discussion of the favorite professions of the *conversos*,
see Chapter II and A. Domínguez Ortiz, "Los conversos de origen
judío después de la expulsión," *Estudios de historia social de España*,
ed. C. Viñas Mey, III (Madrid, 1955), 361–371.

them up to that date. They also received the privilege of going to and trading with the Indies, forbidden to all *reconciliados*.[29] This modus vivendi lasted only a few years for the coming of Charles V to the Spanish throne brought a change in policy. The Hapsburgs found other ways to replenish the royal purse, and the exemptions and privileges given to the *conversos* were soon repealed.

Pedro del Alcázar contributed 800 ducats (one of the largest sums) to the composition of 1510, and he had previously paid 1,000 ducats; in fact, there is evidence that he was one of the leading promoters of the plan. According to C. Guillén, "it almost seemed as if the receivor of the Inquisition, Pedro de Villasís, drew up an agreement for such a composition with several prominent New Christians and then obtained royal approval for it." [30] In any case, Alcázar was one of the three New Christians eventually empowered by the officials of the Inquisition to collect the sums owed by the others.

According to Ortiz de Zúñiga, Pedro del Alcázar married his aunt Beatriz Suárez and their union produced several children, but of these children he names only Francisco, the eldest, and Luis, the father of the poet Baltasar del Alcázar. A third brother, Captain Hernán Suárez, has emerged from the studies of Giménez Fernández. He appears to have been an influential man in Seville, a close collaborator and frequent business associate of Francisco del Alcázar. We have also found traces of a Leonor del

[29] Charles H. Lea, *History of the Inquisition of Spain*, II (New York, 1906), 357.
[30] Claudio Guillén, "Un Padrón de conversos sevillanos (1510)," *Bulletin Hispanique*, LXV (1963), 56, 89.

Alcázar who may have been one of the forgotten daughters
of Pedro del Alcázar. Since she was married to a certain
Alonso Alemán, who bore a well-known *converso* name,
we can understand why Ortiz de Zúñiga did not include
her in his account.[31]

Francisco del Alcázar (d. 1546), the first-born son of Pedro and his wife Beatriz Suárez, occupies an especially important position in the development of my thesis as to the
converso origin of the Alcázars. Francisco del Alcázar held
a succession of official positions during his lifetime—*jurado*
(common councilman) as early as 1504, then *veinticuatro*
(alderman), treasurer of the Mint, and *alcalde mayor* (chief
magistrate) of Seville. Although it has been assumed that
the villa of Palma and the fortress of Alpizar were part of
his inheritance, the documents clearly indicate that he purchased them in 1519 from an impecunious Diego Columbus,
son of the discoverer of America, for the enormous sum of
11,700,000 maravedís, of which he paid 7,500,000 maravedís
immediately. His economic activities were many and varied; they supplied him with the capital that enabled him to
assume a commanding position in Sevillian affairs. He was
active in the transatlantic trade, farmed the customs (*almojarifazgo*) of Seville, and was involved in the grain trade.

[31] Diego Ortiz de Zúñiga, *Discurso genealógico de los Ortizes
de Sevilla* (Cadiz, 1670), p. 152v; RGS, X, nos. 591, 3245: "Pedro
del Alcázar y su mujer Beatriz Suárez, vecinos de Sevilla, por ser
reconciliados." Leonor is a female name frequently used in the
Alcázar family. An Alemán took part in the *converso* conspiracy
of 1480 and was burnt by the Inquisition. Another example is
the novelist Mateo Alemán, whose father, Dr. Hernando Alemán,
was a surgeon. For Captain Hernán Suárez, see Giménez Fernández,
Bartolomé de las Casas, II, 953.

His participation in the trade with the New World was both capitalistic and commercial. He invested in some sea loans, but was more active in shipping merchandise to the Indies. He maintained a number of factors in the New World as early as the first decade of the sixteenth century to take charge of his business there. In 1508 he was part owner of the *San Salvador*, a vessel engaged in the *carrera de Indias*.[32]

Above all, Francisco del Alcázar is a good example of a successful *converso* in the first half of the sixteenth century—prosperous from his investments, politically secure through his municipal posts and the protection of the dominant Guzmán faction (Duke of Medina Sidonia). As such he was the object of combined hatred both on the part of the masses who especially opposed his exportation of wheat from Seville, which caused prices to rise to exorbitant rates, and of a few *hidalgos* of Old Christian origin who were jealous of his wealth and power. The business transactions of Francisco del Alcázar and his *converso* associates were among the basic causes for the uprising of Juan de Figueroa in Seville during the revolt of the Comuneros in 1520–1521. The objective of Figueroa and his fellow conspirators (the younger sons of several families allied to the Ponces) was to

[32] APS, Vallecillo (XV), 3 Nov. 1508, Libro II, fol. Segundo tercio del legajo; freighting contract, *ibid.*, 11 May, Libro único, fol. Tercer tercio del legajo; sales credit, Vallecillo (XV), 6 Nov., Libro II, fol. Tercer tercio del legajo. For the purchase of Palma and Alpizar, see APS, López (X), 7 Nov. 1519, Libro II, fol. 19, as quoted in J. Hernández Díaz and A. Muro Orejón, *El testamento de don Hernando Colón* (Seville, 1941), p. 26, and regarding the grain trade, see Giménez Fernández, *Bartolomé de las Casas*, II, 252–253.

destroy the economic power of the *conversos* and to oust
them from the city government. The anti-*converso* forces
ultimately failed because of the armed intervention of the
Duke of Medina Sidonia, who rallied most of the Sevillian
nobility to his side.[33]

Francisco del Alcázar was involved in still other *converso* affairs. During the early years of the reign of Charles
V, Spanish popular opinion favored some reform in the
judicial procedure of the Inquisition. This shift in public
sentiment coincided with a *converso* plan to reduce the
powers of the Inquisition and to bring about its ultimate
dissolution. From at least 1518 several *conversos* had been
conducting secret negotiations in Rome to achieve these
ends, and Francisco del Alcázar lent both moral and financial support to their cause. In 1519 the *conversos* successfully obtained from Pope Leo X three papal briefs limiting
the authority of the Inquisition, but Charles V prevented
their publication in Spain, and the Inquisition ignored them.
Finally during the revolt of the Comuneros, the *conversos*,
in a last desperate attempt to destroy the Inquisition, tried
to persuade the Comunero leader Juan de Padilla to accept
the papal briefs, but he "refused to consider their request
without expressing his opinion for or against them." [34]
Therefore all the efforts of Francisco del Alcázar and his

[33] This revolt is described in A. Benítez de Lugo, ed., *Discurso de
la Comunidad de Sevilla* (Seville, 1881); see also Giménez Fernández, *Bartolomé de las Casas*, II, 951–971.

[34] José Maravall, *Las Comunidades de Castilla* (Madrid, 1963),
p. 233; Fidel Fita, "Los judaizantes españoles en los cinco primeros
años (1516–1520) del reinado de Carlos I," *Boletín de la Real Academia de la Historia*, XXXIII (1898), 310, 315–317; APS, Castellanos (XV), 25 Feb. 1518, Libro I, fol. 1710.

converso friends were in vain, and their failure meant the disappearance of the last organized opposition to the Inquisition in sixteenth-century Spain.

Gímenez Fernández has suggested the possibility that Francisco del Alcázar's wife, Leonor de Prado, was related to Dr. Juan de Prado, prosecuting attorney for both the Royal Council and the Council of the Indies, whose father was burned by the Inquisition as a *judaizante* (Judaizer). The documents do not indicate that this relationship existed, but they do reveal the activities of the wealthy *converso* Prado family of Seville. Originally neighbors of the Alcázars in the district of Santa Cruz (the ancient *judería* of Seville), the Prados were also their friends and business associates. Notable members of this family in the first half of the sixteenth century were Luis de Prado and his brother Alonso. Luis served as *jurado* and also held the position of lieutenant treasurer of the Mint under Francisco del Alcázar.[35] All members of the Prado family invested in the transatlantic trade. In 1525, for example, the councilman Luis and his nephew Gómez de Prado supplied the funds to outfit and dispatch 24 per cent of the ships that left Seville for the Indies. Most of these sea loans were granted for the dispatch of merchandise rather than for the provisioning of ships.

By the middle of the century, the Prados were involved in the Afro-American slave trade, an activity that enriched many Sevillian elite families in the sixteenth century. In 1551 Luis and Melchor de Prado formed a partnership with a Sevillian merchant, Juan de Villagrán, for the trade of

[35] CDI, 1st ser., XLII, 539. Giménez Fernández, *Bartolomé de las Casas*, II, 953; Alcázar, *Poesías*, p. viii.

merchandise and slaves to the Indies. The total capital of this *compañía* equaled 12,000 ducats, Luis de Prado contributing 3,584. The remainder was divided between the other two parties. Under the provisions of the contract, Juan de Villagrán was "to accompany the investment to New Spain and to sell it there." He was to share equally with the others in the division of the profits.[36]

Like the Prados, Luis del Alcázar, father of the poet Baltasar del Alcázar, also participated in the trade with the New World and served as *jurado* on the city council. Whereas Francisco's marriage to Leonor de Prado joined the Alcázars to the wealthy Prado family, Luis also contracted a favorable marriage to Leonor de León Garabito. The background of the León Garabito family is not clear, but there is considerable evidence that they were also *conversos*. In the first place, Ortiz de Zúñiga, who was so concerned about the origin of all families related to his own, remained silent as to their ancestry. Another contemporary source, Francisco Pacheco, on the other hand, referred to the poet's mother as Leonor de León, omitting the Garabito entirely, and in fact she seldom used her full name.[37] It was standard practice among the *conversos* to obscure their original names, suppressing one or the other and in some cases abandoning them completely and assuming others. Since several members of the family were called Díaz de León Garabito and others Díaz de León, it would appear that the correct family name was Díaz de León Garabito. The surname Garabito (Garavito) is unusual, but the *conversos*

[36] APS, Franco (XV), 9 March 1551, Libro I, fol. 1136.
[37] Francisco Pacheco, *Libro de descripción de verdaderos retratos, de ilustres y memorables varones* (Seville, 1599), p. 62v.

were well known for their rather strange names such as
Gavilán, Bicha (animal names), or objects related to the
market place like Garabato and Garabito. Moreover, their
marriage alliances suggest possible *converso* origin. They
intermarried with the Alcázars twice, for both the poet's
mother and wife were members of that family. The León
Garabito also married into other *converso* families, such as
the Caballero and Cabrera.[38]

Although Luis del Alcázar was apparently not as rich or
successful as his brother Francisco, he made up for these
deficiencies by producing a family of eleven children. All
of these children, with the exception of three daughters
who became nuns, contracted marriages that joined the
Alcázars to several of the most important New Christian
families of Seville. A study of these marriages reveals the
constant intermarriage practiced by the *conversos* in the
second half of the sixteenth century and the close relationship between the Alcázars and other members of the Sevillian elite.

The matrimonial alliances of four of these children can
be traced: Licentiate Gonzalo Suárez de León, Jerónima
de León, Melchor, and Luisa del Alcázar. Licentiate Suárez
de León, who bore the family maternal names, married
Andrea Ponce, the daughter of Pedro Caballero. Pedro and
his more famous brothers, Diego and Alonso, were among
the most active participants in the trade between Spain and
the New World in the sixteenth century. Pedro remained

[38] Pedro Díaz de León Garabito married Francisca Cabrera; their
daughters married into the Caballero family. For a discussion of
converso names, see F. Márquez Villanueva, *Investigaciones sobre
Juan Alvarez Gato* (Madrid, 1960), p. 47.

in Seville where he specialized in the shipment to America of wine and other staples, while Alonso and Diego went to the New World in 1517. After a few years there, during which the brothers were involved in many enterprises, including the trade in Indian slaves, they returned home with a fortune of 3,000,000 maravedís. From this time until their deaths they dedicated themselves to all aspects of the transatlantic trade, especially the shipment of slaves to America. In addition, Diego held several important posts both in Seville and America, such as accountant (*contador*) of the island of Hispaniola and factor of the Casa de Contratación in Seville. He eventually obtained the honorary title of *Mariscal* (Marshal) of Hispaniola (1536) and two *veinticuatrías* on the Seville city council, one of which cost him a million maravedís. In a flurry of wealth and ostentation he built one of the most elaborate tombs in the Seville Cathedral and commissioned the artist Pedro de Campaña to do a portrait of the family for it. This magnificent painting depicting the brothers, Diego and Alonso, their wives, and children, completed in 1560, still hangs over what is popularly called the "tomb of the Marshal," one of the most impressive in the Seville Cathedral.[39]

The Caballero brothers originated from San Lucar de Barrameda and were related to a certain Diego Caballero de la Rosa, secretary of the Audiencia of Santo Domingo, whose parents had been reconciled by the Inquisition as *judaizantes*. Even Ortiz de Zúñiga had difficulty devising a noble ancestry for such an obviously suspect family. Ac-

[39] Giménez Fernández, *Bartolomé de las Casas*, II, 1122–1124. Another brother, Fernando, died at a young age in Santo Domingo in 1529.

cording to the chronicler, the Caballeros were of Portuguese origin, descendants of a noble knight, Alonso González de Meneses, who as a *caballero* of the Order of Santiago was popularly called "el caballero." This nickname eventually replaced his own family name and his children continued to use it. To cover any trace of suspicion resulting from his explanation, Ortiz de Zúñiga made certain to add that the change to the Caballero name was accidental, that is, it was adopted for "far different reasons than that which caused other families in Spain to change their names." [40] Alonso González Caballero went to study in Andalusia in the 1480's and ultimately settled in San Lucar de Barrameda, where he met Andrea Guillén. They produced Pedro, Alonso, and Diego, all of whom took up residence in Seville during the first years of the sixteenth century.

Another member of the Caballero family, Leonor Caballero, probably a sister of the three brothers, married Rodrigo de Illescas, an important Sevillian trader. The Illescas were a large mercantile family with representatives both in Seville and America. Besides Rodrigo other prominent members of the family were Alonso, prior of the Consulado (Seville Merchants Guild) and farmer of the customs of Seville, and his son Alvaro, who was sent to Peru in 1543 to represent the family interests there. He was joined in 1555 by two of Rodrigo's sons, Pedro Caballero de Illescas and Diego de Illescas. After a few years in the New World Pedro returned to Seville where he obtained a seat on the municipal council and married the daughter of his father's partner, the wealthy Luis Sánchez Dalvo. An-

[40] Ortiz de Zúñiga, *Discurso genealógico*, p. 166.

other son, Alvaro Caballero de Illescas, served on the city
council and administered the customs in the 1590's.[41]

The *converso* background of the Illescas can be deduced
from Ortiz de Zúñiga's description of them. Rodrigo de
Illescas' father, a *veinticuatro* of Seville, left the city in the
1480's and settled in Gibraltar under the control of the
Count of Niebla. His move coincides with the establishment of the Inquisition in Seville and the subsequent exodus
of the *conversos* from that city to the lands of neighboring
aristocrats in the hope that feudal jurisdiction would protect them from the Holy Office. On his mother's side, Rodrigo was related to the Marquis of Cadiz, Rodrigo Ponce
de León, whose affection for the *conversos* had resulted in
matrimonial alliances with them in the female line.[42]

The marriage of Rodrigo de Illescas and Leonor Caballero united two prominent *converso* families and created a
new one, the Caballero de Illescas. Leonor's brothers, Diego
and Alonso, married two sisters, daughters of Pedro Díaz
de León Garabito and Francisca Cabrera; the result was another new family, the Caballero de Cabrera. Their niece
Andrea Ponce, daughter of Pedro Caballero, married Li-

[41] APS, Godoy (III), 31 July 1590, Libro I, fol. 756v; Pedro
Caballero de Illescas, *ibid.*; Díaz (XV), 26 Feb. 1577, Libro I, fol.
417, CPI, III, no. 3010; Alonso de Illescas, Cazalla (XV), 7 Aug.
1549, Libro II, fol. 352v; Alvaro de Illescas, Franco (XV), 30 Oct.
1550, Libro II, fol. 332; Rodrigo de Illescas, Cazalla (XV), 2 Sept.
1538, Libro II, fol. 642v. For additional information on the Illescas
and Sánchez Dalvo families, see G. Lohmann Villena, *Les Espinosa,
une famille d'hommes d'affaires en Espagne et aux Indes à l'époque
de la colonisation* (Paris, 1968), pp. 241–243.

[42] Ortiz de Zúñiga, *Discurso genealógico*, p. 168; H. Sancho, "Los
conversos y la Inquisición primitiva en Jerez de la Frontera," *Archivo Ibero-Americano*, IV (1944), 600.

centiate Suárez de León of the Alcázars. These marriages brought about an interrelationship among the following *converso* families that made up the Sevillian elite: the Alcázar, Prado, Caballero, León Garabito, Cabrera, Illescas, Caballero de Illescas, Caballero de Cabrera, and Sánchez Dalvo. It might also be noted that the chronicler Diego Ortiz de Zúñiga was married to Ana María Caballero de Cabrera, a descendant of the Caballero brothers, and that the Caballero de Cabrera were also related through marriage to the well-known *converso* family of Deza, whose most famous member was Fray Diego de Deza, Archbishop of Seville from 1505 to 1523.

In contrast to Licentiate Suárez de León, about whom we know very little except for his marriage alliance, there exists considerable information about the life of his brother Melchor del Alcázar. The artist Francisco Pacheco, who especially admired Melchor del Alcázar for his "administrative abilities, generosity and excellence of character," included a detailed description of his accomplishments along with his portrait in the *Libro de retratos*.[43] Following the family tradition he held several important posts in the Sevillian government. He served as *veinticuatro*, treasurer of the Mint, and lieutenant governor of the Royal Alcázar, and administered the *almojarifazgo*. Melchor's marriage to Ana de la Sal is one of the best examples of the calculated marriage policy followed by the Alcázars and another proof of their *converso* origin. There was actually a double marriage between the Alcázar and Sal families because Melchor's sister Luisa married Ana's brother Diego de la Sal.

---

[43] Pacheco, *Verdaderos retratos*, pp. 70–71v; Ortiz de Zúñiga, *Discurso genealógico*, p. 153.

The Sal like the Alcázars were accused of being *conversos* in the seventeenth century. These charges came to light during an investigation into the qualifications of the poet Juan de Jáuregui for membership in the Order of Calatrava.[44] Jáuregui was related to the Sal through his mother, who was the daughter of Lucas de la Sal, whose brother and sister had both married Alcázars. There was, however, some confusion among the witnesses at the inquiry as to the exact relationship of Jáuregui to the Alcázars, and several of them believed that Melchor del Alcázar rather than Lucas de la Sal was Jáuregui's grandfather. One of the witnesses, Cardinal Zapata, held this opinion and also claimed that both the Alcázar and Sal families were *conversos* and that there was evidence in church records to support this conclusion. Another witness, Juan Antonio de Zapata, choirmaster of the Cathedral, went even further in his denunciation of the Alcázars. He stated that "there existed in the Cathedral of Seville a *sanbenito* belonging to a member of the Alcázar family whose first name was Melchor or Baltazar and who was either the grandfather or great-grandfather of Jáuregui." [45]

As the investigation proceeded, it gradually became clear that Lucas de la Sal rather than Melchor del Alcázar was Jáuregui's grandfather and that unlike his sister and brother

[44] Juan de Jáuregui y Aguilar (1583–1641) was born in Seville and studied in Rome during his youth. Around 1610 he returned to Spain with a reputation as both a painter and poet. He was a friend of Cervantes, whose portrait he painted, and also of Lope de Vega. The testimony in the Jáuregui investigation has been published by Jordán de Urríes y Azara, *Estudio crítico de Jáuregui*, pp. 111–121.

[45] *Ibid.*, pp. 112, 113.

he did not marry into the Alcázar family. Therefore Juan de Jáuregui was only remotely related to the Alcázars—a grandnephew through marriage—but he was still a direct descendant of the Sal through his mother. Juan Antonio de Zapata held the same opinion about the Sal as he did about the Alcázars, "neither of whom had a good reputation in Seville as to 'limpieza.' " [46] The majority of the witnesses, however, tried to purify the Sal at the expense of the Alcázars, and the final consensus of opinion was that the Sal line emanating from Lucas de la Sal was free from intermixture with the suspect Alcázars and that the charges against the Sal were invalid.

The Sal family background is documented. The Sevillian branch of the Sal descended from Pedro González de la Sal and his wife María de Amaya, natives of Vejer de la Frontera (Cadiz) who moved to Seville in the last quarter of the fifteenth century. Pedro González de la Sal became a denizen of his adopted city and also served as *jurado* around the year 1472.[47] The names of two of his sons, Diego and Fernando, appear frequently in the Sevillian Protocols. Both were active participants in the trade with the New World, like most members of the family. A nephew of Pedro González de la Sal, Juan de la Sal, married Isabel Hurtado, and their children Ana and Diego married into the Alcázar family. Several members of the Sal

[46] *Ibid.*, p. 114. Jáuregui's uncle (his mother's brother), Juan de la Sal, Bishop of Bona, was also popularly considered a *converso*.
[47] *Ibid.*, p. 3; CPI, I, no. 1513. According to Ortiz de Zúñiga, the Sal family was of French origin, but he said the same thing about the Alcázars, and he described the Caballeros as being of Portuguese descent. A convenient way to disguise the ancestry of a family was to give it a foreign origin.

served in the New World as agents for their relatives, including Diego, husband of Luisa del Alcázar, who in 1554 went to Tierra Firme as factor for his brother Lucas.[48]

The Sal followed the *converso* practice of intermarrying with families of similar background, such as the Hurtado and the Gutiérrez. Although the origin of the Hurtado was not questioned in the *pruebas* of 1627 (the Juan de Jáuregui inquiry), accusations against them came to light in a subsequent investigation in 1642 for Jáuregui's nephew Miguel de Jáuregui y Guzmán. On this occasion the mother of the poet Jáuregui was accused of being a descendant of a person who was burned in effigy by the Inquisition, and even though it was not clear who this individual was, there was some indication that he belonged to the wealthy merchant Hurtado family. Gómez Hurtado (brother of the Isabel married to Juan de la Sal) was one of the most successful Sevillian *converso* merchants during the first half of the sixteenth century. At his death he left a large fortune that was distributed among his nephews and nieces, one of whom was Lucas de la Sal, Jáuregui's maternal grandfather.[49]

The Gutiérrez are another case in point. Merchant Pedro Gutiérrez (husband of Beatriz de la Sal) and his brother Ruy Díaz de Segura, whose profession of *trapero* (old-clothes dealer) was traditional among the *conversos* and their ancestors, were among the richest Sevillian businessmen at mid-century. Ruy Díaz de Segura owned three ships

[48] CPI, III, no. 2164; another brother Hernando, APS, Cazalla (XV), 18 Aug. 1551, Libro II, fol. 1090v.

[49] APS, León (XX), 1 June 1595, Libro II, fol, 370, as quoted in F. Rodríguez Marín, *Nuevos datos para las biografías de cien escritores de los siglos XVI y XVII* (Madrid, 1923), p. 408; Jordán de Urríes y Azara, *Estudio crítico de Jáuregui*, pp. 3, 112.

engaged in the *carrera de Indias:* the caravel *Santa María del Cabo*, the *Santa María de la Regla* in association with his cousin Pedro de Medina, and the *Santa María de la Consolación*. In 1525 he was one of the three *converso* merchants who tried to purchase the farm of the *almojarifazgo* of Santo Domingo. His brother Pedro Gutiérrez served as his factor in Santo Domingo during the years 1524 to 1527. Upon his return to Seville he devoted himself to the Afro-American slave trade, often in association with Lucas de la Sal.[50]

Returning again to the Alcázars, Jerónima de León, another sister of the poet Baltasar del Alcázar, also married into a suspect family. Her husband Pedro de Ribera was the son of Licentiate Luis Sánchez de Ribera and María de Palma, natives of Cordova. Pedro appears in the Sevillian Protocols along with his brother Diego as an investor in the trade with the Indies. In 1546 he leased the property of Almuedana from the Countess of Gelves, mother of that same Count of Gelves who employed the poet Baltasar del Alcázar as his financial administrator.[51]

The union of Jerónima de León and Pedro de Ribera is just another example of intermarriage among the New Christian families and once again reveals the *converso* origin of the Alcázars. Three generations of Alcázars were linked through marriage to a large group of families of similar

[50] APS, Cazalla (XV), 28 June 1544, Libro II, fol. 127; CPI, III, no. 4252; Ruy Díaz de Segura, APS, Barrera (I), 19 April 1525, Libro I, fol. 622v; owner of the *Santa María de la Consolación, ibid.,* Castellanos (V), 27 Feb. 1524, Libro I, fol. 169; *Santa María de la Regla,* 7 Nov. 1524, Libro II, fol. 389.

[51] *Ibid.,* Cazalla (XV), 5 Feb. 1546, Libro I, fol. 341; Franco (XV), 5 Oct. 1550, Libro II, fol. 306.

background whose wealth was derived from trade. These families constituted the governing, mercantile, and intellectual elite of Seville during this period.

PROFESSIONALS

Clergy

In many ways the Archdeacon of Niebla, Licentiate Alonso Alvarez de Córdoba, was a typical Sevillian churchman in the sixteenth century: he held a university degree and an important benefice in the Seville Cathedral and during his long career served the Archdiocese in both judicial and administrative posts. Not less significant was his *converso* origin and his descent from persons punished by the Inquisition in Cordova at the end of the fifteenth century. There was also the stigma of illegitimacy in his background, for he was the grandson of a priest.[52]

There were many men like the Archdeacon of Niebla in the Spanish ecclesiastical hierarchy in the sixteenth century. The presence of large numbers of *conversos* among the Spanish clergy is not surprising for the church had always kept its ranks open to everyone, regardless of race or social origin. Moreover, a clerical career offered an easy chance of advancement especially for anyone with a university degree. *Converso* students attended all the universities of Spain, and choice benefices and even ecclesiastical sees were reserved for them. By the mid-sixteenth century it was a

[52] Licentiate Alvarez de Córdoba was the grandson of the choirmaster Juan Rodríguez de Baeza. Information about both men and the other members of the Cathedral chapter has been drawn from documentation preserved in the Cathedral Archives and published by Joaquín Hazañas y La Rua, *Maese Rodrigo, 1444–1509* (Seville, 1909), and *Vázquez de Leca, 1573–1649* (Seville, 1918).

well-known fact that the majority of the Spanish clergy in Rome who were seeking ecclesiastical benefices were of *converso* origin.[53]

Although their exact numbers can never be determined, *converso* ecclesiastics made up a substantial part of the Sevillian church throughout the sixteenth century. They could be found in all the religious orders and at every level of the secular clergy from parish priests to Cathedral dignitaries. They were especially numerous in such religious orders as the Jesuits and Hieronymites and among the ranks of the Cathedral clergy. At the opening of the sixteenth century they predominated among the members of the Cathedral chapter and, despite the adoption of a statute of *limpieza de sangre* in 1515, they continued to hold dignities, canonries, and prebends throughout the century. Their continued presence in the Cathedral chapter was actually facilitated by the lenient provisions of the Sevillian statute. In contrast to many of those adopted in other parts of the country, the Sevillian statute did not call for the total exclusion of *conversos*, but only those whose ancestors had been punished by the Inquisition. Furthermore, it was apparent that Archbishop Diego de Deza (also of *converso* origin), on whose initiative the *limpieza* statute was introduced, was motivated by circumstances rather than conviction, for "among the 600 persons burnt and the 6,000 punished by the Inquisition in Seville since its establishment in 1480, there were many clergymen, a considerable number of whom belonged to the Cathedral clergy." [54]

One of the best examples of the ineffectiveness of the

[53] J. Caro Baroja, *Los Judíos en la España moderna y contemporánea* (Madrid, 1962), II, 213–214.

[54] Domínguez Ortiz, "Los conversos," p. 284.

statute (even from the beginning) is the case of Juan Rodríguez de Baeza, a Cathedral choirmaster who was nomi-
nated for a canonry by Archbishop Deza in 1517. A vocal
group within the chapter refused to approve his appointment and called for the application of the *limpieza* statute
since it was widely known that both his parents and grand-
parents had been penanced by the Inquisition as *judaizantes*.
Regardless of the opposition, Rodríguez de Baeza obtained
his canonry, but only through the personal intervention of
Archbishop Deza.[55] That he succeeded in keeping it until
his death in 1546, despite several attempts to remove him,
was also due to the continued protection of Deza and his
successor in the Sevillian See, Cardinal Alonso Manrique
(1524–1538), also of *converso* descent.[56] Both men toler-
ated the existence of *conversos* in high ecclesiastical posts
and even favored them, as can be seen from a study of their
nominations to Cathedral benefices. The same holds true for
Cardinal Rodrigo de Castro (of similar *converso* background), who governed the Sevillian Archdiocese from
1582 to 1600. In addition, all three churchmen were especially known for their flagrant use of nepotism and pluralism.
Not only did they engage in these practices themselves, but
they allowed them to operate throughout their See. One of
the most glaring examples of nepotism occurred in the
1590's when Cardinal Castro secured the three highest dig-

[55] Hazañas y La Rua, *Maese Rodrigo*, p. 327. The family was
originally from Montilla (Cordova), and Baeza's father, Fernando
de Baeza, had served as secretary to the "Great Captain" Gonzalo
Fernández de Córdoba.

[56] For information about the *converso* origin of Cardinal Manrique, see Lea, *History of the Inquisition*, I, 295, and of Archbishop
Deza, Giménez Fernández, *Bartolomé de las Casas*, II, 948.

nities in the Cathedral chapter for his nephews, Diego, Alvaro, and Alonso Ulloa Osorio, who became the Archdeacons of Ecija, Reina, and Jerez. Despite actions like these, Cardinal Castro was very popular in Seville because, in the words of Canon Licentiate Francisco Pacheco, "he understood the Sevillians and gave them what they wanted —preference in ecclesiastical appointment." Both the Cardinal and his nephews were related to the Deza family. All were descendants of Juan Talavera of Toro whose sister was the mother of Archbishop Deza.[57]

The widespread practice of nepotism and pluralism in the Sevillian church enabled certain families to acquire for themselves the best canonries and prebends. In many instances benefices were held consecutively by brothers, uncles, and nephews and even by fathers and sons. Younger family members were provided with coadjutorships that carried succession rights to their relatives' positions. Often three generations of the same family possessed one or more benefices. The Pichardos, for example, secured control over two benefices at the end of the sixteenth century and held them through the middle of the seventeenth century. In 1591 Juan Pichardo obtained prebend number 7; in 1617 he resigned it in favor of his coadjutor and nephew Pedro Andrés Pichardo, but at the same time he took over canonry number 11 (with his brother Antonio Díaz Bejarano as coadjutor), which he held until his death in 1628. Number 11 then passed to Antonio and after the latter's death to

[57] Francisco Pacheco, "Catálogo de los Arçobispos de Sevilla y primado de las Españas," BNM, MS. 5736 = Q-38, folios 28v-29; see Hazañas y La Rua, *Vázquez de Leca*, p. 469; Hazañas y La Rua, *Maese Rodrigo*, pp. 307-309.

his nephew Pedro Andrés Pichardo, who subsequently resigned his prebend number 7 in favor of his nephew Pedro
Pichardo Osorio. All told, the Pichardos controlled prebend number 7 and canonry number 11 for fifty-two and
thirty-one years, respectively.[58]

The perpetuation of a few families, many of whom
were of *converso* background, in rich benefices was further facilitated by the existence of clerical concubinage.
Although the ecclesiastical reform ordinances of 1512
banned this practice and prohibited clergy from keeping
their offspring with them and attending their baptisms or
marriages, these regulations seem to have been ineffective.[59]
Nephews were often sons in disguise; such was the case
with Luis Fernández de Soria el mozo (the younger), whose
father Canon Luis Fernández de Soria was one of the most
influential *converso* members of the Cathedral chapter in
the first decades of the sixteenth century and a close friend
of the Columbus family. The same was true for Fernán
Ruiz de Hojeda, who took over his father's canonry in
1564 with no apparent difficulty even though both his father and his uncle, Luis de Casaverde, had been accused of
Lutheranism, made to abjure publicly in the *auto de fe* of
1562, and suspended from their offices.[60] But the Sevillian
chapter was notoriously lenient in this regard; the canon

[58] The name Pichardo is unusual; it was probably a purposeful
distortion of Pinchón (pigeon), one of the typical *converso* names
mentioned by Márquez Villanueva, *Juan Alvarez Gato*, p. 47.

[59] These ordinances are listed in Armando Cotarelo y Valledor,
Fray Diego de Deza (Madrid, 1922), pp. 200–202.

[60] Hazañas y La Rua, *Maese Rodrigo*, pp. 493–499; for Canon
Luis Fernández de Soria, *ibid.*, pp. 245–246; APS, López (X), 17
March 1520, Registro, Indias, 22.

and preacher Juan Gil, known as Dr. Egidio, was brought to trial on the suspicion of heresy, but let off with light punishment and allowed to resume his place in the chapter. It was not until after Egidio's death in 1556 that the extent of his heresy was discovered and his remains burnt in the *auto de fe* of 1560 along with those of his colleague Canon Constantino Ponce de la Fuente, one of the leaders of the clandestine Protestant community of Seville.[61]

Clerical concubinage also led incidentally to the creation of several important *converso* families whose members formed part of the ruling elite. The Mexía Guzmáns, for example, were descended from Canon Luis Fernández de Soria and his friend the Prebendary Bernal de Cuenca. Cuenca and his Morisco mistress produced the famous Licentiate Andrés de Vergara, alderman and chief magistrate of Seville, who owed his positions to the favor of the Duke of Medina Sidonia. Vergara married Catalina Mexía, the illegitimate daughter of Canon Fernández de Soria and his friend "la Guzmana." Their son Hernán Mexía Guzmán, who inherited his father's aldermanship, married into the wealthy *converso* Cabrera family and in 1542 acccompanied his father-in-law Pedro Luis de Cabrera to Peru where both men acquired large *encomiendas*. They later

[61] For Dr. Egidio, see Hazañas y La Rua, *Maese Rodrigo*, pp. 370–387; for Constantino de la Fuente, *ibid.*, pp. 387–438. See also M. Menéndez Pelayo, *Historia de los heterodoxos españoles*, 2d ed. (Madrid, 1928), V, 75–116; E. Schäfer, *Beiträge zur Geschichte des spanischen Protestantismus und der Inquisition im sechzehnten Jahrhundert* (Gutersloh, 1902), I, 345–367, II, 271–426; P. Hauben, "Reform and Counter-Reform: The Case of the Spanish Heretics," in T. Rabb and J. Siegel, *Action and Conviction in Early Modern Europe* (Princeton, 1969), pp. 154–168.

served as captains in the Gasca campaign of 1548 and after
the war Mexía Guzmán returned to Spain as Gasca's mes-
senger. While he was in Spain he tried to gain entrance into
the order of Santiago for his eight-year-old son Pedro de
Cabrera de Vergara, but in the subsequent inquiry the
family's background was revealed and the candidate rejected. Although this must have been an unpleasant experience for Mexía Guzmán, it apparently did not diminish
his zeal for a *hábito*. Two years later he applied for one for
himself and again the same facts were presented with similar results. It is interesting to note in this connection that
although one of the principal witnesses against the family
on both occasions was the chronicler Pedro Mexía (no
relation), he has somehow come down in history as the
father of Hernán Mexía Guzmán.[62] One possible explanation of this distortion might be that the family simply appropriated him as an ancestor when constructing a false
genealogy in the seventeenth century, due to the similarity
of the name.

The progenitors of the Mexía Guzmán family, Luis
Fernández de Soria and Bernal de Cuenca, were close
friends and colleagues of Rodrigo Fernández de Santaella,
Archdeacon of Reina, who founded the College and University of Santa María de Jesús, which became the University of Seville. Santaella, a graduate of the Spanish College
in Bologna, wanted to establish a university in Seville that

[62] AHN, Ordenes militares, Pruebas de Santiago, nos. 5076, 1357.
Some excerpts from these inquiries have been published by Rodríguez Marín, *Datos*, pp. 407-408. See also CPI, II, no. 5600; III,
2965; and James Lockhart, *Spanish Peru, 1532-1560* (Madison, Wis.,
1968), p. 42.

would contain a small college providing support for a limited number of poor (primarily ecclesiastical) scholars. The result was the College of Santa María de Jesús (popularly called the College of Maese Rodrigo), for which Santaella set aside substantial benefices and rents, including property confiscated from the Jews of Seville that he purchased in 1504. Scarcely had Santaella drawn up the charter for the college when he suddenly died in 1509, leaving the Cathedral chapter supervisory powers over the college and his canon friends the responsibility of putting his plans into operation. The college therefore became an appanage of the chapter and most of those connected with it and the university, especially during the early years, were *converso* ecclesiastics belonging to the Cathedral clergy. The canons Alonso de Campos and Pedro de Fuentes, for example, were the executors of Maese Rodrigo's will, and Campos, who had studied with Santaella in Bologna, selected the first students for the college and drew up the statutes for the university in 1518. Others included the canon Pedro González de Alcocer (an ancestor of the Sevillian poet Gutierre de Cetina) who left his extensive library to the College, the Ruiz de Hojedas; the Casaverdes, including Juan Ruiz de Casaverde who served as College notary, and Iñigo de Rosales, its first rector. The matriculation records also indicate that regardless of the *limpieza* statute adopted in 1537, students of *converso* origin were numerous at the university throughout the century.[63] This

---

[63] University of Seville matriculation records for the years 1570, 1580, 1590, and 1610 (courtesy of Professor Richard L. Kagan). For more information on the College of Maese Rodrigo, see Hazañas y La Rua, *Maese Rodrigo*; Morgado, *Historia*, pp. 138–139;

is not surprising since most of them came from merchant, professional, and *hidalgo* backgrounds and were drawn from the city itself and the surrounding region.

Men like Santaella and his *converso* colleagues owed their influence and power to their positions on the Cathedral chapter whose members represented the most select group within the church. In the sixteenth century the Sevillian chapter consisted of eleven dignitaries: dean, chancellor, treasurer, precentor, six archdeacons, and a prior. In 1579 there were forty canons and forty prebendaries (*racioneros* and *medios racioneros*). The dean enjoyed a lucrative income of 6,000 ducats, while the canonries were worth 2,000 each and the prebends one third of that amount.[64] A survey of chapter members in the sixteenth century indicates that the overwhelming majority emanated from the commercial, *hidalgo*, and *letrado* classes with very few representatives of the high nobility or the peasants. The *hidalgo* character of the chapter is especially noticeable at the end of the century and coincides with the steady ennoblement throughout the period of the *letrado* and merchant classes. This contrasts sharply with conditions early in the century when a substantial number of men of artisan background (many of whom were also *conversos*) were in the chapter. Two good examples are Fernán Ruiz de Hojeda, son of a smith, and Santaella, who came from a poor artisan family.

Chapter members were an elite group not only because

and Antonio Martín Villa, *Reseña histórica de la Universidad de Sevilla* (Seville, 1886), pp. 11–17.

[64] BNM, MS. 732 = D–42, "Relación particular de la santa iglesia y Arçobispado de Sevilla y oficiales del Arçobispo della," fol. 238.

of their wealth and birth, but also because of their education. Of 130 canons in the last two decades of the sixteenth century, almost half held higher degrees, mainly the licentiate and the doctorate. Most were graduates of the universities of Salamanca, Alcalá de Henares, Osuna, or Seville, in that order. The largest number were natives of Seville, its immediate area, and other towns in Andalusia, with a few from Toledo, Burgos, and Madrid. There were also a number of Hispanized foreigners—Genoese, Flemings, and Neapolitans. Several of the most outstanding canons of foreign descent were Genoese, such as the Pinelo brothers, Pedro and Jerónimo, whose father was Francisco Pinelo, a contributor to the Columbian voyages and first factor of the Casa de Contratación. Another was Dr. Luciano de Negrón (1562–1606), son of Licentiate Carlos de Negrón, prosecuting attorney for the Council of Castile. Dr. Negrón achieved prominence in Seville as a preacher, humanist, and poet.[65]

In contrast to the Cathedral chapter the mass of secular clergy consisted of priests of more modest origin. Most came from artisan families and many were of *converso* descent, as can be seen from a study of the names of parish clergy that appear on the meat tax refund lists.[66] Although

[65] For more on the Negróns and Pinelos, see Pike, *Enterprise and Adventure*, pp. 3–5, 10.

[66] AMS, Libro de Propios, siglo XVI, tomo 2, años 1597 a 1599. In contrast to many other Spanish cities, Seville did not have any special shop where those exempt from municipal taxes (nobles, clergy, and holders of university degrees) could buy meat free of purchase tax (*sisa*). Therefore a system was devised whereby a tax refund (one-half a maravedí [*una blanca*] per pound purchase) was returned upon petition to the city council by the interested party.

it was difficult (and it became increasingly more so as the century advanced) for men of humble origins to obtain preferment in the church, there were always opportunities for improvement within the lower ranks. This was especially true in Seville where over one hundred places were devoted to divine worship and prayer. In 1579 the Cathedral alone had 176 chaplaincies, and 812 were scattered throughout the various parishes. Furthermore, it was always possible for the most able to obtain a university degree, which almost always brought some kind of advancement, even if only a transfer from a small or poorer parish to a better one. Indeed a good number of priests in such wealthy and prestigious parishes as San Salvador and Santa Cruz held baccalaureate and licentiate degrees. Assignment to San Salvador was especially advantageous since it had served as a cathedral at one time and its chapter consisted of eight canons, each one with a yearly income of 800 ducats. There were also men with baccalaureate degrees in some of the less wealthy but larger parishes, like Santa Ana in Triana, and some of the pastors of these parishes held higher degrees.[67]

Statistics are practically nonexistent for the number of secular clergy in Seville during the sixteenth century, except for a few unreliable estimates found in the chronicles. The *vecindario* of 1561 lists a total of 229 clergymen, but this figure is clearly too low (only 18 of the 40 canons and 16 of 40 prebendaries are mentioned), and it probably represents less than half the actual number. While the *vecindario* tells little about their numbers, it provides some information about the distribution of the secular clergy.

[67] AGS, Expedientes de hacienda, leg. 170; BNM, MS. 732 = D–42, folios 238–240.

The parishes of Santa María, Santa Cruz, San Vicente, and San Juan de la Palma had the largest number of priests among their inhabitants. Most of the Cathedral clergy lived in Santa María with a few also in Santa Cruz. The presence of a large clerical population in San Vicente and San Juan can be explained by the existence in these two parishes of many noble families whose private chapels they served. Some additional figures can be obtained from the meat tax refund lists. At the end of the century as many as 47 clergymen were connected with a large parish like Santa Ana. Included in this number were both the regular priests assigned to this parish and all others who held chaplaincies in this church. A similar situation existed in San Salvador and Santa María Magdalena with 49 and 44 priests, respectively. Even a small parish like San Bartolomé had 12 priests, and the rest averaged between 15 and 30.[68]

Some clergymen supplemented their incomes by tutoring or by opening private boys' schools in their homes to teach the rudiments of education. Usually they hired laymen, university graduates, or at least men with some years of university training to teach grammar. At mid-century one of the best known of these schools in Seville was run by Juan Rodríguez, a chaplain in the Cathedral. In 1554 Rodríguez hired Lope de Dueñas, a "schoolmaster," to teach in his school for two years, at a salary of two ducats a week payable at the end of each month. In addition Dueñas was to receive room and board and six maravedís extra a day to cover his incidental expenses.[69]

[68] AMS, Libro de Propios, años 1597 a 1599; AGS, Expedientes de hacienda, leg. 170.
[69] APS, Pérez (XXI), 21 July 1554; Libro III, as quoted in Cervantes Saavedra, *Rinconete y Cortadillo* (1905 ed.), p. 18.

If information about the secular clergy is scant and fragmentary, there is still less about the religious orders. The church and monastic archives that could provide a description of the internal life of these monasteries and convents still await investigation. In their absence, chroniclers' accounts, notarial deeds, and government records must serve as the principal sources of information about the regular clergy.[70] In 1579 Seville and its suburbs were covered by a network of some 38 religious houses, 19 male and 19 female, but statistics as to their membership are hard to come by, as are reliable figures for the total population of nuns, monks, and friars. Estimates exist for the male religious orders. The Dominicans reputedly had 230 friars in their four houses: 150 in San Pablo, their principal friary, 40 in both Santo Domingo de Portoceli and Regina Celi, and 20 in Montesión. The Franciscans numbered some 300 with 200 friars in the monastery of San Francisco (the largest in Seville) and 100 in Nuestra Señora del Valle. There were also 200 Carmelites divided between two houses, Santa María de los Remedios in Triana and Santa María del Carmen in the parish of San Vicente.[71] As for the female orders, in 1595 the Carmelite Convent of Belén had

[70] In the Archivo Histórico Nacional (Madrid), section "Clero secular y regular" there are only three legajos (nos. 6676, 6677, and 6678) for Seville. They are an incomplete collection (mainly eighteenth-century) of scattered papers—donations to religious communities and legal transcripts over disputed monastic property. There are also several documents relating to monasteries in Ecija, Marchena, and Osuna.

[71] These figures come from Montoto de Sedas, *Sevilla*, pp. 86–87, but his source is not stated. For the number of religious communities in 1579, see BNM, MS. 732 = D–42, fol. 241.

a total of 59 members—44 professed nuns, 6 lay sisters, and 9 novices; this was one of the more popular communities in Seville. Poverty, not a lack of vocations, created this situation. Almost all female communities were contemplative and cloistered, and there were few opportunities for them to supplement their incomes. Most were totally dependent on small rents and the dowries of their members. Since they performed little or no services to the outside community (teaching and nursing activities by nuns were practically unknown in this period), they attracted far less lay financial support than the socially active friars. Therefore, while most male orders were open to all who felt the call of the religious life, entrance into the female communities was limited and restricted to those whose dowries could provide a minimum of subsistence.[72]

These religious communities owed their existence to the piety and generosity of wealthy Sevillians. The nobility was the most active contributor to the establishment and expansion of the several orders. Large and continued contributions by illustrious Sevillian families enabled the Dominicans, for example, to maintain four friaries and three convents (Santa María de Gracia, Santa María la Real, and the prestigious Madre de Dios) in the city. Occasionally the municipal government also aided the religious orders financially. In 1580 the Franciscans built their new monastery of San Diego and the Jesuits their College of San Hermenegildo with funds donated by the city.[73]

[72] O. Steggink, "Beaterios y monasterios carmelitas españoles en los siglos XV y XVI," *Carmelus*, II (1963), 175; Domínguez Ortiz, *La sociedad española*, II (Madrid, 1970), 113.

[73] Montoto de Sedas, *Sevilla*, p. 85; J. Hazañas y Rua, *Historia de Sevilla* (Seville, 1933), p. 85.

One of the most impressive monasteries in Seville lay outside the confines of the town, along the western bank of the Guadalquivir River. The Carthusian monastery of Santa María de las Cuevas faced the river and was surrounded by its own sweet-scented citrus groves that produced an annual revenue of 1,500 ducats for the community. There were accommodations for 70 monks, and when the German traveler J. Münzer visited it at the end of the fifteenth century, it was occupied by 40 priests and 30 lay brothers in addition to the prior. Within the city proper, the monastery of San Francisco dominated the plaza of the same name. It contained cells for 200 friars, its own workshops, and gardens. Connected to the monastery was the Colegio (College) of San Buenaventura for liberal arts and theology with 40 students, all members of the Franciscan order.[74]

Several other orders—the Carmelites, Friars of San Francisco de Paula, Dominicans, and Jesuits—were also engaged in teaching and were associated with colleges. The two most famous of these schools were the Dominican Colegio mayor de Santo Tomás de Aquino and the Jesuits' San Hermenegildo. The College of Santo Tomás was founded in 1516 by Archbishop Deza for members of the Dominican order, but from the beginning nonecclesiastics were admitted to the faculties of philosophy and Latin. On the other hand, since it was originally a training school for ecclesiastics, its student body remained small and select. In contrast, the Jesuit Colegio of San Hermenegildo was

[74] Caro, *Antigüedades*, p. 62v. For Santa María de las Cuevas, see J. Münzer, "Relación de viaje," in *Viajes de Extranjeros for España y Portugal*, ed. J. García Mercadal, II (Madrid, 1952), 374; Montoto de Sedas, *Sevilla*, p. 87.

probably the largest school of its kind in Spain during the sixteenth century, with some nine hundred students in the 1560's. It was also the most prestigious in Seville, catering to the sons of noble and wealthy merchant families like those described by Cervantes in his *Coloquio de los perros*. For many years both the college and the novitiate were housed together in a building located in the parish of San Salvador that the Jesuits had purchased from Captain Hernán Suárez del Alcázar for 8,000 ducats. In 1580 the college and the novitiate were separated and, with the help of the city government, the college was moved to splendid new quarters in the parish of San Miguel while the novitiate remained on the old site.[75]

The success of the Colegio of San Hermenegildo was due primarily to the teaching ability of the Jesuits (they excelled in Latin and the humanities), but also to support and protection from the governing elite. Throughout the century Sevillians from *hidalgo*, merchant, and office-holding families, many of whom were of *converso* origin, entered the Society of Jesus. One of the first Sevillian members of the Order was Father Basilio de Avila (Alonso de Avila, son of Francisco Fernández de Pineda, an official of the Casa de Contratación), who became a Jesuit while a student at Salamanca in 1550.[76] The popularity of the Je-

[75] For San Hermenegildo see Villa, *Universidad de Sevilla*, p. 22; A. Astrain, *Historia de la Compañía de Jesús en la Asistencia de España*, V (Madrid, 1916), 40–47; Cervantes Saavedra, *El coloquio de los perros*, pp. 238, 242. For Santo Tomás de Aquino, see Diego Ignacio de Góngora, *Historia del Colegio mayor de Santo Tomás* (Seville, 1890), 2 vols.; Morgado, *Historia*, p. 400.

[76] Diego Ortiz de Zúñiga, *Anales eclesiásticos y seculares de la muy noble y leal ciudad de Sevilla, metrópoli de la Andalucía* (Madrid, 1796), III, 419.

suits among the *conversos* was clearly related to the Society's emphasis on intellectuality and its lenient attitude
toward *limpieza de sangre*. The Jesuits did not adopt a
limpieza statute until 1599 and then only after a long internal controversy. Nor did it last long, for in 1618 it was
in effect abrogated. A perfect example of the kind of men
that the Jesuits attracted in Seville was Father Luis del
Alcázar (1554–1614), a member of the well-known *converso* family of that name, and author of a famous treatise
on the Apocalypse. His intellect was of such high order
and he was so totally immersed in his studies that he was
popularly considered an eccentric genius.[77]

Another religious order that drew many *conversos* was
the Hieronymites, again mainly because of their intellectual
orientation. Their monastery of San Isidro del Campo, located a short distance outside of Seville on the road to
Extremadura and Castile, was founded by Alonso Pérez de
Guzmán el bueno, the pater familias of the House of
Medina Sidonia. In view of the relationship between the
Dukes of Medina Sidonia and the *conversos*, it is not surprising that this Hieronymite monastery became a refuge
for New Christians, and in the sixteenth century it was a
clandestine center of Protestantism in Seville. Two of the
most notable figures of Spanish Protestantism came from
San Isidro: Antonio del Corro and Cipriano de Valera, both
of whom were New Christians. They fled Seville for
Geneva in 1557 before their activities were discovered by
the Inquisition. In the *auto de fe* of 1559 six Hieronymites
from San Isidro lost their lives; among them were the Prior,

[77] Pacheco, *Verdaderos retratos*, pp. 10–11v. Luis was a son of
Melchor del Alcázar.

Garci-Arias, known as Maestro Blanco, and Francisco Fox Morcillo, brother of the Sevillian humanist Sebastián Fox Morcillo, both of whom were of *converso* descent.[78]

The monastic orders, like the church as a whole, always contained a wide selection of men and women from all social classes. In the first part of the sixteenth century a substantial portion of the religious community came from artisan families, and like the secular clergy many were *conversos*. A good example is Ana Díaz de Vergara, who entered the Augustinian convent of San Leandro in the first decade of the century with a dowry of only 7,000 maravedís (18 ducats). Her father and sisters were embroiderers and her brother was a scribe, that favorite profession of the New Christians.[79] As the century advanced, the steady growth of the *hidalgo* and *letrado* classes and the inability of society as constituted to absorb them brought more individuals of higher rank into the regular clergy. This was especially true in the female orders, and such convents as Madre de Dios (Dominicans), San Leandro (Augustinians), and Belén (Carmelites) began to cater to women of noble rank. As early as the 1560's the presence

[78] BM, MS. Add. 21.447, "Relación de las personas que salieron al auto de fe que se celebró en la plaça de San Francisco en esta muy insigne ciudad de Sevilla domingo veinte e quatro días del mes de setiembre de 1559 años," fol. 93; Menéndez Pelayo, *Heterodoxos españoles*, V, 105–108; M. Méndez Bejarano, *Diccionario de escritores maestros y oradores naturales de Sevilla y su actual provincia* (Seville, 1922), I, 213.

[79] Gestoso, III, 50. For the regular clergy from artisan and *converso* families, see the entries copied by Muñoz from "Libro de Profesiones del Convento de San Pablo, orden Predicadores de Sevilla desde 1503 a 1545," in RAHM, Colección Juan Bautista Muñoz, MS. 4859, tomo 74, fol. 72.

of greater numbers of such women had begun to cause resentment among those of lower rank; at least this was the situation in the Convent of Belén when Padre Rubeo, the Vicar-General of the Carmelites, visited it in 1566. By the end of the century, *hidalgo* women entered religious orders with large dowries and were accompanied by personal servants and slaves.[80]

Both the regular and secular clergy accumulated large quantities of property in and around the city, the extent of which is difficult to determine. It has been estimated that one-tenth of the urban property of Seville belonged to the church and about one-half of this belonged to the Cathedral chapter. Moreover, church holdings continued to grow through direct donations from laymen in return for chapels and chaplaincies. In addition, many secular priests, especially Cathedral clergy members, owned both urban real estate and country land in their own right. A study of the wills and testaments of chapter members indicates that three or four houses, a store or two, and a few pieces of farm land made up their typical holdings. Santaella's friend, the Canon Alonso de Campos, for example, left all his property to the College of Santa María de Jesús in 1529. It consisted of several pieces of arable land in the Vega of Triana and six or seven houses in the city. Three slaves and a sum of cash (which his executors immediately invested in additional real estate and *juros*) made up the remainder of the estate.[81]

One question remains to be discussed: the role of the clergy in the transatlantic trade. Churchmen were very

[80] Steggink, "Monasterios carmelitas," p. 175.

[81] Hazañas y La Rua, *Maese Rodrigo*, pp. 479–482. See also AHN, Clero, leg. 6676, 6677, 6678.

much a part of the Sevillian world in the sixteenth century and were inevitably drawn into the mercantile concerns of their city. Many clergymen participated in the transatlantic trade, but almost always indirectly. They invested as silent partners in trading ventures or managed the investments of others. It was not unusual for merchants departing for the Indies to entrust their business in Seville to clerical friends or relatives who used their ecclesiastical associations as a business network. The Cathedral clergy, because of their close ties with the trading elite, were especially active in the collection of debts.

Sevillian churchmen did not allow their mercantile activities to interfere with the performance of their religious duties. One notable exception was Canon Alonso Fajardo de Villalobos, Bishop of Esquilache, who so totally dedicated himself to business as to draw the censure of Archbishop Rodrigo de Castro and eventually the sanctions of the papacy. The Villalobos case is indeed a kind of *cause célèbre* in the annals of the Sevillian church. The entrepreneurial undertakings of Canon Villalobos came to light in the *residencia* that Archbishop Castro forced him to submit to in 1582.[82] According to the charges levied against him, Villalobos traded in all kinds of merchandise from grain to pearls both in Seville and the New World. It was further alleged that he had converted his residence into a veritable manufacturing center and store where such di-

[82] BM, MS. Add. 28.358, "Los cargos que resultan de la residencia que se tomó por mandado del Rr^{mo} señor don Rodrigo de Castro Arçobispo de Sevilla . . . contra don Alonso Faxardo de Villalobos Obispo de Esquilache Arcediano y Canónigo de Sevilla," folios 133–134.

verse products as flour, seabiscuit, bricks, and lime were produced and sold. All the witnesses who testified at the hearing gave an unfavorable description of his business methods, claiming that he was totally unscrupulous—buying cheap and selling dear, taking advantage of scarcities in vital goods to raise prices, and selling grain illegally at more than the established price (*tasa*). Finally, he had totally neglected the duties of his religious office, "neither saying mass nor attending church" and, in the colorful language of the period, was "living as a man without conscience on the verge of perdition." [83] Fortunately for the Sevillian church there were few clergymen like Villalobos. The majority of churchmen managed to keep their business and spiritual concerns separate without prejudicing one or the other and to profit from both.

Lawyers

Outside of the clergy, Seville's professional class consisted of lawyers, medical practitioners, and notaries. Great diversity in education, training, and social origins characterized this group. At the top were men with university degrees, most of whom came from *hidalgo, letrado,* and wealthy merchant families; those at the bottom usually had some kind of primary school education, but basically their skills were obtained through apprenticeship or direct practice. There was also a middle stratum—men who had some amount of higher education but had not received their degrees. A classic example is Cervantes' father, who was forced to suspend his medical studies at the University of Alcalá de Henares because of ill health and, as a result,

[83] *Ibid.*, fol. 133v.

fell into the unprestigious category of practicing surgeon (*médico cirujano*).[84] Individuals in the middle and lower groups could originate from the *letrado* class (as did Cervantes' father), but more generally came from artisan and merchant backgrounds.

It is an established fact that many of the professionals were of *converso* origin. This was especially true in medicine, which in addition to the church was one of their favorite fields of endeavor in the sixteenth century just as it had been in previous centuries among their ancestors, the Jews. Less is known about their role as lawyers and notaries. Their participation in the legal profession is amply illustrated by the matriculation records of the University of Seville, which reveal that they made up a substantial proportion of the men studying law there during the sixteenth century, while documents from the Protocols Archive show how many of them were practicing before the several tribunals in Seville as *procuradores* or untitled lawyers. As for their activities as notaries, even a superficial glance at the sources indicates the degree to which they continued to exercise this traditional occupation in sixteenth-century Seville.

Lack of statistics makes it impossible to determine the size of the Sevillian professional class. As for titled professionals, the *vecindario* of 1561 lists 149 men as having the baccalaureate (*bachiller*), licentiate (*licenciado*), and doctorate (*doctor*) degrees, 17 of whom were clergymen. These figures are undoubtedly too low, but it does not appear that the Sevillian titled professional group was a

[84] F. Rodríguez Marín, *Cervantes estudió en Sevilla (1564–1565)* (Seville, 1905), p. 17.

large one. In contrast, untitled professionals seem to have been numerous, especially notaries, whose services were much in demand in a commercial center like Seville. Most of those with the licentiate degree were lawyers (the doctorate in law was a high and uncommon degree), while the holders of the doctorate were medical practitioners. In medicine both the degrees of *bachiller* and *licenciado* were used and very common (one of the *licenciados* in medicine mentioned in the *vecindario* of 1561 was Licenciado Juan Alemán, uncle of the famous novelist Mateo Alemán).[85]

Among the professionals, degrees were highly solicited for they brought both social prestige and tax exemption. The benefits to be obtained from a diploma were so great that many men fraudulently claimed them. Such deception was not difficult in Seville for the whole atmosphere of the town with its large, cosmopolitan, and transient population and its get-rich-quick attitude actually encouraged this kind of mentality. Some who merely attended a university assumed a title; Cervantes' father, for example, during his first years in Seville called himself *Licenciado* although he did not have a degree. More frequently men who held the baccalaureate appropriated the licentiate. Fernando de Almirón y Zayas, who obtained his *bachiller* degree from the University of Seville in 1591, frequently "signed himself licentiate without having that degree," just like Bachiller Pasillas in the *Coloquio de los perros*.[86]

There was no scarcity of opportunities in Seville for men

85 AGS, Expedientes de hacienda, leg. 170.

86 Rodríguez Marín, *Datos*, p. 4; Cervantes Saavedra, *El coloquio de los perros*, p. 284; F. Rodríguez Marín, *Estudios Cervantinos* (Madrid, 1947), p. 57.

trained in law. They could practice before the Audiencia and other tribunals or find a governmental position. Often private practice and a salaried legal post were combined, especially by titled lawyers. Judgeships were available for those with the most talent and connections except on the Audiencia, which was closed to natives of Seville and its district. The prohibition against Sevillians on the Audiencia was dictated by a desire to eliminate conflict of interests and other abuses that had characterized the court of the Jueces de los Grados, its predecessor. On the other hand, positions on the second highest tribunal in Seville, the municipal court of the Alcaldes ordinarios or de la Corte, were open to Sevillians and represented the culmination of success for a Sevillian lawyer. This court exercised jurisdiction over both criminal and civil cases and all those in which the city was a party. Originally the judges were selected annually by the municipal council, but after 1557 these positions became lifetime appointments.[87]

The social prestige surrounding these judgeships contrasts sharply with their modest salaries. In 1536 the Jueces de los Grados received annual salaries of 150,000 maravedís (just six times more than the yearly wages of a mason) and a mere 3,000 maravedís extra for expenses. Some twenty-nine years later their successors on the Audiencia did not enjoy much better financial conditions. In a petition which the judges sent to the king in 1565 requesting higher annual compensation they argued that they "could not sustain themselves on their accustomed salaries in a city like Seville where the cost of living was so high." As proof of the

[87] Morgado, *Historia,* pp. 181–182; Ortiz de Zúñiga, *Anales,* III, 395–396, 419.

urgency of their situation, they noted that three of the most capable judges had resigned their posts because they "became tired of living on credit as most of the judges were forced to do for a greater part of the year" and that a third judge had recently died penniless. But the economic position of the judges was not as bad as they described it for they were tax-exempt and enjoyed countless other perquisites that certainly made them a privileged group. There were also many illegitimate means of augmenting their incomes, which, clearly, many Sevillian judges were willing to use. Finally, in many instances, their precarious financial situation was related to other problems. According to a report of 1589, gambling, women, and ostentatious living played a larger role in corroding the incomes of the judges of the Audiencia than did the high cost of living in Seville or their low salaries.[88]

For most lawyers even a modest steady income was absolutely necessary, and for this reason legal posts with the various governing bodies in the city were much in demand. The city, Audiencia, Inquisition, and Casa de Contratación all employed trained lawyers. Both the Audiencia and the Inquisition had especially large legal staffs, twenty-six lawyers and a prosecuting attorney for the Audiencia and ten lawyers and a prosecutor for the Inquisition. As in the case of judges, salaries were minimal. In 1581 the city paid

[88] AMS, Archivo de Privilegios, Reales Provisiones, carpeta 24, no. 147; BM, MS. Add. 28.349, "Carta del Cabildo de Sevilla al Presidente del Consejo de Castilla sobre los relatores de la Audiencia Real de los Grados," 24 Oct. 1565; *Ibid.*, Add. 28.335, "Carta del licenciado Beltrán de Guevara, regente de Sevilla a Mateo Vázquez con la relación de lo que toca a aquella Audiencia," 20 June 1589.

its four legal advisors a mere 15,000 maravedís a year while
lawyers for the Inquisition received even less—some 10,000
maravedís annually—but the advantages and exemptions related to these posts placed their occupants in favorable economic positions.[89] Licenciado Luis Someño de Porras, for
example, a prominent Sevillian jurist in the last quarter of
the sixteenth century, served as a lawyer for the Audiencia
and also as prosecuting attorney (*fiscal*) for the Inquisition.
His combined income from these two posts amounted to
about 100,000 maravedís, but at the height of his career in
1587 he reputedly had a fortune of over 20,000 ducats. Unfortunately, there is no way to estimate his private practice
(which apparently was substantial), but it seems that the
bulk of his wealth came from *juros*, real estate, and commercial investments.[90]

Some titled lawyers became administrators rather than
court practitioners. One of the most illustrious of these
jurist-administrators was Licenciado Cristóbal Mosquera de
Figueroa, who during his long career served the royal government as auditor in the armada of the Marqués of Santa
Cruz against the Azores in 1582 and that of his native city
as *corregidor* of several towns in the Sevillian district. Mosquera de Figueroa was a most versatile man. He was a humanist who translated Greek and Latin works, a poet whose
verses were eulogized by the leading literary figures of his
day, a soldier renowned for his bravery, and an accom-

---

[89] AMS, Archivo de Privilegios, Tumbo, carpeta 8, no. 131; Morgado, *Historia*, p. 189; Caro, *Antigüedades*, pp. 55v–62v.

[90] Rodríguez Marín, *Datos*, pp. 265–266. Licenciado Someño de
Porras was a son-in-law of the Sevillian physician Dr. Nicolás de
Monardes.

plished musician who played the vihuela with skill and feeling.[91]

Licenciado Mosquera de Figueroa's accomplishments, however, appear to have been more outstanding than his lineage. Although he solicited and eventually received recognition of his claim to *hidalgo* status, it seems suspect, and at least on his mother's side, fraudulent. Documents from the Sevillian Protocols Archive show that his mother came from a family of merchant and *converso* origin. Her three sisters were all married to men of similar backgrounds—one of them, Hernando Rodríguez de San Juan (the husband of her sister María de Palma), was a recently ennobled merchant who administered the *almojarifazgo* in the 1570's and held a seat on the city council.[92] Very little is known about his father's family except that they originated from Badajoz and that they claimed to be related to the Duke of Arcos, Rodrigo Ponce de León. Nevertheless, several witnesses at the official inquiry in 1585 (including a representative of the city) stated that they were not legitimate descendants of the persons they pretended to be. If neither Licenciado Mosquera de Figueroa nor his father paid taxes in Seville, this was not due to their noble status, but rather to their university degrees.[93]

[91] Méndez Bejarano, *Diccionario,* II, 132–135; see also Pacheco, *Verdaderos retratos.*

[92] Rodríguez de San Juan, APS, Palma (XX), 22 Sept. 1570, Libro II, fol. 138. For the rest of the family, see *ibid.,* Pérez (II), 9 June 1555, Libro I, fol. parte 2ª. At one time Mosquera de Figueroa was engaged to his cousin María de Azevedo, daughter of Rodríguez de San Juan, but they apparently did not marry.

[93] Excerpts from the inquiry have been published by Rodríguez Marín, *Datos,* pp. 93–95.

In contrast to the titled lawyers who represented a relatively small and select group were the numerous untitled
lawyers (*procuradores*). Since the titled lawyers were more
active as administrators and legal advisors than as court
practitioners, the untitled men performed most of the routine day-to-day courtroom work in the city. They competed at all levels with the titled lawyers, practicing as they
did before all the various tribunals in Seville. Some of the
most capable, like the well-known Pedro García Tortolero,
were familiar figures at the Audiencia. The documents
show that most of the cases before the Casa de Contratación
were handled by the *procuradores*. These were usually
civil suits, but could also include criminal proceedings. Two
of the most active Casa *procuradores* at mid-century were
Alvaro de Baena and Gonzalo de Molina (both of *converso* origin), who had an impressive list of clients among
the Seville business community.[94] The popularity of the
procuradores was in large part due to their lower fees, but
there was considerable variation depending on the time and
the circumstances of the case.

In addition to their work as court lawyers, the *procuradores* acted as guardians and administrators of the estates
of minors and widows. It was also customary for businessmen and others who were about to travel to the New
World to place their affairs in Seville in the hands of a
procurador for the period of their absence. Some *procura-*

[94] Baena, APS, Cazalla (XV), 1 July 1538, Libro II, fol. 55; Molina, *ibid.*, Franco (XV), 9 Jan. 1551, Libro I, fol. 854. For García
Tortolero, *ibid.*, Cívico (VIII), 3 Sept. 1580, Libro III, fol. 492; in
a criminal case, L. Porras (XXIV), 20 March 1574, Libro I, fol.
1190.

dores conducted the legal business of their clients on a
more permanent basis, that is, for a set salary and over an
established period of time, usually a year. In 1549, for
example, Casa *procurador* Alvaro de Baena entered into
such an arrangement with the New World trader Luis
Sánchez Dalvo, while his colleague Francisco de Aguilar
regularly represented several Genoese merchants during the
1550's.[95]

In the popular mind, lawyers, whether titled or untitled,
had a reputation for dishonesty and trickery. Actually the
profession itself engendered this stereotype because of the
numerous occasions for fraud and illicit gains which it
offered. In Seville this suspicion had a firm basis in reality,
for the whole judicial system was notoriously corrupt. All
contemporary accounts agree that it was difficult to obtain
a fair hearing in a Sevillian court. In the opinion of Luque
Fajardo reals, doubloons, and escudos were worth more
than any law, statute, or decree.[96]

The corruption in the Sevillian courts becomes easier to
understand when one reads a confidential report written in
1589 by a royal commissioner, Beltrán de Guevara, on the
character and qualifications of the judges of the Audiencia.
That such a group of men could hold positions on the highest tribunal in the city is indicative of the sorry state of
Sevillian justice. Three of the magistrates were consummate

[95] Baena, *ibid.*, Cazalla (XV), 8 Nov. 1549, Libro II, fol. 1088;
Aguilar, 26 June 1551, Libro I, fol. 759.

[96] Luque Fajardo, "Fiel desengaño contra la ociosidad," p. 591v,
as quoted in Cervantes Saavedra, *Rinconete y Cortadillo* (1905
ed.), p. 49. For further information on the corruption of justice
in Seville, see BNM, MS. 3207, "Advertencias para su gobierno
(Sevilla)," folios 545–556, undated.

gamblers, one of whom, Licenciado Luis de Molina, "was loaded down with gambling debts and although a married man was seen frequently in the company of women other than his wife." Another gambler was Licenciado Rodrigo Velas, who had a further disability: both his son and son-in-law were Sevillian lawyers and therefore no one trusted his decisions. Licenciado Andrés Fernández de Córdoba, on the other hand, was an honest man with a good education, but was "too lenient, dismissing cases at the first opportunity." Guevara described Licenciado Varela as totally inept, while Licenciado Flores and Jusepe del Castillo lacked the correct dispositions to be judges. In conclusion, out of the twelve men on the Audiencia only four, in Beltrán de Guevara's opinion, were really suited to sit on this tribunal and just one, Licenciado Diego de Valdivia, was outstanding in respect to education, intelligence, and moral qualities. No wonder that Mateo Alemán, who had a good knowledge of Sevillian justice, advised bribing the judge and the notary as the best means to obtain a favorable decision in a Sevillian court.[97]

Medical Practitioners

A large segment of Seville's professional class was made up of medical practitioners. Although incomplete documentation makes it impossible to calculate their numbers, my sources indicate that they were more numerous in Seville than in any other city in Spain.[98] The benevolent

[97] BM, MS. Add. 28.335, folios 150–154; Alemán, *Guzmán de Alfarache*, p. 447.

[98] The *vecindario* of 1561, for example, contains only five names with the designation *médico* (doctor) or *cirujano* (surgeon), but several Sevillian physicians appear as *vecinos* in the various parishes.

attitude of the city government undoubtedly attracted medical men to the city. The rapid growth of the city's population caused urban crowding, and the municipality, fearful of the consequences for public health, openly solicited and encouraged qualified medical practitioners to come to Seville. In 1596, for example, when the chief magistrate of Seville, Andrés de Monsalve, who had been commissioned by the city to "survey the universities and other cities to find one or more surgeons," announced at a *cabildo* meeting that a certain Licenciado Arévalo would be willing to come to Seville and make it his home if the city would finance his move, funds were immediately granted for that purpose. Some four years earlier, the prominent surgeon Dr. Fonseca de Sotomayor had been lured away from Málaga to Seville; one of the principal inducements had been a promise from the city council that he would be allowed to perform an autopsy, but after his arrival the ecclesiastical authorities refused to allow it to take place.[99]

Not only did the city bring medical men to Seville, it also put many of them on the payroll. In the interests of self-protection as well as humanitarianism, the municipality provided some free care for the poor and destitute. Thus the city always employed a sizable and varied group of medical practitioners, ranging from prestigious physicians to primitive folk healers. Typical "town doctors" were Matías de Ayala, a surgeon and bonesetter, who received a yearly salary of 150 ducats in 1597, and Felipe de Tovar,

[99] AMS, Sección Tercera, Escribanías del cabildo, Siglo XVI, tomo 1, no. 76; *ibid*., Actas Capitulares, cabildo de 6 de marzo de 1593. See also Cervantes Saavedra, *Rinconete y Cortadillo* (1905 ed.), p. 27.

a specialist in urinary problems, whose annual salary in the same year was 100,000 maravedís. Even such an outstanding physician as Dr. Bartolomé Hidalgo de Agüero was on the city payroll; he collected a small salary from the municipality for his services to the sick poor in the Hospital of San Hermenegildo (known popularly as the Hospital del Cardenal). The city also employed a medical man at the city jail and another at the officially sanctioned public brothel to take care of the health of the women there. Although salaries for these positions were low (the prison doctor earned a mere 12,000 maravedís a year), for men like Dr. Hernando Alemán (the novelist's father), who held the latter post from 1557 to 1567, it was a welcome addition to rather meager earnings from private practice.[100]

The position of Seville as the principal center for the receipt and distribution of American imports also created a favorable environment for medical men and studies. All the exotic products of the New World came into the city, including many new medicinal plants. Some Sevillian physicians, most notably Doctors Simón de Tovar and Nicolás de Monardes, studied these American products and wrote treatises on their therapeutic value. In addition, both men maintained botanical gardens where they cultivated and experimented with these new medicinal plants. Monardes, for example, mentions how on one occasion he took several sheets of tobacco grown in his garden and applied them to

[100] Cervantes Saavedra, *Rinconete y Cortadillo* (1905 ed.), p. 27; AMS, Libros de Propios, año 1597, 12 June; *ibid.*, año 1600, 25 Sept.; AMS, Papeles Importantes, siglo XVI, tomo 9, no. 32; *ibid.*, Varios Antiguos, Médicos, no. 144. The life and tribulations of Mateo Alemán's father are discussed in F. Rodríguez Marín, *Discursos leídos ante la Real Academia Española* (Seville, 1907).

a sore tooth with the effect, he claimed, of relieving the
pain. Monardes and other Sevillian doctors apparently were
active in the importation of American drug products. Their
partners in this trade were usually pharmacists like Monardes' associate Juan del Valle, who appears as one of the
doctor's biggest creditors at the time of his bankruptcy in
1579.[101]

The Sevillian government encouraged medical men, but
it also regulated their activities. Municipal decrees against
quackery and dishonesty in the practice of medicine and
the dispensing of drugs were frequent, and compliance was
enforced by the courts. Furthermore, a municipal commission periodically examined and licensed physicians, surgeons, and druggists and inspected apothecary shops. Service
on this body was honorary, but apparently so time-consum-
ing that in 1597 Dr. Agustín Gudiel felt obliged to petition
the city council to compensate him for the time and money
lost from his private practice while a member of the commission.[102]

In plague times doctors were expected to work closely
with city authorities. Municipal law required them to remain in the city caring for the afflicted in plague hospitals
and private homes. They were paid for their services, but
the city's generosity hardly compensated for the dangers
involved. During the plague of 1580–1582 the municipal
account books show repeated payments to Tomé Sánchez

[101] Francisco Guerra, *Nicolás Bautista Monardes, su vida y su
obra* (Mexico City, 1961), p. 82. Regarding Tovar, see Cervantes
Saavedra, *Rinconete y Cortadillo* (1905 ed.), pp. 25–26; Guerra,
Monardes, pp. 16, 21.

[102] AMS, Escribanías del cabildo, siglo XVI, nos. 78, 79.

Ronquillo, a surgeon, and Doctors Gómez and León for their work in attending plague victims in the Carretería and Arenal districts of the parish of Santa María. There is also a payment of 50,000 maravedís (dated December 4, 1581) to Dr. Monardes for his services during this contagion. The frequency of epidemic disease in the sixteenth century made the medical profession a hazardous one. Doctors often met premature deaths during these epidemics, as did the uncle of the novelist Mateo Alemán, Licenciado Juan Alemán, who lost his life in the plague of 1568 while attending the sick in the Hospital de las Cinco Llagas.[103] On the other hand, considering the risks they ran, they were extraordinarily immune from the infection.

In addition to their care of the plague-stricken, doctors advised the municipality regarding measures to prevent the spread of disease and to lessen its impact. In 1579, at the first signs of the plague, the Asistente of Seville, Count of Villar, convoked a meeting of the city's medical men to discuss whether an epidemic was imminent and, if so, how to deal with it. Copies of their written opinions were then sent on to the Council of Castile. Some of the collective measures that they advised included cleaning all streets and public places, an embargo on the entrance of goods and persons from plague-infected areas, isolation of the afflicted in specially designated plague hospitals, destruction of the clothing of plague victims, and the burning of aromatic

[103] *Ibid.*, Libro de Propios, año 1581, 4 Dec.; for Ronquillo and Drs. Gómez and León, see *ibid.*, Autógrafos de hijos ilustres de la ciudad, carpeta 3. These three documents have been published by Rodríguez Marín, *Datos*, pp. 261–262. See also AMS, Escribanías del cabildo, siglo XVI, tomo 11, no. 71.

plants in various parts of the city so as to purify the air. Individuals could ward off infection through a combination of special diets, pomanders, and "fumes." Several of those who attended this meeting eventually incorporated their views in treatises on the pestilence, with publication subsidized by the city.[104] A host of medical works were also occasioned by the plague of 1599–1601, with the city again bearing the costs of publication.[105] Moreover, on several occasions during the century one or two prominent medical men were formally commissioned by the city to write such books. This occurred during the epidemic of 1568, when Doctors Andrés Zamudio de Alfaro and Francisco Franco were both asked to prepare treatises about the pestilence of that year.[106]

Regardless of their vital role during plague periods and their importance to society as a whole, doctors had little social prestige and were often the objects of popular criticism. In the sixteenth century the survival of a seriously ill person was more often the result of his own curative powers than the prophylactic measures taken by physicians. The fact that medical men were powerless to prevent death and that many patients died while under their most attentive care laid them open to the charge of quackery and turned

[104] AMS, Papeles Importantes, siglo XVI, tomos 5, 6; *ibid.*, Escribanías del cabildo, tomo 7, no. 14; J. Velázquez y Sánchez, *Anales epidémicos* (Seville, 1866), p. 71; BNM, MS. 9372 = Cc–42.

[105] AMS, Escribanías del cabildo, siglo XVI, tomo 7, no. 17, contains many documents dealing with the plague of 1599–1601.

[106] Velázquez y Sánchez, *Anales*, p. 71; Matute y Gaviria, *Noticias*, p. 66. Dr. Zamudio de Alfaro's work was entitled *Tratado de Peste* (Seville, 1569) and that of Dr. Franco, *Libro de las enfermedades contagiosas* (Seville, 1569).

the populace against them. Literature attests to the low opinion of contemporaries for the medical profession, for satire against doctors is commonplace in the sixteenth century just as it was in the Middle Ages. Even Mateo Alemán and Cervantes, both offspring of medical men, had harsh words for them, although Cervantes was careful to distinguish between what he called "the 'bad doctors,' the curse of the state (that is, the quacks) and the 'good doctors' who deserve palms and laurels." In *Don Quijote* he created one of the best caricatures of a sixteenth-century physician—Dr. Pedro Recio de Agüero, the governor's official doctor on the island of Barataria who, according to Sancho, "gets a salary for killing all the governors who come here." [107]

Popular antipathy toward medical men was, of course, not peculiar to Spain during this period, but existed in most European countries. In Spain, however, this popular image had two sides: quackery and dishonesty on the one hand, anti-Semitism on the other. In the Middle Ages Jews monopolized the medical profession, while in the sixteenth century *conversos* predominated. For the majority of Spaniards the term "medical practitioner" became synonymous with Jewish descent.[108] The coming together of these two ideas—Jewish descent and lack of professional integrity—created the popular concept of the medical man that was held into the eighteenth century. It is therefore not difficult to comprehend the reluctance of the upper classes to enter the field of medicine in the seventeenth and eighteenth cen-

[107] Miguel de Cervantes Saavedra, *Don Quijote de la Mancha*, ed. Martín de Riquer (New York, 1966), 887, 913.

[108] Domínguez Ortiz, "Los conversos," p. 369.

turies, for to do so would immediately cast suspicion on one's origins.

In addition to projecting a negative image, the medical profession was not very remunerative. The income of most doctors was no more than double that of a master mason. Quite typical was Mateo Alemán's father, who had great difficulties making a living and was frequently in debt. Even some of the most successful physicians, like Bartolomé Hidalgo de Agüero and García Pérez de Morales, lived on modest incomes and never became wealthy in spite of their skill and reputation. Dr. Hidalgo de Agüero held the chair of surgery at the University of Seville and practiced at the Hospital del Cardenal. It was there that he developed a special method for the treatment of wounds called the *vía particular* as opposed to the commonly used *vía común* that brought him wide acclaim. No wonder the ruffians of Seville "commended themselves to Dr. Hidalgo de Agüero as well as to God before fighting." Yet despite his fame he never became wealthy; at his death in 1597 he left an insignificant estate—some property and a small amount of cash—to his daughter and physician son-in-law, Dr. Francisco Jiménez Guillén.[109] The same was true for Dr. García Pérez de Morales, personal physician to the Count of Ureña and an early occupant of the chair of medicine at the University of Seville, whose total fortune at death amounted to 1,238,527 maravedís (3,302 ducats). This sum included his daughter's dowry, a house in the Calle de la Sierpe which had served as his residence and of-

[109] Méndez Bejarano, *Diccionario*, I, 320–321; Rodríguez Marín, *Datos*, p. 495.

fice, some olive groves, and one-quarter of an oil press in Aznalcázar.[110]

Only one Sevillian physician really achieved both fame and wealth—Dr. Nicolás de Monardes, who at his death in 1588 left a fortune of over 30,000 ducats.[111] Monardes was a capable doctor, but he was also a skillful businessman, a quality that enabled him to obtain larger rewards from his profession than did many others. His talents in this respect came naturally, for he was of Genoese origin, the son of a Ligurian bookseller who had settled in Seville at the end of the fifteenth century and had married the daughter of a local *converso* surgeon, Bachiller Martín de Alfaro. Their son Nicolás studied at the University of Alcalá de Henares and after receiving his baccalaureate there, transferred to the University of Seville for his licentiate and doctorate degrees in medicine. He began his professional career in Seville as an assistant to Dr. García Pérez de Morales and married the doctor's daughter. At his father-in-law's death, Monardes inherited his practice and then built up a profitable one of his own, which included aristocrats like the Duchess of Béjar and the Duke of Alcalá; ecclesiastics (the Archbishop of Seville, Cristóbal de Rojas y Sandoval, and the Cathedral chapter); and municipal officials (the Asistente of Seville, Count of Barajas, and members of the city council). There is no way to estimate his income from private practice, but it must have been substantial. On one

[110] J. Hazañas y La Rua, *La Imprenta en Sevilla,* II (Seville, 1949), 91; Rodríguez Marín, *Datos,* p. 243; Méndez Bejarano, *Diccionario,* II, 220.

[111] Information on Dr. Monardes has been drawn from Guerra, *Monardes.*

occasion, for example, the Duchess of Béjar gave him 600 ducats for his services.

Besides his private practice Monardes received money for his services to the city, as during the plague of 1580–1582. In addition, he frequently "sponsored" candidates for medical degrees at the university; it was customary on such occasions to reward sponsors (*padrinos*) with gifts, usually cash. Finally, the doctor made money from his writings, especially those dealing with the prophylactic uses of the recently introduced American medicinal plants. Popular interest in these new drug products was high, and Monardes took advantage of it by writing several books on American pharmacopoeia. These works enjoyed wide circulation both in Spain and abroad, and through them Dr. Monardes' name became known outside of his country.

Although it is clear that Monardes made an excellent living from his profession, the bulk of his fortune was drawn from his varied business dealings. He speculated in real estate both in the city and surrounding countryside, bought and sold *juros*, and invested in the transatlantic trade. In 1554 he formed a commercial partnership for the trade of merchandise and slaves between Seville and the New World with a merchant named Juan Núñez de Herrera, who soon after took up residence in Panama. After his partner's death in 1563, Monardes associated himself with his son-in-law Rodrigo de Brizuela in a new company specializing in slaves (in 1564 alone they sent 349 slaves to Vera Cruz), cochineal, and hides. A series of economic reverses, however, ruined the enterprise, and in 1567 they went bankrupt. In March 1568, Monardes, fleeing from his creditors, took sanctuary in the monastery of Regina

Celi, but he did not remain there for very long. Timely bullion shipments from America enabled him to settle with his creditors and leave his sanctuary. Within a few years he completely recovered from his bankruptcy and at his death in 1588 was generally regarded as a famous doctor and wealthy trader.

Physicians like Dr. Monardes represented the elite among medical men; they held university degrees and practiced mainly among the wealthier classes. Although they had to be knowledgeable about all kinds of diseases, as scholars and theoreticians, they did not work with their hands as did surgeons. The latter were trained by apprenticeship and by hospital instruction and rarely held degrees. Surgeons dealt with structural emergencies, superficial growths, and skin diseases, but since their work was peripheral to the art of medicine (even though it was required on all social levels), their status was inferior to that of physicians. Specialization was frequent among surgeons; some like Maese Francisco Díaz, who offered his services to the city in 1589, were specialists in removing cataracts; others in treating fractures and dislocations (Marco Antonio Parga, for example, whose work for the city brought him an annual salary of 24 ducats at the end of the century).[112] Although most surgeons did routine bleeding, some actually specialized in phlebotomy. After 1507 the phlebotomists had their own guild and were examined and licensed by the city to practice their trade. In addition, some of them were dentists and herbalists on the side. A good example of a man who practiced all three professions of phlebotomist, dentist, and

[112] AMS, Libro de Propios, año 1602, 21 Aug.; *ibid.*, Escribanías del cabildo, siglo XVI, tomo 5, no. 35.

herbalist was Juan de Peralta, a resident of the district of Santa María in 1541.[113]

Besides the regular practitioners of medicine in Seville there was no scarcity of irregular ones—quacks, charlatans, and folk healers—who claimed to be able to cure all kinds of infirmities. They had at their disposal various exotic ingredients of supposed medicinal virtue like bezoar, dissolved pearl, potable gold, or the philosopher's stone. Some of these impostors were audacious enough to seek the protection of the municipality, Juan de Herbio, for example, who, after exalting the curative powers of the philosopher's stone in a petition to the city council, asked them to allow him to practice with it and to put him on the payroll.[114] Among the most unusual of the folk healers were the *saludadores*, or those who cured with "Divine Grace" (*gratis data*), for which Seville and its district were famous. It was generally believed that certain persons (male and female) were endowed with special God-given powers to cure various illnesses, especially rabies. Treatment consisted of giving the afflicted party small pieces of bread that had been moistened in the mouth of the *saludador;* the curative powers were presumably in the saliva. Another method, used mainly in cases of gout, was for the *saludador* to spit in the face of the patient.[115]

[113] J. Gestoso y Pérez, *Curiosidades antiguas sevillanas, serie segunda* (Seville, 1910), pp. 136–137.

[114] Cervantes Saavedra, *Rinconete y Cortadillo* (1905 ed.), p. 28.

[115] Alonso Sánchez Gordillo, "Memorial de las Grandezas ecclesiásticas de la ciudad de Sevilla y catálogo de sus ilustrísimos arzobispos, año 1632," RAHM, Colección Salazar, MS. R-2; Sebastián de Covarrubias, *Tesoro de la Lengua Castellana o Española*, ed. Martín de Riquer (Barcelona, 1943), p. 923. See also Gestoso y Pérez, *Curiosidades*, p. 133.

Despite their picturesque behavior, folk healers and other irregular practitioners operated freely in the city and reaped a rich harvest among the gullible. Nor did they ply their trade only among the poor and ignorant. Since medical men could do little in some cases, even the wealthier and better educated might turn to them in desperation. The *saluda-dores* received a sympathetic hearing from the city government which, it seems, on occasion paid them a salary for "treating persons afflicted with rabies in this city and its district."[116] Furthermore, friction between regular medical men and these irregular practitioners was rare. Physicians and surgeons might call their irregular colleagues impostors and charlatans, but never disputed their existence. Even the municipal licensing system was not devised to exclude them, but rather to label the qualified practitioners. This was a tolerance born of reality, for in the sixteenth century even among the best physicians fortune often prevailed more than skill.

Notaries

Notaries occupied the lowest stratum of the Sevillian professional class, but their position in the social scale contrasted sharply with their important role in the community. The legalistic sense of the Spaniards in the sixteenth century called for the notarization of all important acts in both private and public life. This whole mass of documentation, from marriage contracts and powers of attorney to official ordinances and petitions, was drawn up by notaries who were experts in legal formulas and terminology. Their training was strictly vocational. It involved the completion

[116] Gestoso y Pérez, *Curiosidades*, p. 134.

of a grammar-school education and a relatively short period of apprenticeship after which application was made to the royal court for a notary's title: *escribano de su Majestad* (His Majesty's Notary). This title, however, did not bring the right to open an office. Appointments were made on the basis of royal patronage, and the number of offices in the municipalities was fixed by law. In reality, municipal authorities had large powers over these appointments and generally positions were freely bought and sold with royal approval coming after purchase. Since positions had to be purchased and prices were high, most beginners worked in the office of an established notary until they had secured enough money and connections to obtain an office of their own. Notarial offices therefore tended to be large; in addition to the chief notary there were usually two or three others and several apprentices. Quarters were rented rather than owned and had to be spacious enough to accommodate a substantial working group. In 1525, for example, two notaries, Rodrigo Sánchez de Porras and Miguel Díaz, with their respective staffs, rented a whole row of stores in the Plaza de San Francisco and converted them into offices.[117]

In Seville there were twenty-four public notaries (*escribanos de número*) with offices scattered throughout the city, but most of the prominent men (those with the largest following) were located either in Gradas (the business area near the Cathedral) or on the Plaza de San Francisco in the proximity of the city hall.[118] Their principal duties con-

[117] Morgado, *Historia*, p. 188; Antonio Xavier Pérez y López, *Teatro de la legislación universal de España e Indias*, XI (Madrid, 1796), 161–170; APS, A. R. Porras (III), 23 Oct. 1525, Libro II, fol. 6.
[118] Morgado, *Historia*, pp. 188–189.

sisted of drawing up and notarizing public contracts, but since Spanish trials and investigations were mostly written affairs, a considerable amount of time was spent preparing trial transcripts. Some notaries specialized in commercial documents, which in a port like Seville was an important and lucrative business. A successful notary could command a large mercantile clientele that regularly frequented his office.

There is considerable evidence to indicate that the Sevillian merchants had favorite notaries whom they selected on the basis of family and business connections. A survey of the leading Sevillian public notaries during the sixteenth century shows that a majority were related in one way or another—through blood, marriage, or close business ties—to the outstanding trading families of the city. This includes such successful notaries as Pedro Fernández, Manuel Segura, Antón Ruiz de Porras, Alonso de Cazalla, and Alonso de la Barrera. A perfect illustration is Alonso de Cazalla, who came from a large and well-placed *converso* business family that included wealthy merchants and municipal councilmen. The Cazallas were also bound through marriage to other *converso* trading families: the Ruiz (Councilman Antón Ruiz), the Virués (Beatriz de Virués was the wife of Gaspar de Cazalla), and the Dávilas (Rodrigo Dávila, cousin and partner of Gaspar de Cazalla in Panama).[119] With such family connections, it is not surprising that Alonso de Cazalla was one of the most popular notaries of his period, the mid-century.

[119] Isabel de Cazalla was the wife of Councilman Ruiz, APS, Cazalla (XV), 11 Nov. 1551, Libro II, fol. 1940; for the Virués and Cazallas, see *ibid.*, 13 Nov., fol. 1938; Dávilas, fol. 1961; in slave trade (including Alonso de Cazalla), 9 Nov., fol. 1921.

Like other professionals, the notaries originated in the merchant and artisan classes; there were also quite a few from families (generally *converso*) in which the office was traditional, passing from generation to generation. Three generations of the Segura family occupied the same office: Bartolomé Segura (1488–1492), Francisco Segura (*c.* 1500), and Manuel Segura (1506–1534). The same was true for the Farfáns: Pedro Farfán (1525–1544), his father Martín Rodríguez Farfán (*c.* 1506), and his grandfather Martín Rodríguez (*c.* 1467). In addition, one of Pedro's sons, Martín Rodríguez de Alfaro, was trained as a notary and had he not died young would have continued the line. Of the two remaining sons of Pedro and his wife Ana, Alonso went into the church and held a dignity (Archdeacon of Reina) in the Seville Cathedral and Pedro obtained a doctorate in law and served as a judge in the Audiencia of Mexico.[120]

In general notaries were considered good marriage partners because of the possibilities for enrichment inherent in the office. Pedro Farfán's wife Ana de Alfaro was the daughter of a wealthy and prominent Sevillian printer, Juan Varela de Salamanca, and she brought him a dowry of 400,000 maravedís. Even better opportunities were open to the daughters of successful notaries. Farfán's daughter Isabel de Sandoval married the famous Sevillian banker Domingo de Lizarrazas, while Diego de Porras, the chief notary of the Casa de Contratación, married his daughter to

[120] For the Farfáns, see Hazañas y La Rua, *La Imprenta*, II, 136–137; Rodríguez Marín, *Maese Rodrigo*, p. 463; for Seguras, Hazañas y La Rua, *La Imprenta*, I, 7; APS, F. R. Porras (III), 30 Oct. 1520, fol. Registro de Indias.

Juan López de Arechuleta, a ship captain and trader who had become wealthy in the transatlantic trade.[121] It is significant that both men were nonnatives (Basques) and relative newcomers to Seville; they probably were not aware of the *converso* background of these families.

Besides the duties regularly connected with their office, notaries also performed tasks that were similar to those carried out by the *procuradores*. They collected debts and salaries and administered the estates of absentee persons, widows, and minors.[122] Some notaries devoted themselves entirely to government work, serving as clerks and secretaries in the courts, Casa de Contratación, Inquisition, and the various branches of the municipal government. A large number of such positions were available in Seville, but they were both expensive to purchase and competitive. The office of chief notary of the Casa was worth 150,000 maravedís and that of clerk of the city council even more; there were two of them and each had an assistant. Some of the most responsible posts were with the courts—most notably *escribanos de la justicia* (clerks of the investigating judges), who took all testimony in writing before presentation to the judges. In Seville there were seven such notaries for criminal cases and four for civil suits, all of whom had their offices in the Plaza de San Francisco. Not only were these positions costly (they were worth some 187,500 maravedís each at the end of the century), but the men who held them had great influence over the outcome of legal cases.

[121] Hazañas y La Rua, *La Imprenta*, II, 138–139; APS, Segura (IV), 5 Nov. 1518, Libro V, fol. 447.

[122] APS, J. Cuadra (I), 20 Oct. 1517, Libro II, fol. 455; *ibid.*, Castellanos (V), 8 Aug. 1525, Libro III, fol. 211.

Mateo Alemán put it as follows: "For the quill of their pen
is more dangerous against whom it is bent, than a brass
cannon with all its batteries." [123] Moreover, the court clerks
had a reputation for dishonesty and there were few, it
seems, who did not take bribes. An anonymous memorial
on misgovernment in Seville dating from the last years of
the century described them as a "special kind of highway
robber who when they took testimony wrote down whatever they wanted (depending on the size of the gift) and
in this way perverted justice." [124] Nor were only the court
clerks under attack; notaries in general were not held in
high esteem. Contemporary opinion held that they customarily "delayed litigation, failed to advise the parties involved, charged excessive prices for their services, made it
their business to pry into other people's lives in order to
entangle them in the web of the law and plotted with the
judges on the principal of 'you scratch me and I'll scratch
you.'" [125] In view of all the possibilities for graft and corruption in this profession, no wonder it was such a popular
calling.

In addition to their professional duties, notaries, like other
professionals, were involved in all kinds of business ventures. Such activities were absolutely necessary, for most
professionals were caught in the squeeze between their

[123] BNM, MS. 18225; Morgado, *Historia,* pp. 188–189. For chief
notary of the Casa de Contratación, APS, M. Segura (IV), 5 Nov.
1518, Libro V, fol. 447. Mateo Alemán, *Guzmán de Alfarache,*
p. 308.

[124] BNM, MS. 3207, fol. 545.

[125] Cervantes Saavedra, *El coloquio de los perros,* p. 269. Similar
complaints can be found in the MS. mentioned in the preceding
note.

modest salaries and the need to maintain a standard of living commensurate with their rank in society. Only income derived from sources outside their profession could bridge this gap, and in Seville this meant first and foremost investment in the transatlantic trade. In the last analysis, professionals occupied a fluctuating and insecure status in the social hierarchy—those at the top close to the nobility, those at the bottom near artisan level—and most of them had to work hard just to maintain themselves.

MERCHANTS

There were two parallel currents that operated in Seville during the sixteenth century: one was the commercialization of the nobility, and the other the ennoblement of rich merchants. The desire for nobility was an especially powerful force. Merchants used their accumulated wealth to purchase *hidalguías* and to create entailed estates. Much of the capital from the trade with the New World was invested in landed estates in Aljarafe and Sierra Morena, out of which the Sevillian merchants established rich *mayorazgos* for their children.[126] This passion for *hidalguía* was not merely the result of empty vanity on the part of rich commoners, but rather a reflection of economic and social realities. In the aristocratically structured society of sixteenth-century Spain wealth, even though it was the principal instrument of social mobility, did not in itself bring social prestige or honor.[127] Only nobility insured the individual of

[126] Pike, *Enterprise and Adventure,* pp. 6–7.

[127] For a perceptive analysis of honor in Spanish society of the sixteenth century, see Julio Caro Baroja, "Honor y vergüenza,

these and other important privileges and benefits such as the all-important exemption from taxation. Furthermore, for men of suspect origin noble status offered security (the final liquidation of a "tainted" background) and the opportunity to attain power and reputation, which otherwise would have been denied them in a society dominated by the doctrine of *limpieza de sangre*. Under these circumstances the merchant class became an intermediary stage in the social hierarchy to be abandoned as soon as possible.

The boom-town atmosphere of Seville also contributed to the transitional nature of the merchant class. In rank the traders stood between the nobility and the artisans, but lines were not distinctly drawn in a city where chances for enrichment through trade seemed endless and miracles of social mobility were being performed every day. Merchants were constantly moving up to join the nobility, and the very success of commoners in acquiring titles and estates encouraged others to do the same. On the lower levels, the division between merchants and artisans was often blurred since artisans sold their products at retail and frequently invested surplus funds in trade. In the early years of the sixteenth century some of the most active Sevillian traders were either former artisans or men who combined both activities. Two outstanding examples of artisans turned merchants are Antón Bernal and Juan de Córdoba. Bernal was a goldbeater who through hard work and inconspicuous consumption accumulated enough capital to invest in the transatlantic trade. As early as 1506 he granted sea loans and

examen histórico de varios conflictos," in J. G. Peristiany, *El concepto del honor en la sociedad mediterránea* (Barcelona, 1968), pp. 77–126.

sold merchandise on credit to merchants and shipmasters. He also sent shiploads of goods to the New World and by the second decade of the century was the owner of one-half of the *Santa María de la Merced,* a vessel engaged in the Afro-American slave trade. At the same time he began to lend money to certain impecunious members of the aristocracy who were in constant need of cash. Diego Columbus received many of these loans. In 1523 the bankrupt son of the discoverer of America was forced to turn over a piece of jewelry worth 6,000 ducats to Bernal as a pledge for a loan. Several years passed before Columbus was able to repay the loan, during which time Bernal served as Don Diego's guarantor, an excellent way to secure his investment.[128]

Antón Bernal's rise from the artisan class into the nobility was accomplished in less than ten years, an indication of the fluidity of the class structure in Seville during this period. Although the notarial deeds continue to designate him as "goldbeater" throughout the first decade of the century, it is clear that he did not practice his trade and that he had assumed the role of a merchant-capitalist. The culmination of his career came in 1512 when he purchased a seat on the city council and thus joined the ranks of the ennobled commoners who governed the city.[129] Success stories such as Antón Bernal's were not unusual in Seville during the sixteenth century.

[128] APS, Ruiz (XII), 14 Feb. 1506, Libro I, fol. Principio del legajo; *ibid.*, Cuadra (I), 3 Dec. 1516, Libro II, fol. 792; Barrera (XV), 3 Dec. 1523, Libro I, fol. 1173; Castellanos (V), 23 Jan. 1526, Libro I, fol. 283v.

[129] *Ibid.*, Cuadra (I), 11 Feb. 1512, Libro I, fol. 232.

Like Bernal, silversmith Juan de Córdoba granted sea loans and sales credit and shipped goods and slaves to America in the first decades of the sixteenth century. In fact he was one of the first Sevillian businessmen to trade with the New World. As early as 1502 he sent out four caravels to Hispaniola with provisions for the starving colonists.[130] He also had business dealings with several New World captains. The names of some of the most important participants in the Spanish overseas expansion—Columbus, Pedrarias, Diego Velázquez, and Cortés—appear in the Sevillian Protocols as debtors of Juan de Córdoba. His relations with Cortés were especially significant; in 1519 at a critical point in Cortés' career he lent him a large sum of money and in doing so contributed to the completion of the conquest of Mexico.[131]

Besides their artisan beginnings, Juan de Córdoba and Antón Bernal had something else in common: their *converso* origin. Both men were attached to the party of Medina Sidonia and were supporters and associates of Francisco del Alcázar and other *converso* members of the Sevillian government. As such they played an active role in the opposition to the Comunero revolt, which in Seville was directed against the *conversos*. As we have seen, the Comu-

[130] *Ibid.*, F. Segura (IV), 8 Jan. 1502, Libro I, fol. Principio del legajo; freighting contract, Vallesillo (XV), 12 Nov. 1515, Libro II, fol. 924; slaves, 12 May, fol. 379.

[131] M. Giménez Fernández, "El alzamiento de Fernando Cortés según las cuentas de la Casa de la Contratación," *Revista de historia de América*, XXXI (1951), 1–58; APS, M. Segura (IV), 15 Sept. 1520; Libro III, fol. 2986; for Pedrarias, *ibid.*, Vallecillo (XV), 13 Jan. 1513, Libro único, fol. Primer tercio del legajo; Columbus and Velázquez, Giménez Fernández, *Bartolomé de las Casas*, II, 963.

neros led by Juan de Figueroa wanted to oust the *conversos* from the city government, but they also planned to stimulate the masses to attack them and to destroy their property as had been done to the Jews in 1391. The situation during the initial stages of the revolt was so turbulent and threatening that a group of frightened *converso* businessmen met in Juan de Córdoba's house and drew up a pact for mutual protection, pledging themselves to defend, with arms if necessary, their lives and property, and calling upon the Sevillian authorities to aid them. Fortunately the timely intervention of the Duke of Medina Sidonia doomed the Comunero revolt in Seville and prevented it from turning into the wholesale massacre of the *conversos* that its leaders had projected.[132]

One of the most important reasons for the failure of the Comunero revolt in Seville was its hostility to the *conversos* which alienated the influential elements of the population. This situation is not difficult to understand in view of the composition of Sevillian society, that is, the large *converso* representation among the nobility, merchants, and artisans. The *conversos* predominated in certain professions and trades; significantly, they were the same ones that the Jews were identified with in the Middle Ages. The chronicler Andrés Bernáldez, of *converso* descent himself, noted that most of them were "merchants, salesmen, tax gatherers, stewards of the nobility, cloth-searers, tailors, shoemakers, tanners, weavers, grocers, silk mercers, jewellers and other like trades; none were farmers, but all sought after com-

[132] For more on the Comunero revolt, see Chapter II. The meeting at Juan de Córdoba's house is described by Giménez Fernández, *Bartolomé de las Casas*, II, 963–964.

fortable posts and ways of making profit without much labor." [133] A glance at the professions mentioned in the Sevillian composition of 1510 confirms Bernáldez' opinion. A variety of occupations are listed, including all those described by Bernáldez, but by far the largest number of Sevillian New Christians were silversmiths, silk mercers, grocers, rag and old-clothes dealers, merchants, taxgatherers, and moneychangers.[134] Furthermore, these same *converso* businessmen, their descendants, and others like them were among the most important members of the Sevillian trading community in the sixteenth century. They were the famous Sevillian merchants whose wealth and enterprise amazed contemporaries.

Two of the most active *converso* traders in the first half of the sixteenth century were the moneychangers Pedro de Jerez and García de Sevilla. Both men participated in the Sevillian composition of 1510; Pedro de Jerez appears as number 124 on the list and García de Sevilla as number 341. Although these two businessmen shipped goods and slaves to the New World and were shipowners in their own right, their investment in the transatlantic trade was primarily capitalistic.[135] Like the Genoese, the Sevillian *con-*

[133] Andrés Bernáldez, *Historia de los Reyes Católicos* (Seville, 1869), I, 341.

[134] The *Padrón* of 1510 contains 390 names, and although it includes individuals of both Jewish and Moslem descent, the overwhelming majority are Jewish. See Guillén, "Padrón de conversos," pp. 89–98.

[135] Pedro de Jerez, freighting contract, APS, F. Segura (IV), 5 Oct. 1504, Libro II, fol. Mitad del legajo; sea loan, *ibid.*, Quijada (I), 22 Sept. 1505, Libro I, fol. 768, Cuaderno 27; owner of the *Santa María de la Antigua*, Vallecillo (XV), 24 Jan. 1508, Libro I, fol. Principio del legajo; slave trade, M. Segura (IV), 13 June 1513,.

versos played a vital role in financing the trade between Spain and America during the first decades of the sixteenth century when capital was scarce, the risks were great, and freight rates were high. They granted credit or cash in the form of the sea loan to persons departing for the New World, helping them to arm their ships or to cover the cost of merchandise.[136]

Often these merchant-capitalists delivered goods on credit instead of advancing cash. In this case, the interest was included in the higher valuation of the goods which served to compensate the delay in repayment. The borrower depended on the profits from the sale in America to provide him with the funds to repay the debt. In general, the *converso* merchants preferred to grant loans rather than sales credit, although some of the wealthiest *conversos* during the first decades of the sixteenth century, such as Diego de Sevilla el mozo (number 15 of the Sevillian composition of 1510), Gonzalo Fernández (number 3), and Manuel Cisbón (number 1), invested heavily in such credit transactions. Rodrigo de Sevilla (number 5) and Francisco de Jerez (number 278) also divided their investment between loans and credits.

Another important part of the *converso* participation in the transatlantic trade was the shipment of goods to America. Some idea of the extent of their enterprise can be obtained from a study of the ships' registers for the fleet of

Libro II, fol. Carece "Indias," 7; García de Sevilla, sea loan, Aguilar (VII), 11 March 1504, Libro único, fol. Tercer tercio del legajo; owner of the *Santa Cruz*, Vallecillo (XV), 11 Sept. 1508, Libro II, fol. Segundo tercio del legajo.

[136] For a discussion of these loans, see Pike, *Enterprise and Adventure*, pp. 48–83.

Diego Columbus in 1509. The names of some of the most
important *converso* merchants in the first decades of the
sixteenth century appear on this list: Alonso de Burgos
(number 180 in the Sevillian composition of 1510), Fernán
Jiménez (number 21), Diego de Rojas (number 168), Fernando de Sevilla (number 16), Gonzalo de Baena (number
375), Pedro de la Palma (number 364), and the previously
mentioned Juan de Córdoba, among others. One vessel
alone, the *Santa María Magdalena*, carried merchandise belonging to seven of these traders. The following shipment
sent on the same vessel by Alonso de Burgos and Diego de
León is typical of the kind of goods that these merchants
shipped to the New World in the early years of the sixteenth century. It included "220 *arrobas* of flour, 380 *arrobas* of white wine, 21 *fanegas* of chick-peas, 13 jars of
olives, 50 *arrobas* of olive oil, 6 *botijas* of honey, 18,500
walnuts, 100 wax candles, 225 embroidered shirts, 97 pairs
of coarse linen breeches, 57 *varas* of wool cloth, 24 trimmed
hats, 40 pairs of cordovan leather shoes, 220 pairs of *al-
pagates* [hempen sandals], 1 ream of paper." [137]

The family was the basis of business organization in sixteenth-century Seville. One of the most typical *converso*
mercantile families in the first half of the century was the
Jorges. The founder of the Jorge firm was Alvaro Jorge, a
silk mercer (number 323 on the Sevillian composition) who
became wealthy from his investments in the transatlantic
trade. His sons Gaspar and Gonzalo were among the most
prominent Sevillian traders at mid-century. They were especially active in the Afro-American slave trade in the

[137] Enrique Otte, "La Flota de Diego Colón—Españoles y Genoveses en el comercio transatlántico de 1509," *Revista de Indias*, 97–
98 (1964), 484.

1540's and 1550's. Not only did they send large numbers of slaves into the colonies, but they also owned several of the vessels that ran slaves between Africa and Vera Cruz, one of the main ports of entry for slaves on the mainland. During the years 1545 to 1551 five ships owned by the Jorge brothers made regular runs between Africa and America. These vessels also carried merchandise in lots up to one hundred *toneladas* belonging to the two brothers.[138]

The Jorges, like the rest of the Seville traders, maintained a network of agents in the New World. Whenever possible, younger family members—sons or nephews—were sent to represent these firms in America. Two sons of Gaspar Jorge, Gonzalo and Juan Rodríguez Jorge, served as family agents in Mexico in the 1540's. When it was necessary to employ someone from outside the family, every effort was made to obtain persons of confidence, that is, of similar origins. A study of the factors used by these traders reveals the tendency of the *conversos* to form business associations within their own group. Their partners and associates both in Seville and the New World all had the same background. Most of the Jorge factors, for example, bore well-known *converso* names like Diego Alemán in Vera Cruz, Andrés de Loya in Mexico City, and Gonzalo Fernández de Loya in Lima.[139] In addition, many of their business associates were related to them through marriage. Four

---

[138] The five ships were: *Nuestra Señora de Guadalupe, Santiago, San Gonzalo, Santa María de Begoña,* and *Santa María de la Luz.* The number of contracts in the Sevillian Protocols involving the Jorges is too large to be listed.

[139] Diego Alemán, APS, Cazalla (XV), 16 Nov. 1549, Libro II, fol. 1166; Gonzalo Hernández de Loya, *ibid.*, 13 Jan. 1550, Libro I, fol. 92; Andrés de Loya, Franco (XV), 21 Nov. 1550, Libro II, fol. 612.

mercantile families closely allied with the Jorges in both
marriage and business were the Segura, Núñez, Jerez, and
Baeza. Gonzalo Jorge was married to a member of the
Segura family and Gaspar to Isabel de Baeza; their sister's
husband was Juan Núñez, an official of the Consulado and
farmer of the customs with Alonso de Illescas in the 1540's
and 1550's. Núñez' sister Inés was married to Fernando de
Jerez who was his partner in many ventures, including the
purchase of two ships, the *Santiago* in 1543 and the *Victoria*
in 1548.[140]

The endogamy practiced by the Jorges and other Sevillian *converso* families may be interpreted as an expression of insecurity. Despite their assimilation and apparent
religious orthodoxy, it seems that they felt threatened by
the general hostility of society and the very existence of an
institution like the Inquisition. Their psychological state
has been appropriately described as a kind of *zozobra* or
permanent tension. One of the best expressions of this psy-
chosis of fear can be found in Mateo Alemán's *Guzmán de
Alfarache* when he relates the tale of the wealthy *converso*
merchant who became just skin and bones because an inquisitor moved next door to him.[141] Nevertheless, regardless of any feelings of insecurity and tension that they may
have had, the Sevillian *converso* merchants cannot be con-

[140] *Santiago, ibid.,* Cazalla (XV), 5 Feb. 1543, Libro I, fol. 359;
La Victoria, 8 Sept. 1548, Libro II, fol. 565; Núñez as *almojarife,*
Franco (XV), 30 June 1550, Libro II, fol. 54; and Consul, Cazalla
(XV), 15 Nov. 1549, Libro II, fol. 1157v. In 1545 Jerez also owned
the *Santa Barbola,* 2 Dec. 1545, Libro II, fol. 1319.

[141] Claudio Guillén, "La disposición temporal del Lazarillo de
Tormes," *Hispanic Review,* XXV (1957), 276; Alemán, *Guzmán
de Alfarache,* p. 567.

sidered marginal men because they were fully incorporated into the life of their city. Having successfully blotted out their "tainted origins" they became part of the power structure that controlled Seville.

Neither their practice of endogamic marriages nor their tight-knit organization could prevent these family firms from dissipating after one or two generations. Economic conditions in Seville were not favorable to the creation of merchant dynasties. The year 1567 saw the failure of the Jorges along with a large group of traders whose combined assets were worth half a million ducats.[142] Risk and speculation governed the Sevillian market, dependent as it was on American bullion. Any delay in the arrival of the silver fleets caused such tightness on the money market that the solvency of the traders was threatened. Moreover, the fiscal policies of the government, such as the confiscation of private capital for royal needs and the repayment of debts in annuities rather than ready cash, deprived the merchants of the fluid capital needed to transact their business.[143] Under these circumstances prolonged commercial enterprise was difficult if not impossible. Even temporary success, on the other hand, brought enormous profits, which explains the willingness of all to keep investing.

Social factors also operated against the continued exis-

[142] Henri Lapeyre, *Une Famille de marchands, Les Ruiz: Contribution à l'étude du commerce entre la France et l'Espagne au temps de Philippe II* (Paris, 1955), p. 483.

[143] For a discussion of the disastrous effects of government fiscal policies, see R. Carande, *Carlos V y sus banqueros* (Madrid, 1943), pp. 156, 208; and C. Haring, *Trade and Navigation between Spain and the Indies in the Time of the Hapsburgs* (Cambridge, Mass., 1918), p. 173.

tence of family firms. In the beginning of the sixteenth century sons traditionally followed their father's calling, including those belonging to the most prosperous business
families. Two good examples are Juan de Herver and Juan
Pérez Cisbón, offspring of two of the most outstanding
converso merchants in the first decades of the century, Juan
de Córdoba and Manuel Cisbón. Both men entered trade
early, served as their fathers' agents in the New World,
and eventually took over the family business.[144] But as the
century advanced and the social prejudice against trade and
toward nobility grew stronger, fewer merchants' sons went
into business, and more began to enter the professions,
church, and government. Nevertheless, the mercantile tradition of these families was not lost, for although their descendants ceased to be merchants by profession, they did not
disengage themselves from trade. They successfully combined their chosen professions with commercial investment.
The third generation of the Jorge family amply illustrates
this point. Of the six male children of the brothers Gonzalo
and Gaspar Jorge, Diego went into the church, Gonzalo
and Juan Rodríguez Jorge were landowners in Mexico, Salvador Jorge de Segura lived off his property in Seville, and
Alvaro and Rodrigo were in the armed forces.[145] None of
these men were professional traders yet all traded, that is,
they invested funds in the transatlantic trade, as the docu-

[144] Juan Pérez Cisbón (no. 1 with his father on the Sevillian
composition of 1510); in the New World, APS, M. Segura (IV),
4 April 1514, Libro II, fol. 141v; Juan de Herver, *ibid.*, Vallecillo
(XV), 26 Feb. 1516, Libro único, fol. 157; Cazalla (XV), 15 Dec.
1526, Libro II, fol. 919.

[145] *Ibid.*, León (XIX), 25 Nov. 1580, Libro VII, fol. 205.

ments preserved in the Sevillian Protocols clearly show. Thus it was that the mercantile vocation of the Jorges continued even though the family firm no longer existed.

In addition to the transatlantic trade, Sevillian businessmen found a profitable outlet for their capital in real estate. The increase of rents under the stimulus of the price revolution and the rise of land values due to the growth in population stimulated a building boom in Seville. There was a frantic scramble among wealthy speculators to buy up available city lots and to erect new buildings. Some like Martín López de Aguilar built entire blocks of houses for speculation, and in their enthusiasm these builders often appropriated public streets and plazas, a practice that was condemned by city authorities in 1556. Some idea of the extent of the Sevillian building boom can be obtained from figures drawn from the censuses of 1561 and 1588 (Table 4). Between 1561 and 1588 approximately 2,456 new houses were constructed in the city.[146] The largest increases were registered in the parishes of Santa Ana (Triana) and San Vicente (900 and 742 new buildings respectively) and it is likely that a good proportion of them were multiple dwellings, that is, tenement-like buildings known as *casas de vecindad*.

Besides building for speculative purposes, businessmen erected new homes for themselves. In the first half of the sixteenth century they transformed the appearance of the

[146] Domínguez Ortiz, *Orto y Ocaso*, pp. 44–45. Figures are lacking for San Telmo and the Compás de San Juan de Arce in 1588, and it is not clear whether or not they were included in any other parish.

city by constructing impressive town houses that stood as
visible signs of their good fortune. Pedro Mexía, in his
Coloquios y Diálogos published in 1547, noted that Seville
was a veritable beehive of construction activity, its streets
and public thoroughfares covered with building mate-

Table 4. Number of houses, 1561 and 1588

Parish	1561	1588
Santa María	1,995	2,292
Santa Ana (Triana)	948	1,848
San Salvador	988	1,085
San Ildefonso	199	209
Santa María la Blanca	84	86
Santa Cruz	199	215
Santa María Magdalena	896	1,000
San Miguel	184	208
San Bartolomé	198	218
San Esteban	168	168
San Pedro	216	200
San Nicolás	175	106
San Juan de la Palma	282	326
San Martín	217	372
San Vicente	793	1,535
San Lorenzo	574	746
Santa Catalina	399	349
San Marcos	223	250
San Andrés	188	222
Santiago	267	130
San Isidro	233	268
San Román	240	292

Omnium Sanctorum	710	854
Santa Marina	195	250
San Julián	163	179
Santa Lucía	193	124
San Gil	342	445
Compás de San Juan de Arce	56	—
San Telmo	196	—
Total	11,521	13,977

Source: AGS, Expedientes de hacienda, leg. 170; González, *Censo de población,* p. 334.

rials.[147] Moreover, these new dwellings with their ornate facades and elaborate gratings reflected a revolution in architectural design. For centuries after the reconquest of their city from the Moslems, Sevillians had continued to follow Moslem building concepts—concentration on the interior parts to the neglect of the exterior—but in the sixteenth century the new opulence of the age called for a conspicuous display of worldly wealth in the outward decoration of homes.

Most rich traders were as concerned about their resting places after death as their style of life in this world. They built magnificent tombs for themselves in endowed chapels in the Cathedral and in the many churches and religious houses throughout the city. The best artists and sculptors were employed to decorate their chapels and tombs. One of the most noteworthy of these tombs was erected in the Church of Santa Cruz by the wealthy *converso* merchant

[147] Pedro Mexía, *Diálogos o Coloquios de Pedro Mexía,* ed. M. Mulroney (Iowa City, Iowa, 1930), pp. 21–22.

Hernando de Jaén. In 1547 Jaén endowed a chapel in that church for the express purpose of "obtaining a final resting place for himself and his descendants." At the same time he commissioned the artist Pedro de Campaña to paint a mural depicting the Descent from the Cross with the proviso that it would include a life-size portrait of the donor kneeling before a crucifix. This remarkable painting has been universally praised; in fact it is said that the great Bartolomé Esteban Murillo so fervently admired it that he repeatedly went to the Church of Santa Cruz to view it.[148]

Finally, and most important, Sevillian merchants spent large sums of money on the maintenance and education of their children. In general, these businessmen did not display their wealth on their own persons and were extremely modest in what they spent on themselves. According to Cervantes in his *Coloquio de los perros*, their impulse for ostentation found an outlet in their sons, "whose fathers spent as much upon them as if these youths were the heirs of some prince—and indeed, they do sometimes procure titles for them and place upon their bosoms the mark that so distinguishes people of importance from the common herd." Since education was looked upon as the first step to an eventual rise in status, every effort was made to send children to the best schools. The merchant's sons in the *Coloquio de los perros* attended the prestigious Jesuit Academy of San Hermenegildo. They went off to school each day with great pomp and circumstance, while their father "went to the Exchange to transact his business attended by no other ser-

[148] Argote de Molina, "Aparato de historia," p. 288; Gestoso, III, 276–277.

vant than a Negro and sometimes mounted on a poorly caparisoned mule." [149]

Such exaggerated attention and indulgent treatment had disastrous results for some of these children. The prodigal son is a frequent theme in the plays and novels set in Seville during this period. Several Golden Age writers mention the so-called *gente de barrio*—idle, good-for-nothing wastrels, young men about town, the sons of the wealthiest residents of the various parishes. They were "worthless, presumptuous, and well-spoken" and like Feliciano in Castillo Solórzano's *Garduña de Sevilla y anzuelo de las bolsas* dissipated their families' newly found fortunes on wine, women, and gambling.[150] One of the best examples of these prodigal sons was the ruffian-poet Alonso Alvarez de Soria, whose father was the rich *converso* merchant and councilman, Luis Alvarez de Soria. Not only was Alonso dissipated and licentious, he was also rebellious, for he openly rejected the values of his class and the society of his day. All of his poems were violent diatribes against the existing establishment, both persons and institutions. So great was his alienation that he sought out the friendship and company of the lowest elements in the city—ruffians and prostitutes—whom he treated with sympathy and understanding in his poetic compositions. A combination of his bitter pen (slanderous insults against the then Asistente of Seville,

[149] Cercantes Saavedra, *El coloquio de los perros*, p. 239.
[150] Alonso de Castillo Solórzano, *La Garduña de Sevilla y anzuelo de las bolsas* (Madrid, 1942), p. 125; Miguel de Cervantes Saavedra, *El celoso extremeño*, in *Novelas ejemplares*, ed. F. Rodríguez Marín, II (Madrid, 1957), 104–107.

Count of Avellaneda) and his association with criminals and undesirables brought him to an early death on the gallows in 1603.[151]

Elegant homes, splendid tombs, quality education for their offspring were all part of a life style cultivated by the Sevillian traders. Although this conspicuous display required large amounts of money, the Sevillian merchants did not seem to find it difficult to maintain themselves on a level that came close to equaling that of the nobility. No wonder contemporaries believed that their wealth was extraordinary. Merchants could be found, according to Morgado, who "could afford to purchase three good villas outside of Seville, provide a dowry of 240,000 ducats for their daughters while at the same time keep their arms free for greater concerns." [152] Morgado may have had in mind the famous Juan Antonio Vicentelo de Leca, whose daughter received a dowry of this size when she married the Count of Gelves and who in 1597 declared in his testament that he was worth 1,600,000 ducats.[153] Nevertheless, a study of testaments and property inventories belonging to the Seville merchants suggests that there was wide variation in wealth and that only a few of them left estates equaling 200,000 to 400,000 ducats. Among those in the upper bracket were Alonso de Espinosa and Juan de la Barrera, both of whom were worth 400,000 ducats at time of death. Lesser businessmen left anywhere from 20,000 to 100,000

[151] The life and deeds of Alonso Alvarez de Soria have been studied by F. Rodríguez Marín, *El Loaysa de El celoso extremeño: Estudio histórico-literario* (Seville, 1901).

[152] Morgado, *Historia*, p. 172. This same example is repeated by Rodrigo Caro, *Antigüedades*, p. 67.

[153] Montoto de Sedas, *Sevilla*, p. 218.

ducats. In general, cash represented only an insignificant part of their estates; most of their money was invested in their business, real estate (both urban property and rural land), *juros*, and personal possessions. The merchant and councilman Luis Alvarez de Soria, for example, left an estate in 1595 of some 23,679 ducats (in *juros* and real estate) in addition to three houses, including the one he lived in, and a "portion of jewels, furniture and clothing." [154]

Merchants' wills and testaments always included substantial donations to religious and charitable institutions. These included the different religious orders, especially the Mercedarians, who devoted themselves to the task of obtaining the redemption of Christian captives held by the Turks and North African pirates, and the various hospitals and asylums that abounded in Seville for the care of orphans, the aged, and the sick poor. Gifts varied in size; one of the largest single contributions came from the estate of Juan de la Barrera—some 200,000 ducats that was divided among several charitable foundations. Other unusually large donations included 50,000 ducats left by Diego de Yaguas for pious works, and 6,000 ducats to the foundling hospital from the estate of Hernando de Luna. The numerous foundations that provided dowries for "poor but honorable" girls were also very popular. Juan de la Barrera alone left funds to provide annual dowries for twenty such needy women. He also established a fund to provide yearly scholarships for seven poor boys to study at the University of Salamanca.[155]

[154] Rodríguez Marín, *El Loaysa*, p. 330. For Alonso de Espinosa, see Lohmann Villena, *Les Espinosa*, p. 38.

[155] Caro, *Antigüedades*, p. 69; Morgado, *Historia*, pp. 319–321.

A good proportion of the *converso* merchants of Seville
during the sixteenth century were *indianos*, men who had
gone to the New World early in the century, made their
fortunes, and returned home to Seville where they continued to invest in the transatlantic trade. In contrast to
the rank-and-file Sevillian merchants, the *indianos* had extensive real estate holdings in America and large investments in such New World industries as sugar production,
mining, herding, and pearl fishing. Two of the most notable
indianos during the first half of the sixteenth century were
Juan Fernández de las Varas and the previously mentioned
Juan de la Barrera. Fernández de las Varas resided on the
island of Hispaniola as early as 1510 where, according to
the chronicler Gonzalo Fernández de Oviedo, he was
among the first settlers to construct a permanent home
made of stone in the city of Santo Domingo.[156] With his
son Alonso he farmed the *almojarifazgo* of Hispaniola and
Puerto Rico during the years 1513 to 1518. He was also
one of the most active Indian slave traders, both in the
Lucayas and the coast of Paria, but despite his wealth and
influence Fernández de las Varas found himself surrounded
by powerful enemies, specifically the treasurer of Hispaniola, Miguel de Pasamonte, who was determined to ruin
him at all cost. Failing everything else, Pasamonte finally
accused his enemy of adultery and denounced him to the
Inquisition. He charged that Fernández de las Varas had
refused to bring his wife from Spain (as he was required
to do in accordance with royal decrees) so that he could

[156] Gonzalo Fernández de Oviedo, *Historia general y natural de
las Indias,* ed. Juan Pérez de Tudela Bueso, CXVII (Madrid, 1959),
78; CPI, I, nos. 523, 2292.

continue to "live in concubinage" on the island. Regardless of this denunciation and a subsequent embargo of his property, Fernández de las Varas, through his friendship with the Inquisitor General, Bishop Alonso Manso of San Juan, was able to return to Seville in 1522 and eventually to obtain a rescinding of the embargo order.[157]

Like Juan Fernández de las Varas, Juan de la Barrera also went to America in the first decade of the sixteenth century; after having enriched himself there, he returned to Seville in the late 1530's and assumed the role of a merchant-capitalist in his native city. During the following years he invested in sea loans and extended credit to needy shopowners and merchants. In the 1540's he was especially active in the shipment of merchandise and slaves to Mexico. By mid-century he was concentrating on the Afro-American slave trade and was part owner of a slaver, the *Santa Catalina*, that made regular trips between Seville, Africa, and Vera Cruz. A freighting contract for the *Santa Catalina*, dated October 29, 1549, mentions 120 slaves, 70 males and 50 females, to be taken on in Africa and sold in the Indies.[158]

Another aspect of the entrepreneurial activity of Juan de la Barrera was his investment in such New World enterprises as cattle raising. The latter was a profitable industry on Hispaniola and Puerto Rico. Oviedo noted that herds of

[157] Giménez Fernández, *Bartolomé de las Casas*, II, 1168; J. Toribio Medina, *La Primitiva Inquisición americana (1493–1569)* (Santiago de Chile, 1914), pp. 10–12; testament of daughter Juana married to Councilman Ruy Pérez de Esquivel, APS, Fernández (IX), 20 June 1523, Libro I, fol. 888v, 894 (inventory of property).

[158] APS, Cazalla (XV), 29 Oct. 1549, Libro II, fol. 1012; *ibid.*, 19 Sept. 1537, fol. 970; 21 Feb. 1548, Libro I, fol. 413.

42,000 head could be found on Hispaniola and that 20,000 head was the average. Hides and sugar made up the chief exports from the Caribbean area during the whole colonial period. As early as 1538, Juan de la Barrera found it necessary to send two herdsmen from Spain to assist his New World employees in watching over his herds in Puerto Rico.[159]

Pearl fishing off the island of Cubagua along the Venezuelan coast also interested Barrera. In 1536 he directed his factors, Francisco de la Reina and Diego Almonte, to purchase one-quarter of a pearl-fishing business in Cubagua from Luis Sánchez, a resident of the island. The investment was indeed profitable, for in 1548 Barrera sold 400,057 maravedís' worth of pearls to a single individual, the treasurer Francisco de Castellanos, councilman of the city of Los Remedios (Río de la Hacha).[160]

Another converso family of *indianos* were the Gibraleóns, who were close associates of Juan de la Barrera and large investors in the Cubaguan pearl-fishing industry. Rodrigo de Gibraleón, a prosperous Sevillian merchant and shipowner, and his son Antonio arrived in Cubagua in the early 1530's. The pearl fisheries were at the height of their production, which meant that capital for investment was eagerly sought and profits were high. Indian slaves, vital to the operation of the enterprise, were scarce and a valuable commodity for trade, whereas the terrain of Cubagua was so dry that it could not be cultivated without intense irrigation, forcing the islanders to depend on imports of

[159] *Ibid.*, 14 Oct. 1538, Libro II, fol. 1129; Oviedo, *Historia*, I, 79.
[160] APS, Portes (X), 28 April 1548, Libro II, fol. 360, cuaderno suelto; *ibid.*, Barrera (I), 30 May 1536, Libro I, Sin folio, Registro núm. 1.

food and other necessities. The Gibraleóns, father and son, were deeply involved in the slave and commodities trade, in addition to their other investments in the pearl-fishing industry.[161]

The boom on the island of Cubagua did not last long, however, for careless and unscientific methods of exploitation soon exhausted the oyster beds. Thus began a gradual depopulation of the island that gained momentum with the discovery of new banks at Cabo de la Vela along the mainland to the west of Cubagua in 1538. Significantly, Rodrigo de Gibraleón was one of the first residents of Cubagua to receive a royal license permitting him to send a ship to Cabo de la Vela to engage in pearl-fishing activities there, but by this time it was quite clear that the period of initial enthusiasm and gain was over. About this time Rodrigo returned to Seville, while his son Antonio took up residence in Nombre de Dios (Panama) as the family agent. The younger Gibraleón remained in Panama until the death of his father in 1550, after which he returned home to assume direction of the business. In 1555 he sent his mestizo son Rodrigo (the product of an illicit union with an Indian woman) to take his place in Panama, an unusual example of the incorporation of a mestizo offspring in a Spanish firm during this period.[162]

Two other active members of the Gibraleón family were

[161] *Ibid.*, Castellanos (V), 7 Nov. 1524, Libro II, fol. 390; *ibid.*, 26 March 1526, fol. 91v; 6 April 1526, fol. 172; 3 Jan. 1528, Libro I, fol. 8; Barrera (I), 29 April 1536, Libro I, fol. Sin foliar, cuad. suelto; E. Otte, ed., *Cedularios de la Monarquía española relativos a la isla de Cubagua, 1523–1550* (Caracas, 1961), II, 49–51, 145, 148, 155.

[162] CPI, III, no. 2824; Otte, *Cedularios*, II, 142; APS, Cazalla (IV), 12 May 1539, Libro I, fol. 881; *ibid.*, Franco (XV), 25 Sept. 1550, Libro II, fol. 277.

Juan and Ruy Díaz de Gibraleón. Both men resided in the
Indies for many years—Juan in Mexico and Ruy Díaz in
Peru. The latter was a partner of Francisco Núñez de Illes-
cas (another member of that famous Illescas family), who
had first operated in Panama and then enriched himself in
Peru. Núñez de Illescas returned home in 1535 leaving Ruy
Díaz de Gibraleón to represent him in Peru. In the mid-
1540's Ruy Díaz returned to Seville where in association
with his partner and other members of the Gibraleón and
Illescas families he purchased and operated ships engaged
in the *carrera de Indias* and sent merchandise and slaves to
Mexico and Peru.[163]

Another close business associate of the Gibraleóns and
the Illescas was Fernán Pérez Jarada, who as early as 1525
received royal permission to ship goods directly from Seville to Cubagua without making the customary stop at Hispaniola and to participate in the slave trade along the Venezuelan coast.[164] Jarada was originally from Toledo and was
among that group of northern merchants—Castilians and
Basques—who migrated to Seville in the last decade of the
fifteenth and first years of the sixteenth centuries to take
advantage of the opening of trading relations with the New
World. Many of the Castilian families were of *converso*
origin, Fernán Pérez Jarada, for example, whose family
name was among those specifically mentioned by Sebastián
Horozco as commonly found among the *conversos* of Toledo. The famous mercantile family of Espinosa (originally

[163] *San Nicolás*, APS, Cazalla (XV), 23 Oct. 1549, Libro II, fol.
962v; *La Trinidad, ibid.*, Franco (XV), 6 March 1551, Libro I, fol.
1126; Cazalla (XV), 20 March 1540, Libro único, fol. 655v. See also
Lockhart, *Spanish Peru*, p. 87.

[164] Otte, *Cedularios*, I, 4; APS, Castellanos (V), 4 July 1525, Libro II, fol. 524v.

from Medina de Ríoseco), who operated one of the most successful banks in Seville and whose members engaged in all aspects of the transatlantic trade, are another example. There was also the Burgos family, who bore the name of their native city; outstanding members included Alonso de Burgos and the brothers Jerónimo and Francisco de Burgos. Alonso participated in the Sevillian composition of 1510 (number 180) and all three men were wealthy and important traders in the first half of the century.[165]

Three other prominent families of Burgos merchants resident in Seville were the Islas, Astudillos, and Medinas, all of whom were probably of *converso* origin. Such a conclusion seems reasonable in view of their tendency to form mercantile and matrimonial alliances with well-known Sevillian *converso* families. The Medinas and Astudillos were business associates of the Jorge family and intermarried with them; Juan Alonso de Medina was the husband of María Jorge de Segura, daughter of Gonzalo Jorge, and Gaspar de Astudillo married one of Gaspar Jorge's daughters. The Islas were closely associated with a whole group of *converso* traders—men like Juan Pérez Cisbón and Pedro de Jerez—and were related through marriage to the Vergaras descendants of Luis de Vergara, old-clothes dealer and overseas trader.[166]

[165] The list of *converso* names mentioned by Licenciado Sebastián Horozco has been published by F. Fita, "La Inquisición Toledana: Relación contemporánea de los autos y autillos que celebró desde el año 1485 hasta el de 1501," *Boletín de la Real Academia de Historia*, XI (1887), 309–310. For the origin of the Burgos family, see Carmen Carlé, "Mercaderes en Castilla (1252–1512)," *Cuadernos de historia de España*, XXI–XXII (1954), p. 288; Otte, "La Flota de Diego Colón," pp. 479–480.

[166] APS, Cívico (VIII), 16 Jan. 1580, Libro I, fol. 978; *ibid.*, Toledo (II), 29 Feb. 1580, Libro I, fol. 292; *ibid.*, Barrera (I), 5 Oct.

The head of the Isla family in the first half of the six-teenth century was Bernardino de Isla, who held a seat on the Seville city council and was particularly active in the shipment of goods to America. He sent several cargoes of twenty to forty *toneladas* each year, often in association with his brother García. He also invested in real estate in the city of Santo Domingo and in the carrying business on the island. At his death in 1520, an inventory of his prop-erty lists "houses in the city of Santo Domingo that were built by the said councilman and his factors and several mule teams." [167]

Councilman Isla's investments in the New World were cared for by two younger family members, his nephew Fernando and his cousin Pedro de Isla. The lives of these two men contrast sharply, but both are indicative of the problems that the Seville traders faced in dealing with their agents in America even when they were members of the same family. When sons and relatives were sent to the New World under partnership agreements (*compañías*) the sit-uation did not change. The distance and the opportunities available in the colonies proved to be, in many instances, overpowering.[168]

This was particularly true in the case of Fernando de Isla, who after 1509 received large shipments from Seville to be sold in the islands. By 1510, however, his relatives and other Sevillian merchants he represented began to sus-

---

1523, Libro I, fol. 978; Segura (IV), 19 Aug. 1513, Libro III, fol. 481; *ibid.*, 7 April 1514, Libro II, fol. 141.

[167] *Ibid.*, 13 Nov. 1520, Libro IV, fol. Registro de Indias; freight-ing contract, Vallecillo (XV), 7 Nov. 1510, Libro II, fol. Segundo tercio del legajo.

[168] Pike, *Enterprise and Adventure*, pp. 68–69.

pect that Fernando was not faithfully carrying out his duties and that he was using the funds he collected for his
own benefit. To cover his fraudulent activities, he simply
stopped sending the records of his transactions back to Seville. For several years members of the Isla family tried to
force Fernando to pay his debts and, when this was not
forthcoming, to show his books to representatives sent from
Spain. During the course of this struggle, Fernando suddenly died. Finally, in 1527, the Isla family sought the aid
of the crown. The king directed the governor of Puerto
Rico (Fernando's last place of residence) "to investigate
the accounts of the deceased Fernando de Isla and order
his executors to pay his debts." [169]

Pedro de Isla's name first appears in the Sevillian Protocols in 1509 when he was serving, along with his relative
Fernando, as a family representative on Hispaniola. In fact,
in 1510 García de Isla (brother of the councilman Bernardino de Isla) ordered Pedro to collect 602,000 maravedís
that Fernando owed him "for merchandise that he sent him
to sell in the Indies." [170] Pedro's activities up to this point
were those of a regular commission agent. Nevertheless,
during the period 1510–1514, his life changed radically. He
apparently underwent a religious conversion, abandoned his
commercial obligations, and began actively to champion the
cause of the mistreated Indians of the Caribbean. His efforts
on behalf of the natives became so pronounced that he at-

[169] APS, Tristán (XVII), 22 Feb. 1527, Libro I, fol. 359; Vallecillo (XV), 29 Jan. 1509, Libro I, fol. Primer tercio del legajo;
ibid., 10 Oct. 1512, fol. Tercer tercio del legajo.
[170] *Ibid.*, Vallecillo (XV), 7 May 1510, Libro I, fol. Segundo
tercio del legajo.

tracted the attention of the future defender of the Indians, Bartolomé de las Casas. According to Las Casas, Isla tried to save the remaining Indians of the Lucaya Islands from extinction by bringing them to Hispaniola and settling them there in a colony. To accomplish this plan, he financed an "expedition of from eight to ten men who spent three years in the Islands," peacefully persuading the Indians to join the colony. The experiment failed not because of the method —peaceful persuasion—but because they could not find enough Indians left to form the projected settlement. Pedro de Isla eventually entered the Franciscan Order, living out the rest of his life in humility, asceticism, and devotion.[171]

One of the most active members of the Medina family during the second and third quarters of the century was Alonso de Medina. Councilman Medina owned the vessel *San Salvador* and was a slave trader in the 1530's and 1540's. Like the rest of the Sevillian business community he made large investments in marine insurance during the years around mid-century. Sea loans had by this time become less frequent as there was no longer an urgent need for cash among the enriched shipowners and merchants. Insurance contracts could be had on easier terms and served to cover the risk. A document of 1551 mentions an insurance policy of 30,000 ducats which Medina and twenty other Sevillian traders placed over a cargo of slaves on the *Santa María de Guadalupe*, lost off the Mexican coast.[172]

[171] Bartolomé de las Casas, *Historia de las Indias*, ed. Agustín Millares Carlo (Mexico City, 1951), II, 353–354. In the years following the discovery of America all of the Lesser Antilles in addition to the Bahamas and Bermuda were called the "islas de los lucayas."

[172] APS, Franco (XV), 19 Feb. 1551, Libro I, fol. 1059v; Cazalla (XV), 16 Sept. 1546, Libro II, fol. 700v.

In contrast to the Castilians, the Basque merchants were fewer and less assimilated. Whereas the Castilians generally intermarried with the Sevillian trading families, and in so doing eventually became indistinguishable from them, the Basques in general continued to marry within their own group.[173] Yet among the Basques were some of the most active mechant-capitalists in the city, any one of whom could have easily served as the inspiration for one of the characters in Lope de Vega's *Premio del bien hablar*—a Basque trader who became wealthy selling iron in America. The Jáureguis (the father and grandfather of the poet Juan de Jáuregui), for example, reputedly made their fortunes in the iron trade.[174] But Basque enterprise went beyond the importation and exportation of iron; most were involved in a broad and diversified range of economic activities. Two examples of prominent Basque businessmen in sixteenth-century Seville were Domingo de Lizarrazas and Pedro de Morga. Both men operated successful banks in the city, shipped merchandise and slaves to the New World, and owned vessels in the *carrera de Indias*. In addition Morga farmed the *almojarifazgo* for several years with Rodrigo de Illescas, who was a partner in his bank along with other members of the Illescas and Sánchez Dalvo families. Lizarrazas, on the other hand, was closely associated with the Genoese merchants of Seville—they guaranteed his bank and were his secret partners.[175]

[173] Exceptions such as those mentioned in Chapter II, and the Jáureguis existed, but were not frequent.

[174] Félix Lope de Vega Carpio, *El premio del bien hablar*, Act I, in *Obras de Lope de Vega Carpio*, ed. Emilio Cotarelo y Mori, XIII (Madrid, 1930), 375.

[175] For information about the Lizarrazas and Morga banks, see Pike, *Enterprise and Adventure*, pp. 92–94.

While the importance of the Basque, Castilian, and Genoese merchant-capitalists in providing the initial capital and entrepreneurship for the creation of the Spanish Empire in the New World cannot be denied, it must be remembered that these three groups always represented a minority within the Sevillian business community and one that became smaller as the century advanced. In the case of the Genoese, who were by far the most outstanding among them, I have pointed out elsewhere that by mid-century they had already begun to move toward a greater involvement in royal finance, which lessened their participation in the transatlantic trade. On the other hand, the Sevillian Protocols inform us that from the beginning of the century a group of native merchant-capitalists of *converso* origin existed, whose operations in the early period, although more numerous than those of the foreigners and non-Sevillian Spanish merchants, were on a much smaller scale. By the 1540's, however, the situation had been reversed. As the role of the Genoese, Basques, and Castilians declined, that of the Sevillians grew until their investments far exceeded those of the others. By mid-century the great shippers of Seville were natives who belonged to powerful merchant dynasties like the Jorges, Illescas, and Sánchez Dalvos, among others. Moreover, the enterprise and continued mercantile vocation of these families seriously challenges the oft-repeated assumptions about the Spanish lack of aptitude for business and the total abandonment of trade by the descendants of wealthy and ennobled merchants for the aristocratic way of life. No wonder that contemporary writers frequently rebuked the Sevillians for their desire to serve Mercury more than Mars. In any event, they can hardly be blamed, for was not the transatlantic trade, in the words of Mercado, "one of the richest that the world had ever seen"? [176]

[176] Mercado, *Tratos y contratos*, p. A2.

III

Working Classes: Artisans and Unskilled Laborers

Workingmen made up the largest part of the population of sixteenth-century Seville, but despite their numbers and economic importance, we know very little about them. Spanish society of this period believed that manual labor was degrading, and workers, confronted by a prosperous nobility whose status was eagerly coveted by wealthy commoners, had visible evidence of this viewpoint. Therefore, craftsmen lost confidence in the dignity of their labor and in work as a means of advancement. They worked because they had no alternative, but they were fully conscious of their inferior position. The aristocratic nature of Spanish society and the ignominious status of the working class come through very clearly in the literature of the period. In the theater of the Golden Age artisans almost never appear, although they probably made up much of the audience, and many of the most famous playwrights originated from this class. When they are mentioned in contemporary novels, it is usually in a disdainful and satirical manner.[1]

[1] Charles Aubrun, *La comedia española, 1600–1680* (Madrid, 1968), pp. 70–71.

In such an aristocratically dominated society, workers remained a submerged majority who expressed discontent by rioting in times of economic distress, but who otherwise lived out their lives anonymously. In a city like Seville, where there were ample opportunities for enrichment through trade, many craftsmen climbed the social ladder. These are the exceptional few whose names have been recorded; the rest are forgotten.

Although we know very little about workingmen as individuals, a great deal of information is available about the organization of Sevillian industry and labor in the sixteenth century. The transatlantic trade made Seville one of the most attractive markets in Europe, but Sevillian industry never produced enough to provision that market. Even the clothing industry, which was the most highly developed, could not meet the demands of both the city and the overseas trade. Moreover, there was great emphasis on the manufacture of luxury goods. Sevillian industry was oriented toward quality production, catering to the lavish demands of the elite—nobility and rich merchants. Among the largest crafts were those of the embroiderers, painters, silversmiths, engravers, and sculptors.[2] This luxury production was organized along guild lines typical of the period. Division of labor was occupational as far as possible, not through transverse division of the process. The guilds insisted that a worker produce a product from beginning to end by himself. Specialization related to final products; one worker produced vests, another hose. Most trades were divided into numerous specialties. There were, for example, four or five kinds of shoemakers, including

[2] Carande, *Carlos V*, p. 253.

clogmakers, pumpmakers, cobblers, and children's shoe-makers. Even the more menial trades had their special divisions, like the shad and prawn specialists among the fishermen.[3]

The continuous subdivision of the crafts led to the creation of some sixty guilds. They ranged from such craftsmen as skinners, basketweavers, and fishermen at the bottom of the hierarchy to silversmiths and pharmacists at the highest levels. In education, skill, and training, the practitioners of the two top trades were closer to the professional class than to other artisans. The difference was clearly not between the mechanical and nonmechanical trades, for the silversmiths were technically manual workers, but they enjoyed more prestige than did pharmacists. Another group of craftsmen who were greatly respected in the Sevillian guild hierarchy were the carpenters. Their favored position can be seen as a reflection of religious beliefs and the origin of their guild as a confraternity dedicated to Saint Joseph.[4]

The guilds were supervised by the city, which had the authority to approve their ordinances and oversee their operations, and by internal officials known as *alcaldes* (magistrates) and *veedores* (inspectors), who were elected annually by the membership. The powers of the guild officials were large and their duties varied; they managed the finances and courts of the organization, made police regulations, visited workshops, imposed penalties and fines, administered the master's oath, and presided at ceremonies

[3] Montoto de Sedas, *Sevilla*, pp. 114, 127–128.
[4] *Ibid.*, p. 119; J. Vicens Vives, *Historia social y económica de España y América*, III (Barcelona, 1957), 124.

and feasts. Elections were by majority vote and usually took place on the feast of Saint John the Baptist.[5] The qualifications of candidates for these positions were carefully scrutinized: the principal requirements were good character, reputation, and skill, and conflict occurred if these criteria were not followed. In 1562, for example, a group of swordmakers sent a petition to the municipal council contesting the election of a certain Martín de Acosta as *veedor* on the grounds that he did not meet the character qualifications for the post because he was "universally known as a dissolute, argumentative and quick tempered man."[6]

Within the guild hierarchy there were three distinct social classes: apprentices, journeymen, and master craftsmen. Documents from the Protocols Archive make it clear that both apprenticeship and journeymen arrangements were much the same in every trade. Apprenticeship contracts covered a period of from four to five years, during which time the master was obliged to teach the apprentice his trade and to feed, clothe, and house him. At the end of the stipulated term the apprentice received a suit of clothing (often they had to be new clothes like those the painter Antonio Pérez gave his apprentice Pedro Rodríguez Palomino), a sum of money such as the 3,000 maravedís that the apprentice embroiderer Francisco Fernández accepted in 1503 instead of a new outfit, or both clothes and money.[7] Most of these Sevillian apprentices came from

[5] Antonio Rumeu de Armas, *Historia de la Previsión social en España* (Madrid, 1944), pp. 188–195.

[6] Gestoso, I, 236.

[7] *Ibid.*, II, 78; III, 28.

the city itself with a small number originating from towns and villages in the surrounding countryside.

Journeymen also contracted their labor with master craftsmen through formal agreements. These contracts ran for periods lasting from a few months to two years, and the obligations on both sides were very explicit. A typical example of a journeyman contract is the one drawn up in 1560 between Cristóbal Rubio, a master embossed leather-maker, and Luis de Torrejón, a journeyman in the same trade. This agreement was valid for eight months; Torrejón was required to emboss twenty pieces of leather a day and in return to receive one *real* for every ten pieces that he finished. If he completed his daily quota, his earnings would amount to two *reales* or 68 maravedís a day, some three to four times the daily sum paid to unskilled laborers at that time.[8] If free room and board were included in these arrangements the journeyman's monetary compensation would be far less. Such was the case in 1528 when the printer Juan Varela de Salamanca hired Nicolás Dibón, a pressman, for two years at a salary of 938 maravedís a month plus food and lodging.[9]

The number of workers in each shop was determined by the volume of business rather than the kind of goods produced. In 1572, Martín de Acosta, a swordmaker, had two journeymen working for him, while Juan de Trujillo, an embroiderer, employed four journeymen and three apprentices.[10] In general, two to four journeymen and two apprentices was the rule in most shops. Masters labored

[8] *Ibid.*, III, 214.
[9] Hazañas y La Rua, *La imprenta*, II, 277.
[10] Gestoso, I, 40, 236.

alongside their workingmen, taking part with their own hands in the more important operations of their craft, but they also played an important role as foremen and trainers. Artisans could increase their productivity by hiring temporary unskilled laborers, many of whom were free Negroes or slaves.

Regardless of the social distinctions among artisans, there existed a sense of community among craftsmen, symbolized by their cooperation in public ceremonies, with their dignitaries clad in brilliant liveries, their banners, and the insignia of their trades. Within this larger community were the single crafts representing spontaneously cohesive groups, whose members met together on regular occasions for brotherly comfort and cheer, to elect the officers of their guild, and to formulate the ordinances for the conduct of their trades. They possessed a spirit of brotherhood and charity, which was embodied in their fraternities, hospitals, and organizations for the help of the sick, widows, and orphans. With their trade as a center, they fabricated their whole lives in cooperation and friendly rivalry with other guilds.[11]

Common interests and objectives promoted artisan solidarity, but governing authorities also encouraged association among craftsmen for purposes of regulation, control, and taxation. After the reconquest of Seville from the Moslems in 1248, King Ferdinand III of Castile decreed that men of the same craft should be settled in specific areas and the streets where they resided should bear their names. As early as the fourteenth century, however, modifications

[11] For a discussion of confraternities and hospitals see Montoto de Sedas, *Sevilla*, Chapter III.

in the original plan began to appear, and although the designated districts (barrios) and streets continued, on the whole, to carry their assigned names, they began to reflect a more diversified population. In the sixteenth century Sevillian craftsmen (with the exception of a few like the skinners who were required by municipal law to confine themselves to a specific area because of the foul odors connected with their work) were scattered all over the city, but members of the same trade still tended to dwell together.[12]

Artisans like most Sevillians rented rather than owned their homes. Most city property was owned by the church and the city government and rented to private individuals on long-term (ninety-nine-year) leases. Rent was minimal, but tenants were required to make all necessary repairs at their own cost, a system that opened the door to serious abuses. Over the years, tenants were forced to undertake all kinds of improvements and repairs so that in many instances they practically remade their homes. Moreover, since a large number of dwellings had been hastily constructed to meet the needs of the city's expanding population, they were defective to begin with and deteriorated within a few years. Some of them had to be rebuilt from the foundations upward. The plight of the engraver Francisco Ortega, who spent 100,000 maravedís to fix up a house for which he only paid 1,000 maravedís rent a year, is typical. Furthermore, it was almost impossible to determine the real value of a building. Some of the problems

[12] Peraza, *Historia*, as quoted in *ibid*., pp. 24, 117; R. Carande, "Sevilla, fortaleza y mercado," *Anuario de historia del derecho español*, II (1925), 292.

involved in drawing up appraisals are discussed by Diego López de Arenas in his *Tratado de carpintería de lo blanco*. According to the author (a successful carpenter and one of the few Sevillian craftsmen to write a manual for his trade), a house that rented for 792 *reales* a year was really not worth more than 2,988 *reales* after deductions were made for maintenance.[13]

The Sevillian building boom encouraged artisans, like other members of the business community, to invest in urban property. A study of wills and property inventories indicates that artisans actively engaged in real estate speculation. Houses and stores were acquired with the objective of subletting them at higher rents for income purposes. It was not unusual for an artisan to own two or three houses besides his own residence; the silversmith Luis de Ribera owned all the houses on one block of the Calle de Vírgenes at the end of the century. Nor was this speculation confined to the more prosperous or to those at the top of the craft hierarchy; it also involved moderately placed craftsmen. A good example is the previously mentioned engraver Ortega, who left three houses and two stores to his heirs in 1575, or the embroiderer Gabriel Carvajal, whose possessions at the time of his marriage in 1523 included three houses.[14]

Rural land provided another investment opportunity in which artisans of different economic levels participated, especially in the first half of the sixteenth century when American demand for oil and wine from the Andalusian countryside caused the market value of land to rise. A

[13] Domínguez Ortiz, *Orto y Ocaso*, pp. 43–44; Gestoso, I, 60, 395.
[14] Gestoso, III, 30; I, 395.

surprising number of artisans held land in the Vega of Triana and the rest of the surrounding countryside during this period, but their holdings were small, often no more than a quarter or half of a parcel of farm land or a portion of a vineyard. The possessions of Diego de Estrada, a saddler, can be considered representative of most artisan holdings during these years. They consisted of part of a small vineyard and half of a piece of cultivated land with a total value of 10,000 maravedís. Often the investment included the funds of two craftsmen, like the vineyard in the Vega of Triana that was acquired by Juan Rodríguez, an armorer, and Diego Sánchez, a quilt maker, in 1548.[15]

Most of the capital that artisans invested in real estate came from savings. Although the returns from their crafts fluctuated with economic conditions, in normal times when their services and products were in demand, there were opportunities to save. One of the most important factors in most crafts was operating costs. Some of them required elaborate equipment; others required costly materials or a combination of both. Furthermore, salaries had to be paid to journeymen, and apprentices had to be maintained. These expenses, plus overhead (rent, taxes, and fees) and living costs all cut into their profits. It is very difficult, given the dearth of documentation, to determine the incomes of artisans as individuals or as a group. Some idea of the amount of business done by a few Sevillian crafts can be obtained from their *alcabala* payments for the years 1554–1555. The *alcabala* was a tax on sales, which was compounded with each guild paying a fixed sum. According-ing to these statistics, the largest volume of business in

[15] *Ibid.*, II, 332, 376.

Seville was done by the cordagemakers, shoemakers, pot-
ters, and leather workers, with the painters and sieve-
makers at the bottom of the list. Few craftsmen earned
more than 1,000 ducats from their trade, and the majority
made far less. The hosiers and the hatters, for example,
two of the largest clothing guilds in Seville, registered a
mere 64,218 ducats' and 22,940 ducats' worth of business,
respectively, during this two-year period.[16]

Wills and property inventories bear out the *alcabala*
figures. Even those at the pinnacle of the craft hierarchy
left little cash and few possessions of real value. One of the
few exceptions was the silversmith Alonso de Medinilla,
whose fortune in 1618 totaled 11,850 ducats, but most of
it was inherited wealth obtained through trade and speculation. More representative was the silversmith Miguel de
Monegro, who served as prior of his guild and was one of
the best-known members of his craft during the last quarter
of the sixteenth century. At his death in 1572 his heirs
inherited some 82,477 maravedís (around 220 ducats, all in
juros), several houses, and two female slaves. Even the
enterprising silversmith Juan de Oñate, who was so active
in the transatlantic trade during the first part of the century, left an estate consisting of 541,420 maravedís in

[16] BNM, MS. 3449, folios 184–188. These statistics should be
viewed with caution since the guilds probably reported lesser figures so as to reduce their tax. This document has also been published by Domínguez Ortiz, *Orto y Ocaso*, pp. 103–105. A similar
account is in the manuscript "Censo estadístico y tributario de
España desde 1550 a 1556," folios 18–19v, in the Escorial Library
(Biblioteca de El Escorial). I was able to use the copy made by
Señor Ramón Paz through the courtesy of the Instituto Juan Sebastián Elcano in Madrid.

credits (1,444 ducats), but debts of 675,000 maravedís (1,800 ducats), no real estate besides the house he lived in, and the tools of his trade described as "very old and well used." [17]

The contributions of artisans to charity also reflect their limited means. Even the prosperous Alonso de Medinilla only left 156 ducats for charitable purposes: 56 ducats to be divided evenly among four religious orders and 100 ducats to the Confraternity of San Eloy to help defray the costs of a statue of Saint Eligio, patron of the silversmiths. Among their favorite charities were the Mercedarian and Trinitarian Orders, who ransomed Christian captives from the Turks and North African pirates, and the leper hospital of San Lázaro in Seville. The donations of the sculptor Pedro Millán are typical: 10 maravedís to the Church of San Esteban which contained his tomb, 5 to the Santa Cruzada, 5 to the Trinitarians and Mercedarians for the redemption of captives, 2 to the Hospital of San Lázaro, and 6 for the completion of the Seville Cathedral, a total of 28 maravedís.[18]

Some of the capital that artisans invested in real estate was apparently drawn from dowries. Two houses and a store belonging to the sculptor Millán were obtained with the dowry of 27,000 maravedís brought to him by his first wife. The same was true for the embroiderer Nicolás Martínez, who invested his wife's dowry of 30,000 maravedís in their residence and other properties. Marriages were contracted with an eye to obtaining as large a dowry as possible and were considered an important part of an ar-

[17] Gestoso, III, 171–172, 255–256, 431–432.
[18] Ibid., p. 225.

tisan's wealth. There was wide variation, but in general dowries ranged from 20,000 to 80,000 maravedís. Dowries above 80,000 maravedís occurred infrequently and among the daughters of artisans at the top of the craft social scale, the majority of whom had augmented their fortunes through investment in trade or whose talent had brought them prominence, such as painters and sculptors. A good example is the famous painter Pedro de Campaña, who gave his daughter Catalina a dowry worth 108,870 maravedís (75,000 in cash and the rest in household furnishings). On the other end of the scale, anything under 20,000 maravedís was equivalent to poverty status and on the same level as the dowries that were distributed yearly among orphans and poor girls by several Sevillian charitable organizations (usually between 15,000 and 18,700 maravedís). Servants traditionally received 10,000 maravedís, as did Constanza de Ribera, a maid in the house of the noble Ribera family, upon her marriage to Diego Fernández, a swordmaker, in 1501.[19]

Artisans as a group were active participants in the transatlantic trade. As has been pointed out, many of the early Sevillian merchants were originally artisans who combined commercial activities with their craft. Some of them eventually gave up artisanry and became full-time traders, but a larger number continued to labor at their crafts while augmenting their income through trade. Those at the top of the craft hierarchy (silversmiths, printers, pharmacists) invested in sea loans, gave sales credit, and shipped slaves

[19] *Ibid.*, pp. 50, 163, 283. For information about dowries distributed by charitable organizations, see Morgado, *Historia*, pp. 377–379.

and merchandise to the New World; their enterprise differed little from that of professional merchants. An especially lucrative business for Sevillian pharmacists was the sale of established European drugs and medicines in America. One of the most active pharmacists in this trade in the first half of the century was Juan Bernal, who was closely associated both in trade and professionally with the prestigious Sevillian physician Dr. Alvarez Chanca. Together they shipped medicinal products to their representative in Santo Domingo, Ordoño Ordóñez, also a pharmacist.[20]

In contrast to the well-rounded entrepreneurial activities of the upper echelons of artisanry, the participation of average craftsmen was primarily commercial, that is, shipment of small quantities of merchandise to the New World, often in association with other artisans. Very few craftsmen had the funds to sustain continuous or large-scale enterprise; their investments tended to be occasional. Shipments consisted of inexpensive staple goods, such as the 102 *varas* of coarse frieze that Miguel Martínez, a tanner, sent to Santo Domingo in 1536 and the 29 *arrobas* of honey, 1 quintal of soap, 7 quintals of wax, and 11 *arrobas* of olive oil bound for the New World in 1508 in the name of Salvador Martín, a candlemaker.[21] Participation in the

[20] APS, M. Segura (IV), 6 Oct. 1513, Libro IV, fol. Carece "Indias, 2." Dr. Diego Alvarez Chanca accompanied Columbus on the second voyage as the fleet's physician. His account of the trip is in M. Fernández de Navarrete, *Vida y Obras de Martín Fernández de Navarrete*, in *Biblioteca de Autores Españoles*, LXXV (Madrid, 1954), 183–196.

[21] APS, Becerra (IV), 2 March 1536, Fragmento de un libro, fol. Tercer tercio del legajo; *ibid.*, Vallecillo (XV), 18 Oct. 1508, Libro II, fol. Segundo tercio del legajo.

transatlantic trade was confined to certain kinds of craftsmen. Most of the artisans whose names appear in the documents were shoemakers, clothiers, and leather workers, all of whom belonged to the most prosperous crafts in the city. Members of the building trades (carpenters, masons), for example, are almost never found, and painters, sculptors, and workers in ferrous metals occur infrequently.

Many of the artisans who were most active in the transatlantic trade were of *converso* descent. We can never determine the exact proportion of Sevillian artisans with this background, but they were widely represented in most crafts and in some, such as the silversmiths, clothiers, and pharmacists, they made up a majority. In general they predominated in the trades that required more skill and education, and few were in the heavier and more manual crafts. Some sixty-one different trades and professions are mentioned in the Sevillian composition of 1510, but with few exceptions they are the more skilled and less menial occupations. None of the 390 individuals included in this list, for example, was employed in the construction industry, an important but strenuous and low-paid craft.[22]

The *conversos* were most numerous in the clothing trades. As tailors, hosiers, and doublet makers they belonged to one of the largest industries in Seville. Their guild, the Confraternity of San Mateo, was among the wealthiest in the city, and the brothers enjoyed many privileges, not least of which was a preferred place in the Corpus Christi celebrations. The clothiers were active guildsmen—they met regularly for social, religious, and business purposes and maintained two hospitals and a chapel in the prestigious

[22] Guillén, "Un Padrón de conversos," pp. 89–98.

Monastery of San Francisco. The members of the Confraternity of San Mateo were also among the most conspicuous participants in the many receptions and processions that were a part of the ceremonial life of the city. In 1579, for example, two hundred guild members (mainly tailors) took part in the procession accompanying the remains of King Ferdinand III of Castile that were being transferred from their traditional place in the Cathedral to a new location in a chapel built expressly for that purpose. All were lavishly dressed in gold-trimmed velvet breeches with matching hats. These outfits reputedly cost the brothers from 200 to 300 ducats apiece, but given the economic position of the guild, these expenses were not considered exorbitant.[23]

A representative member of the clothiers' guild during the first half of the sixteenth century was Hernando Morcillo, grandfather of the famous Sevillian humanist Sebastián Fox Morcillo.[24] The Morcillos were a large family of *converso* artisans, five of whom, including Hernando, appeared as residents of the Calle de Génova in the district of Santa María in the census of 1534. Like other New

[23] Francisco de Sigüenza, *Traslación de la imagen de Nuestra Señora de los Reyes y cuerpos reales a la real capilla de la Santa Iglesia de Sevilla*, p. 14v, as quoted in Montoto de Sedas, *Sevilla*, pp. 132–133.

[24] Sebastián Fox Morcillo was born in Seville between 1526 and 1528. Around 1548 he studied at Louvain and published commentaries on Plato and Aristotle, in which he endeavored to reconcile their teachings. His numerous works on philosophy and style brought him wide acclaim, and in 1559 he was appointed tutor to Don Carlos, son of Philip II. He did not live to assume his post, however, for he was lost at sea on his way to Spain in 1560. The following discussion is based on R. Pike, "The *Converso* Origin of Sebastián Fox Morcillo," *Hispania*, LI (Dec. 1968), 877–882.

Christians, Hernando, a hosier by trade, participated in the Sevillian composition of 1510 (number 221 on the list), along with another family member, Alvaro Morcillo, a silversmith (number 91). Hernando Morcillo and his wife Isabel de Carmona were the parents of several children whose names appear frequently in Sevillian documents. Among them were Gonzalo, married to Leonor de Burgos, who followed the trade of his father, and Juan, also a hosier. A third brother, Francisco, was a silversmith, which meant that he occupied a higher social position than his father and brothers.[25]

Besides engaging in their respective crafts, the Morcillos, like other well-to-do artisans and businessmen, took advantage of the opening of commercial relations between Spain and the New World to increase their fortunes. They granted loans in the form of money and credit to needy persons departing for the Indies. In addition, both Juan and Gonzalo traveled to the New World to sell merchandise there. The first of these undertakings, a joint enterprise, occurred in 1513. Several years later Juan crossed the ocean again, leaving Gonzalo in charge of all his affairs in Seville. Whether or not Juan remained in the New World or returned to Spain is not known since no further trace of his career can be found among the Sevillian documents. We can assume that Gonzalo continued to interest himself in the transatlantic trade, for in 1534 his son Alonso went to the New World to take care of his father's business there.[26]

[25] AMS, Varios Antiguos, carpeta 125, p. 46; Gestoso, II, 261, 430.
[26] APS, J. R. Porras (III), 20 March 1515, Libro I, fol. 4360; *ibid.*, Aguilera (VII), 22 Aug. 1520, Libro II, fol. 27 del cuaderno 12; CPI, I, nos. 1162, 4040.

Like his two brothers, Francisco Morcillo also invested
in the transatlantic trade, but he preferred to devote most
of his time to his craft. In 1541, for example, he fashioned
several elaborate silver ornaments for the Cathedral. During this same period he played an active role in the organization of the Confraternity of San Eligio, the silversmiths'
guild. He signed a document containing the original statutes for the guild in 1554. Three years later he participated
in a guild lawsuit against the city government.[27]

Silversmith Morcillo and his wife Violante de Fox were
apparently the parents of Sebastián Fox Morcillo and his
brother Fray Francisco Fox Morcillo. Sebastián was probably born to the couple while they were still living in
Gradas, the business district of Seville located in the Santa
María quarter. The family apparently moved frequently.
In 1534 they are listed as residents of San Ildefonso Parish;
five years later they were again living in a rented house in
Gradas. Both Sebastián and Francisco received excellent
primary and secondary school training in their native city.
They studied Greek and Latin under the renowned classi-
cist Fray Alonso de Medina, whom Sebastián later ac-
knowledged as one of his most important teachers.[28] As we
have seen, it was not unusual in sixteenth-century Seville
for prosperous merchant and artisan families like the Morcillos to spend considerable sums of money on the educa-

[27] Gestoso, I, 261.
[28] S. Fox Morcillo, *De philosophici studii ratione,* as quoted in
U. González de la Calle, *Sebastián Fox Morcillo* (Madrid, 1903),
p. 17; Gestoso, II, 261. Regarding Alonso de Medina, see Justino
Matute y Gaviria, *Hijos de Sevilla señalados en santidad, letras,
armas, artes o dignidad* (Seville, 1886), I, 125.

tion of their offspring since a good education was a means to social and economic advancement.

While the Sevillian documents give us some information about Fox Morcillo's paternal line, we know almost nothing about his mother's family. Undoubtedly they were also New Christian artisans, but compared with his father's family were relative newcomers to Seville. There is probably some truth to Fox Morcillo's own account of the migration of his family from Catalonia to Seville during the reign of the Catholic kings. In 1487 King Ferdinand introduced the Inquisition into Aragon, Catalonia, and Valencia, and as a result many *conversos* left the country or moved to other parts of Spain. The family of Violante de Fox may have fled to Seville at that time. The only reference to the Fox name in Seville in the sixteenth century is a Foz or Fox, a painter who appeared as a witness at the marriage of a fellow artist, apparently also a *converso*, in 1582.[29]

The Fox family was closely related to the Abregos, also *conversos*. Luisa, a sister of Violante de Fox, was married to the silversmith Antonio de Abrego, a friend and colleague of her sister's husband. Antonio's brother Luis was a scribe, who in 1546 was commissioned by the Cathedral clergy to copy an illuminated choir book for them. He received 1,500 maravedís on account, the rest to be paid on completion of the work.[30] In fact, the Abregos, as scribes, silversmiths, and merchants in sixteenth-century Seville, practiced all the favorite professions of the New Christians.

[29] Gestoso, II, 65; Lea, *History of the Inquisition*, I, 183.

[30] Gestoso, I, 207; II, 127. Luis de Abrego perished in the *auto* of 1559 as a Lutheran along with his relative Fray Francisco Fox Morcillo (BM, Add. 21.447).

The large number of *conversos* among the artisan class, especially in the upper ranks, was one of the reasons for the failure of the Comunero revolt in Seville. Since Figueroa and his followers were against the *conversos*, they alienated the artisans (as they had the nobles and merchants), whose support was essential for a successful revolt. It is significant that the only artisans who rallied to Figueroa's cause belonged to the lower crafts, specifically those with the least number of *conversos*. One of these men, Francisco López, a cheese maker, was eventually tried and condemned to death as a traitor for his participation in the revolt. He took part in the seizure of the Alcázar under the orders of Figueroa and, once taken, it was alleged that with sword in hand and in the presence of a large multitude, he raised the cry: "Long live the King and the *Comunidad*." It was further charged that he personally seized the *vara* (symbol of office) from the chief magistrate of Seville and throughout the revolt made strenuous but unsuccessful efforts to stimulate the masses to rise up in support of Figueroa and his cause.[31]

All Sevillian artisans, *conversos* or not, were vulnerable to periods of economic depression when their services were in little demand and their incomes correspondingly low. Agricultural conditions were a determining factor, for crop failures could produce disastrous food shortages in the cities. Although the Andalusian countryside was one of the most fertile agricultural areas in Spain, comparatively little grain was grown, and drought, floods, and locusts were common occurrences. There was hardly a year in

[31] BNM, MS, 3449 = K-165, "Sevilla: Varias noticias y documentos," fol. 171; Giménez Fernández, *Bartolomé de las Casas*, II, 970.

which there was not a serious shortage of wheat in Seville, caused either by these natural phenomena or by the manipulations of speculators, who often included members of the city council. The situation was made more critical by the city's demographic increase during the course of the sixteenth century. Higher food prices affected the artisans as consumers—they had to spend more of their income on basic necessities; higher prices also led to a general curtailment of their production, since all elements of the population reduced their expenditures. Under these conditions artisans often expressed their discontent by rioting, which drew attention to their grievances and brought about some immediate redress. The threat of rioting kept city officials ready to control prices and to distribute wheat and foodstuffs in times of acute scarcity. By the establishment of a public granary in 1505 the municipality hoped to meet the frequent subsistence crises that caused rioting.[32]

One of the most famous of these mass uprisings, known popularly as "la Feria y Pendón Verde" occurred in 1521 and was brought on by a combination of food shortages (wheat was selling at 700 maravedís a *fanega* as compared to 70 maravedís the year before) and unsettled conditions resulting from Juan de Figueroa's Comunero revolt. Driven into the street by hunger, the residents of the impoverished Feria district (parish of Omnium Sanctorum), with those of San Gil and San Martín, seized a quantity of arms from the palace of the Duke of Medina Sidonia and, taking as their standard a green Moorish banner that had been preserved in the parish church of Omnium Sanctorum, ran riot through the city attacking the homes of the rich and open-

[32] Ortiz de Zúñiga, *Anales*, III, 206.

ing the jails. After three days of continuous violence and disorder, they were put down by the armed nobility.[33]

Since journeymen and members of the lower crafts were most severely affected by fluctuations in prices and by food shortages, it is not surprising that they usually formed the leadership and the nucleus of any movement of mass protest. Unskilled laborers also joined the rioters as well as criminal elements out for loot, but these groups, oppressed by intense poverty and the hopelessness of their position, were incapable of starting or sustaining a riot. They merely followed the leadership of the artisans, whose collective power helped to keep a corrupt and ineffective municipal government responsive to their immediate needs.[34]

Although vital to the city's economy, the unskilled laboring population was isolated, disorganized, and largely ignored by other urban classes. Without resources, organization, or sense of purpose in society, they eked out a miserable day-to-day existence. In Seville the position of the Old Christian laborers was especially difficult because of competition from other depressed elements at the bottom of the social scale—slaves, freedmen, and Moriscos—who virtually monopolized the limited number of unskilled jobs. Moreover, the steady flow of migrants from the countryside into town during the course of the sixteenth century flooded the labor market and caused chronic unemployment. The streets of the city were soon overrun with

[33] *Ibid.*, pp. 325–326; BNM, MS. 3449 = K-165, "Feria y Pendón Verde en Sevilla," fol. 172.

[34] Artisans also played a dominant role in the two seventeenth-century revolts of 1623 and 1652; these uprisings also were centered in the Feria district.

beggars, vagabonds, and unemployed who wandered from
one monastery to another in search of food. Begging, thiev-
ing, and prostitution became their only means of liveli-
hood.[35]

Both trade and industry employed unskilled workers in
the lesser capacities. They did hauling and digging in construction work and carried goods within the city. They
worked as stevedores on the docks and porters in the public
granary and market places. They also did odd jobs around
the city—mainly in the slaughterhouse and port area.
Wages were low—just enough to meet their basic needs—
and work was temporary, usually on a daily or seasonal
basis, especially in the construction industry. Low pay and
frequent unemployment kept workers at subsistence level
and dependent on charity. Furthermore, guild regulations
effectively prevented them from rising higher than unskilled, low-paid jobs. The expense of going through a
period of apprenticeship and of fulfilling the requirements
related to entrance into the guilds was beyond the means
of the unskilled laboring population. As a result, they remained trapped in a vicious cycle of infrequent, low-paid
employment, poverty, and destitution.

Outside of the construction trades only one other Sevillian industry employed substantial numbers of unskilled
workers—the soap industry. Since the Moslem period, the
abundance of oil had fostered the development of soap
manufacturing in Seville, and in the sixteenth century it
was an important export item. There were two factories in
operation during this period, one in the San Salvador parish
and the other in Triana. The Triana factory, owned by the

[35] These groups are discussed in Chapter IV.

Dukes of Alcalá, was leased for periods of ten years at
20,000 ducats a year, but this did not include the cost of
materials and the slaves and other workers necessary for
production.[36]

Personal service also absorbed a portion of the unskilled
laboring class, although there were fewer opportunities for
this kind of work in Seville due to the existence of so many
slaves. Although servants (especially lackeys) could be
hired for short periods of time (by the day, week, or
month), most of them were employed on a more permanent
basis. The relations between masters and servants were
determined by formal contract agreements. Servants
pledged themselves to be continuously at the command of
their masters and to carry out all orders, provided that
they were "licit and honest." In return they received
free room and board and some kind of monetary compensation.[37] Generally the conditions provided were meager
and salaries low, but service in a noble household, even if it
meant being underpaid and poorly fed, was preferable to
no employment at all. Besides it offered security—a steady
job and care in times of sickness and old age—and a sense
of personal importance. Servants of the wealthy and noble
shared in the prestige of their employers, for some of the
luster of the master inevitably rubbed off on the servant.
In Castillo Solórzano's *Bachiller Trapaza*, for example, the
servants of the *pícaro* Trapaza deserted him when they
discovered that he was not the nobleman don Fernando de

[36] Morgado, *Historia*, p. 156.
[37] Domínguez Ortiz, *La sociedad española*, pp. 277–279; J. Beneyto, *Historia social de España y de Hispanoamérica* (Madrid,
1961), p. 226.

Quiñones that he claimed to be, for "they were ashamed at having served someone who was lower than themselves." [38] Finally, contemporary opinion held that, in contrast to trade and the crafts, personal service was honorable, since it was often performed by people of noble rank. Many impoverished *hidalgos* served in the households of wealthier and more important lords, but despite their lineage, their position and duties were not very different from those of other servants.

For those not absorbed in industry, trade, or domestic service, there was nothing left to do but peddle flowers, fruits, and like goods on the streets and in the public markets. If this should fail, begging or crime were all that remained. Many unskilled workers lived by doing occasional labor and the rest of the time by begging and thievery which seemed to go hand in hand.

Although the poverty and misery of the Old Christian laborers was acute, there were other groups in Seville whose position was even more desperate. Moriscos, slaves, and freedmen suffered the same economic hardships as the Old Christians, but were also subjected to prejudice and discrimination that made them veritable outcasts, especially the Moriscos because of their unassimilable character. They were above all the most depressed elements in Sevillian society.

[38] A. de Castillo Solórzano, *Aventuras del Bachiller Trapaza* (Madrid, 1944), p. 33.

IV

Social Outcasts and
Unassimilated Classes

MORISCOS

The foundations for the Morisco community of Seville were laid at the opening of the sixteenth century. Between 1502 and 1505 the Sevillian Moslems (*Mudéjares*) were converted, their mosque turned into a Christian church, and their ancient *morería* disbanded. In the Middle Ages these native Moslems had been confined to their own walled quarter known as the Adarvejo, located in the southeastern portion of the city.[1] In 1483 the city fathers, anxious to open more land in a central part of town and to make the Moslems less conspicuous, moved them to the outlying parish of San Marcos. But the old Adarvejo continued to exist, and so there were in effect two *morerías* in Seville during the last years of the fifteenth century. The new converts, known as Moriscos, were free to live in any area of the city, but the two former *morerías*, especially San Marcos, continued to attract them throughout the century.

While these native Moriscos formed the nucleus of the Morisco community of Seville, in the second half of the sixteenth century they were far outnumbered by refu-

[1] For a description of the Adarvejo, see C. López Martínez, *Mudéjares y Moriscos sevillanos* (Seville, 1935), p. 12.

gees from Granada. The unsuccessful Alpujarras Rebellion (1568–1570) resulted in the dispersal of the Granadine Moriscos throughout Castile, with New Castile, La Mancha, and Andalusia receiving large numbers. Within these areas the Moriscos gravitated toward the towns where there were greater opportunities for work and anonymity. Seville with its large population and highly transient society served as a natural magnet to them. The 1570's and 1580's saw a steady influx of Granadine Moriscos into the city where by the last years of the century they became the dominant Morisco element.

Sources for a study of the Moriscos in Seville are relatively few, and they tend to be hostilely prejudiced. Fortunately, our knowledge of this important urban minority has been increased by the discovery in the Sevillian Municipal Archives of a census of Granadine Moriscos that apparently escaped the attention of past historians and was not utilized up to this time.[2] This account was compiled in 1580 after the abortive Morisco conspiracy of that year and was part of a larger effort by Sevillian authorities to place the Moriscos under stricter controls. Although much of this document has been lost, figures for five parishes are complete. Regardless of its fragmentary character, it provides valuable information about the Moriscos of Seville in the last quarter of the sixteenth century.

The extant parts of the census of 1580 contain the names, ages, marital status, and physical descriptions of all Grana-

[2] AMS, Varios Antiguos, no. 334, "Padrón de los Moriscos del Reino de Granada que residen en esta ciudad de Sevilla." C. Guillén noted the existence of this document in his "Padrón de conversos," pp. 49–89, but he did not use it.

dine Moriscos residing in the parishes of San Ildefonso, San
Pedro, San Marcos, San Andrés, and San Gil. This information was obtained by means of a street-by-street, house-
by-house count in a door-to-door canvass of households by
specially appointed officials under the supervision of the
common councilmen of each parish. Most of the census
takers carefully listed all the required data, but some were
careless. In San Ildefonso, for example, the ages of women
and children were often omitted, and several people were
listed twice, although they were only counted once. Official totals are given for San Gil, San Andrés, and San Ildefonso. Statistics for San Marcos have been deduced by a
direct count, but the deteriorated character of the document regarding San Pedro makes it impossible to obtain
more than approximate figures.

There were, then, according to the census of 1580, some
812 Moriscos in the five parishes under study, out of a total
Morisco population of over six thousand.[3] Only a small
percentage of this number were slaves, for the overwhelming majority of Sevillian Moriscos were free. In general,
females outnumbered males, but when the slave and free
Moriscos are considered as separate groups, the pattern
changes. Among the free Moriscos, males had a slight edge
on females, while the reverse was true for slaves. The
typical free Morisco was a male between the ages of twenty
and forty, and the majority, male and female, were over
twenty and under sixty years of age. There were more
males than females in the forty-to-sixty age group, and
many of them were married to females between the ages

[3] Figures for the total Morisco population of Seville in 1580 are
an estimate based on those given by Lapeyre for 1589. See H. Lapeyre, *La Géographie de l'Espagne morisque* (Paris, 1959), p. 135.

of twenty and forty. Married people predominate. The few single individuals were usually male and under twenty-five years of age. Widowers were rare (only two are mentioned), but widows with small children were common.

Most striking is the large proportion of children under five years of age, in contrast to the smaller number of older children and young adults. Crude birth rates in this period were high, but life expectancy at birth was very low. The same is true at the other end of the scale; there were few people over sixty years of age and only one mention of a really old person—a man of ninety years. Among a group that lived at subsistence level like the Moriscos, disease and malnutrition wiped out substantial numbers each year, especially the old and the young. In times of plague the demographic losses must have been disastrous so that without a high birth rate the Moriscos could not have survived. But it does not appear that they were any more prolific than the rest of the population, although contemporary opinion held this to be true.[4] The census of 1580 gives an average of two children per Morisco family, and in some parishes where there were numerous slaves it was lower. There were only 18 families out of a total of 121 in the four parishes of San Ildefonso, San Andrés, San Marcos, and San Gil who had three children and just 5 with four children. There was not one example of a family with more than four children.[5]

[4] In 1590, for example, the Council of State seriously considered a plan to force all able-bodied Moriscos to serve a period of paid service in the galleys so as to reduce their prolificness (Braudel, *La Méditerranée*, p. 128).

[5] After studying a census of Segovian Moriscos of 1594, C. and J.-P. Le Flem concluded that the average Morisco family consisted of four persons. In Segovia there were 2.04 children per family,

Clearly the difference between the Moriscos and the
Old Christians was not in the number of children born to
either group, but rather in the career orientation of their
offspring. In Old Christian families a substantial number of
the surviving children remained celibate; they entered the
church or remained single for lack of a dowry or some
other reason. Some emigrated to the New World and others
served in the armed forces, where they lost their lives early.
The Moriscos did not go into the army or the church. The
majority married at a young age, so that in the long run
they had a demographic advantage over the Old Christians.[6]

The living habits of the Moriscos also contributed to the
widely held contention that they bred more rapidly than
others. In Seville most Moriscos lived in substandard hous-
ing—tenement-like dwellings (*casas de vecindad*) and
rooming houses located in the *corrales* (back yards) scattered throughout the poorer sections of the city. Crowded
conditions typical of ghetto existence prevailed, with many
people living together in narrow and inhospitable quarters.
In the parishes of San Gil and San Marcos an average of
from 15 to 20 Moriscos lived in a single dwelling. One

2 in Salamanca, 1.99 in Valladolid, and 1.77 in Avila (Claude and
Jean-Paul Le Flem, "Un censo de Moriscos en Segovia en 1594,"
Estudios Segovianos, XVI [1964], 437).

[6] In 1588 a Sevillian official, Alonso Gutiérrez, had a clear understanding of the problem: "Ansí considerando que como no ay saca
de esta gente tienen en grandísima multiplicación lo qual es en los
cristianos viejos por la ordinaria que hay de ellos para Ytalia,
Flandes, Yndias y jornadas hordinaria" (A. Gutiérrez, "Informe
acerca de la cuestión morisca," 6 de septiembre de 1588, as quoted
in P. Bornat y Barrachina, *Los moriscos españoles y su expulsión*
[Valencia, 1901], p. 634).

house on the Calle de Parras in San Gil contained 20 people, 9 of whom were children. Since 8 of these children were under five years of age, it is not surprising that popular opinion, sharpened by economic rivalry and intolerance, held that the Moriscos multiplied faster than the rest of the population.

Group solidarity among the Moriscos was very strong, as shown by their communal living patterns and their practice of endogamic marriages. There are only three instances of mixed marriage in the census of 1580, and in each case the man was an Old Christian and the wife a Morisco, an arrangement that seems to have been more frequent than the reverse.[7] Two of these couples lived in the same house in the parish of San Gil, and both men bore the same name, indicating a family relationship. All three couples were in the twenty-to-thirty age group and lived in dwellings occupied by several other Morisco families. The refusal of the Moriscos to marry outside their numbers was one of the sources of contention between them and the Old Christians. It was alleged that they used intermarriage to preserve Moslem rites and practices and to prevent any real religious assimilation. This opinion appears in most of the official documents of the period, and available evidence seems to verify it.[8]

[7] C. and J.-P. Le Flem found a similar situation in Segovia where out of a total Morisco population of 1,049 there were only 11 Old Christian men married to Morisco women, and 4 Old Christian women married to Morisco men (Le Flem, "Moriscos en Segovia," p. 439). See also A. Domínguez Ortiz, "Notas para una sociología de los Moriscos españoles," *Miscelánea de estudios árabes y hebráicos* (1962), pp. 39–54.

[8] It is a constant theme in the reports of the common councilmen (*jurados*) (AMS, Varios Antiguos, Moriscos). A. Gutiérrez

The majority of the Moriscos in Seville were poor and unskilled; the popular stereotype of the "rich and avaricious Morisco" has little basis in reality.[9] Some of them were employed as domestic servants; others worked in the *huertas* (orchards) and *hornos* (baking establishments) in and around the city, where they performed unskilled and semiskilled tasks. Gardening was one of their favorite occupations, and there are frequent references to "Morisco gardeners" in the literature of the period. In the *hornos* they kneaded the bread and mixed the ingredients, and there is also indication that some did the actual baking. The vast majority of Moriscos earned their living as stevedores, carriers, and occasional farm laborers.[10] In the parish of San Gil, for example, quite a few young men were engaged in seasonal agricultural labor—carting and reaping in the surrounding countryside—and in temporary construction projects.

There were also Morisco *tenderos* (small retail tradesmen) who peddled food products such as bread, oil, fruits, and vegetables through the city streets or set up temporary stands in the market places of the outlying parishes. Other typical Morisco businessmen were the *buñoleros* (fritter

also held this opinion (as quoted in Bornat y Barrachina, *Los moriscos españoles*, p. 635).

[9] "Estos moriscos poseen grandes riqueças, aunque no lo muestran exteriormente por ser como son generalmente mezquinos, y el real que una vez entra en su poder no saven trocarle." (Gutiérrez, quoted in Bornat y Barrachina, *Los moriscos españoles*, p. 635). This same idea is similarly expressed by Cervantes; see *El coloquio de los perros*, p. 317.

[10] AMS, Varios Antiguos, Moriscos; *ibid.*, Escribanías del Cabildo, siglo XVI, tomo 4, no. 45; Gutiérrez, as quoted in Bornat y Barrachina, *Los moriscos españoles*, p. 635.

sellers) who, along with the Morisco women who sold buttercakes, roasted chestnuts, and sweets, were a common sight on the streets of Seville.[11] None of these occupations was very remunerative, but the fact that the Moriscos managed to make a living from them at all aroused popular indignation and resentment. They were accused of cornering the market in vital supplies and charging higher prices for goods than they were worth. Since they were basically parsimonious, they were able to survive and even prosper, but supposedly at the expense of the Old Christians.[12] Jealousy of the success of the Moriscos, sharpened by religious intolerance and fear, made them objects of popular hatred.

Although the census of 1580 does not mention any Moriscos as skilled artisans, some of them were. Other sources indicate that some Granadine Moriscos worked in the ceramic industry in Triana; others fashioned objects out of hemp and esparto grass, including the popular *alpargates* (hempen sandals).[13] Nevertheless, it seems that the majority of skilled workers were native rather than Granadine Moriscos. The basic picture of the Granadine Moriscos in Seville remains one of an impoverished, unskilled people whose standard of living was lower than that of the Old

[11] Matute y Gaviria, *Noticias*, p. 53; BNM, MS. 18735, "Informe de Sevilla para su magested sobre los moriscos que ay en ella."

[12] This was the opinion of the city council (AMS, Varios Antiguos, Moriscos). See also BNM, MS. 18735, and Gutiérrez, as quoted in Bornat y Barrachina, *Los moriscos españoles*, p. 635.

[13] AMS, Varios Antiguos, Moriscos; Gutiérrez, as quoted in Bornat y Barrachina, *Los moriscos españoles*, p. 635. For information about Morisco artisans, see Gestoso and, by the same author, *Historia de los Barros vidriados sevillanos* (Seville, 1903).

Christians and whose very survival under such adverse conditions was both puzzling and insulting to most Spaniards.

Despite their feelings of group consciousness, the Moriscos conformed outwardly to Sevillian life. In daily life they mingled freely with the Old Christians in a way that surprised many contemporaries, like the Marquis of San Germán, who in 1609 remarked that "they were very well mixed (*mezclados*) with the Old Christians." [14] But this apparent integration was deceiving, for the Moriscos were indeed different. They retained their own language (*algarabía*) and such traditional customs as abstention from pork and wine that set them apart from the rest of the population. Finally, in what to most Spaniards was the basic fact of existence—their faith—the Moriscos remained unconvinced. In 1588 a Sevillian official, Alonso Gutiérrez, claimed that they were real Moslems like those in North Africa and that they exercised the Christian religion only when forced and for purposes of subterfuge.[15] In the last analysis, their religion made the Moriscos different from other Spaniards. There was no room in Spain in the sixteenth and seventeenth centuries for Spaniards of different faiths. Spanishness was equivalent to Catholicism, and since the Moriscos seemingly refused to accept Christianity, they remained unassimilated.

[14] Lapeyre, *L'Espagne morisque*, p. 151.

[15] Gutiérrez, as quoted in Bornat y Barrachina, *Los moriscos españoles*, p. 635. Their feelings of repugnance toward pork and wine became a frequent pun in the literature of the period as did the distorted Spanish that many of them spoke. A good example of their typical speech is in the *Entremés del Gabacho, Nueva Biblioteca de Autores Españoles*, XVII, 185-b.

At the opening of the seventeenth century the structure and composition of the Morisco community of Seville had not changed substantially since the 1580's. Even the population had grown little, for in 1609 there were a total of 7,503 Moriscos in the city, just 848 more than twenty years before.[16] The Morisco population, like that of Seville in general, reached its height in the 1580's and then leveled off in the 1590's. The plague of 1599–1601 must have attacked the Moriscos with great fury due to the crowded and unsanitary conditions under which they lived. This epidemic especially ravaged Triana and several other districts in which they were congregated, and it must have so decisively reduced their numbers that they had not recovered by 1609.

Triana, the second largest Sevillian district, contained in 1609 the greatest concentration of Moriscos in the city, some 2,179, or roughly 29 per cent of their total number in Seville. Unfortunately, statistics are lacking for Triana in 1580, but other sources indicate that a similar concentration existed there in the sixteenth century. In 1580, for example, sailors from the Sicilian fleet, which had been anchored in the Guadalquivir off Triana, invaded the quarter, attacking the Moriscos, and carrying many of them off as galley slaves. The Sevillian authorities, angered and shocked by this incident and fearful of its consequences for public order, decreed the immediate freeing of the Moriscos

[16] Statistics for the Morisco population in 1609 have been taken from BNM, MS. 9577, "Sumario general de los moriscos que habían en las distintas colaciones de Sevilla (1609)." This document has also been published by M. Serrano y Sanz, "Nuevas datos sobre la expulsión de los moriscos andaluces," *Revista contemporánea,* XC (1893), 120.

and the restoration of their property. Furthermore, they wrote a detailed account of the episode to Philip II, who eventually directed the commander of the fleet to comply with the orders of the Seville city council.[17]

Outside of Triana, the second largest contingent of Moriscos lived in the parish of San Lorenzo (603), followed by San Julián (541), Omnium Sanctorum (537), and Santa María (492). With the exception of Santa María (the business section of the city), all were periphery parishes whose total population increased enormously in the second half of the sixteenth century. These four parishes and Triana contained 67 per cent of all the Moriscos in Seville in 1609. The remaining 33 per cent were distributed throughout the poorer parishes in groups of from 200 to 400 each with the largest contingents in the parishes of San Gil and Santa Marina.

The separateness and distinct existence of the Moriscos in Seville was of grave concern to both municipal and ecclesiastical authorities, who realized that under such conditions assimilation would be difficult, even impossible. Attempts were made by the city government to break the inner coherence of the Morisco community through legislation, for example, prohibiting the cohabitation of more than a specific number of Moriscos in one building or in certain city districts and by strictly enforcing existing royal decrees against the practice of Moslem customs. These regulations were also aimed at combating crime in areas of Morisco concentration where it apparently flourished. The reports of the common councilmen (*jurados*) during the second

[17] This incident is described in López Martínez, *Mudéjares y Moriscos,* pp. 64–66.

half of the sixteenth century contain frequent references to Morisco outlaw bands that terrorized their own sections and were responsible for countless crimes of violence— murder, robbery, and assault—all over the city and sur- rounding countryside.[18] But the municipality lacked the men and resources to enforce effectively its laws, and as a result its efforts were in vain.

The church did not follow a consistent policy toward the Moriscos; they were alternately ignored due to apathy and persecuted with vigor. Sizable numbers of them could be found at every *auto de fe* held in Seville during this period. It was generally agreed that most Moriscos were ignorant of the basic tenets of the Catholic faith and that a program of indoctrination was badly needed, but while much was said, little was done until 1604. In that year Archbishop Niño de Guevara assigned special priests to teach the Moriscos and to guide their religious life, but it was too late to overcome the barrier of hatred and indiffer- ence created by years of neglect and intolerance.[19]

The resistance of the Moriscos to assimilation was but one part of the total problem; of equal importance was what the city fathers believed to be the security problems arising from their presence and numbers. It was feared that such conditions would ultimately lead to a Morisco rebellion,

[18] AMS, Varios Antiguos, Moriscos.

[19] In the Seville *auto de fe* of 1559 three Moriscos were burned and eight reconciled with *sanbenito* and prison; of these, six were also scourged, including three women (BM, MS. Add. 21.447, fol. 93, "Relación de las personas que salieron al auto de fe que se celebró en la plaça de San Francisco en esta muy insigne ciudad de Sevilla domingo veinte e quatro días del mes de setiembre de 1559 años"). See also Domínguez Ortiz, *Orto y Ocaso,* pp. 57–58.

aided by the Turks and Barbary pirates who, it was assumed (and with sufficient evidence), were in contact with
the Moriscos. In 1580 the worst fears of the city government became a reality when a Morisco conspiracy abetting
invasion from North Africa was uncovered. The leader of
this abortive revolt was Fernando Enríquez, also known as
Fernando Muley, who is described in the documents as "a
clever man of medium height, with dark hair and slightly
bald, whose polished speech and manner belied his Morisco
origin." [20] Enríquez held numerous secret meetings in his
home attended by Moriscos from Cordova, Ecija, and other
towns. According to the official accounts in the Sevillian
Archives, the plotters expected to seize Seville and several
neighboring cities and then to extend their control over the
rest of Andalusia with the aid of the North Africans and
Turks. In case of failure they planned to escape to Portugal
or to the mountains around Granada, from where they
could eventually make their way to North Africa. After the
discovery of the plot, Enríquez and several of his associates
tried to flee, but were quickly apprehended and punished.[21]
Although nothing more serious than stricter police regulations for the Moriscos resulted from this event, it inflamed
public opinion and convinced most Sevillians that the Moriscos did indeed harbor treasonable intentions.

The possibility of a Morisco insurrection continued to
obsess Sevillian governing authorities in the 1590's. The

[20] AMS, Varios Antiguos, Moriscos; López Martínez, *Mudéjares
y Moriscos,* p. 64.

[21] The Count of Villar, Asistente of Seville in 1580, mentions
this conspiracy and the dangerous situation it created in Seville in
his "Relación de sus servicios y méritos," BNM, MS. 9372 = Cc–42.

English attack on Cadiz in 1596 created a new crisis. When the news of this event reached Seville, the city fathers took immediate steps to prepare the city against what they believed was an imminent Morisco uprising in collusion with the English. A curfew was established for Moriscos, and armed men were stationed in the districts where they were concentrated.[22] Two years later, with the threat of another English attack and Morisco collaboration with the enemy still present, the city council seriously considered a plan to draft all able-bodied Moriscos into the army and to force the whole Morisco population of Seville to wear some kind of identifying badge, but these proposals were shelved in face of royal opposition.[23]

In 1600 tensions were again brought to the breaking point when rumors circulated through the city that the Moriscos in Triana were ready to rise up in a coordinated effort with those of Cordova and that both groups had assurances of English aid. If this incident passed quickly and peacefully, it was only because several well-known Moriscos, led by a certain García Montano, succeeded in convincing the city council that there were no foundations to the rumors.[24] By this time, however, many prominent Sevillians began to insist that the Moriscos' movements should be restricted along the lines of the proposals of 1589. In 1601 the Marquis of Montesclaros, Asistente of Seville, wrote the king that many responsible people in Seville favored the drafting of the Moriscos as a means of control-

[22] Serrano y Sanz, "Nuevos datos," p. 119.
[23] Gestoso y Pérez, *Curiosidades*, p. 307.
[24] Francisco de Ariño, *Sucesos de Sevilla de 1592 a 1604* (Seville, 1873), p. 112.

ling them and also of filling the Sevillian quotas, but that he
did not agree with this idea. He suggested instead that their
wealth should be tapped, and he presented a plan to accomplish this through dissimilation. He proposed to ask
the Moriscos to contribute a contingent of men for the
army, knowing full well that they would refuse and offer
money instead. The suggestions of Montesclaros were avidly
accepted by Philip III, who in August 1601 gave him permission to effect his plan. At the same time the king reiter-
ated his position that he was interested in "the money not
the person of the Moriscos" and that since it was not fea-
sible to use them in the army, they should be made to support it financially, especially if the money would be used
to equip the Sevillian levies.[25] But just a few years later,
not even the Moriscos' money could influence the king and
his advisers to reverse what they believed was the only solu-
tion to the problem of a potentially treasonous and unassimilated minority—their expulsion from Spain.

The great exodus from Seville began in January 1610,
when all Moriscos, except slaves who were excluded from
the expulsion decree, were given twenty days to arrange
their affairs and leave the country. As far as we know, some
7,503 Moriscos left Seville at this time, although a few of
the more prosperous had abandoned the city earlier. Padre
Bleda reported seeing a large group of Sevillian Moriscos in
Narbonne (France) much before the expulsion decree.[26]

[25] BNM, MS. 3207, "Cartas del Marqués de Montesclaros,
Asistente de Sevilla," folios 618, 658–659.
[26] J. Bleda, *Coronica de los moros de España* (Valencia, 1618),
p. 1042. Figures for the expelled Moriscos come from BNM, MS.
9577, and are the same ones given by Serrano y Sanz and Lapeyre.

Most Moriscos went directly to North Africa, but because of the royal prohibition against taking children under seven years of age to non-Christian lands, others were forced to go first to Marseilles or some other European port. But the risks and hazards of such a journey through other Christian countries seemed so great to some Moriscos that they were willing to give up their young children rather than undertake it. A total of three hundred Morisco children abandoned by their parents were turned over to the ecclesiastical authorities, who distributed them among the clergy and pious laymen.[27]

The harsh terms of the expulsion decree reflected the mood of the Spanish people, for there was great joy at the departure of the Moriscos. The consequences of this event have never fully been determined. Most contemporaries believed that the expulsion of the Moriscos had little effect on the economy of the country, but the judgment of history has been different. Historians have generally held that their removal was a grave mistake from an economic viewpoint, but this opinion was often based more on subjective reasoning than on facts. Since the economic importance of the Moriscos varied from one area to another, no real evaluation can be made until more is known about them on a regional basis. The majority of Sevillian Moriscos were not rich, nor did they represent the most enterprising members of the community. They were mainly engaged in menial and unskilled tasks, but since many of these jobs were indispensable, especially in the port area, their removal from the scene must have created a short-lived labor crisis. In the long run, however, Sevillian economic life was only tem-

[27] Hazañas y La Rua, *Vázquez de Leca*, pp. 254–256.

porarily affected by their departure, for their places were
taken by other marginal groups, such as slaves (Negro and
Moorish), who continued to be numerous in Seville and
who had always done most of the menial labor anyway,
and displaced peasants from the surrounding countryside.
Even the Morisco vendors of chestnuts and sweets were
soon replaced by gypsies.[28] On the other hand, the expulsion, coming as it did just ten years after the great plague
of 1599–1601, accelerated the demographic crisis that the
city was facing at that time. In the last analysis, the economic disruptions caused by the expulsion of the Moriscos
from Seville seem to have been far less than the demographic ones, which were permanent and irreversible.

SLAVES AND FREEDMEN

In the sixteenth century, Negro, Moorish, and Morisco
slaves made up a sizable and conspicuous part of the population of Seville. Throughout the century slaves abounded
among the crowds that filled the streets of this teeming
metropolis. They could be found in all the focal points of
the city—along the wharves, in the Arenal, and in the public squares and market places. To many contemporaries, the
presence of so many slaves did much to create the cosmopolitan atmosphere for which the city was well known.
Some observers even claimed that there were almost as
many Negro and Moorish slaves as free citizens. Others
compared the city to a giant chessboard containing an
equal number of white and black chessmen.[29]

[28] Matute y Gaviria, *Noticias*, p. 53; BNM, MS. 18735.
[29] Antonio Domínguez Ortiz, "La esclavitud en Castilla durante
la Edad Moderna," *Estudios de historia social de España*, II (1952),
377–378.

People usually referred to the Moorish and Morisco slaves as *esclavos blancos*. The Moors were most often North African prisoners of war. The conflict in the Mediterranean between Spain and the Turks and their allies, the Barbary pirates, brought a steady stream of North African slaves into Seville during the sixteenth and seventeenth centuries. In 1508, for example, the Spaniards took eight thousand prisoners at Oran, and in 1535 Charles V's campaign against Tunis netted eighteen thousand captives. Most of the Moriscos came from Granada. The wars against Granada at the end of the fifteenth century resulted in the seizure of many prisoners who were eventually enslaved. In addition, an undetermined number of Moriscos became slaves during the course of the sixteenth century, mainly after the uprisings of 1500 and 1568–1570.[30]

Some information about Morisco slaves in Seville appears in the census of 1580. In that year there were 148 such slaves in the five parishes of San Pedro, San Ildefonso, San Gil, San Andrés, and San Marcos. The largest contingent was in San Andrés (47), followed by San Ildefonso (43); the smallest number were in San Gil which, as has been noted, contained a large free Morisco population. In general, female slaves outnumbered males, and there were few captive children. The overwhelming majority of slaves—male and female—were between twenty and forty years of age. There were almost none over the age of sixty and a very small number of youths and older children, clearly a reflection of the low birth rate and limited life span among slaves. The frequent practice of manumission also helped

---

[30] Domínguez Ortiz, *Orto y Ocaso*, p. 62; M. A. Ladero Quesada, "La esclavitud por guerra a fines del siglo XV: El caso de Málaga," *Hispania*, XXVII (1967), 80.

to reduce the numbers of slaves in the older group (forty to sixty years) and among the children. Most Morisco slaves in Seville were women between the ages of twenty and forty years.[31]

While contemporary writers often exaggerated the size of the unfree population of Seville, there is no doubt that in the sixteenth century Seville harbored the largest slave community in Spain. We can never know their exact numbers throughout the century, but we do have fairly satisfactory statistics from a census taken by church officials in 1565. In that year Seville had 6,327 slaves out of a total population of 85,538 people, that is, one slave for every fourteen inhabitants.[32] Although this account does not tell what proportion of these slaves were Negroes, Moors, or Moriscos, other sources indicate that Negroes outnumbered the other two groups, especially in the second half of the century.[33] The majority of slaves in Seville, therefore, would appear to have been Negroes.

Sixteenth-century Sevillians found nothing new or unusual about the existence of numerous slaves in their city. Negro slavery, especially, had been a part of its life for many centuries. We do not know when the first Africans were introduced into Seville after its reconquest from the Moslems in 1248, but the chroniclers state that by the end

[31] AMS, Varios Antiguos, no. 334. In 1589 there were 381 slaves (98 males, 283 females) in Seville out of a total Morisco population of 6,655. See Lapeyre, L'Espagne morisque, p. 135.

[32] Matute y Gaviria, Noticias, p. 51. In comparison, Lisbon had some 10,000 slaves out of a population of 100,000 in 1552 (João Lúcio Azevedo, Épocas de Portugal económico [Lisbon, 1929], p. 75).

[33] The deeds of purchase and sale involving slaves among the Sevillian Protocols give ample proof of this statement.

of the fourteenth century many Negro slaves had been brought there by merchants engaged in the trans-Saharan trade. During this period the municipal authorities tried to ease the rigors of servile life by allowing the Negroes certain privileges, such as the right to gather together on feast days and perform their own dances and songs. Eventually it became customary for one of them to be named by city officials as *mayoral* (steward) over the rest, with authority to protect them against their masters, defend them before the courts of law, and settle their quarrels.[34] In a similar manner the church, although primarily interested in conversion, also tried to ameliorate the physical conditions of slavery. During the last years of the fourteenth century the church expressed its charitable intentions by establishing the Hospital of Our Lady of the Angels in the parish of San Bernardo to serve the Negro population. A short time later the church made a further gesture toward incorporating Negroes into the spiritual fold by creating a Negro religious confraternity to run this hospital. In subsequent years many wealthy Sevillians helped to maintain Our Lady of the Angels; a notable donor was the Duke of Medina Sidonia, who at his death in 1463 left 1,000 maravedís for the poor of this institution.[35]

The duke's donation to the Hospital of Our Lady of

[34] Ortiz de Zúñiga, *Anales*, III, 78. On slavery in medieval Spain, see Charles Verlinden, *L'esclavage dans l'Europe médiévale, I: Péninsule Ibérique—France* (Bruges, 1955), and on the trans-Saharan trade, see Antonio Rumeu de Armas, *España en el Africa Atlántica* (Madrid, 1956), I, 163–166.

[35] José Bermejo y Carballo, *Glorias religiosas de Sevilla* (Seville, 1882), p. 381. The exact date of the construction of the Hospital of Our Lady of the Angels is not known, but it occurred during the period in which Gonzalo de Mena was Archbishop of Seville, 1393–1401.

the Angels came at a time when Seville had already begun to feel the effects of the opening of West Africa by the Portuguese. Greater numbers of Negro slaves were entering the river port, as Andalusian shipowners, including members of the highest nobility, competed with the Portuguese in organizing raiding expeditions on the West African coast. It was not until 1479 that the Spaniards finally recognized the Portuguese monopoly, and even then they did so reluctantly. Throughout the second half of the fifteenth century, Negroes were brought directly into the ports of southern Spain by Spanish shippers. Others were transported overland from Lisbon by Spanish and Portuguese merchants, a practice which accounts for the presence of Negro slaves in such frontier towns as Huelva, Badajoz, and Jerez de los Caballeros. By the reign of Ferdinand and Isabella, the Negro population of Seville had grown so large that the Catholic kings decided to place them under greater royal supervision and control. In 1475 Juan de Valladolid, a royal servant, who was known popularly as the "Negro count," was appointed *mayoral* of the Seville Negro community.[36]

After the discovery of the New World the constant demand for a source of cheap labor to work the mines and plantations of America increased the flow of Negroes into Seville during the sixteenth century. The city soon became one of the most important slave centers in Western Europe, second only to Lisbon. In fact the first Negro

[36] Rumeu de Armas, *España en el Africa*, pp. 123–128, 149–154; Domínguez Ortiz, "La esclavitud en Castilla," p. 372; AMS, Archivo de Privilegios, Tumbo, carpeta I, no. 197. See also Ortiz de Zúñiga, *Anales*, III, 78.

slaves introduced into the New World came from Seville, and some of them had been born in that city. During the first decades of the sixteenth century, the Spanish monarchs, anxious to keep the colonies free from religious taint, insisted that the slaves sent to America be Christians—that they should have been born in Spain or have resided there long enough to be baptized. In 1510, for example, King Ferdinand gave permission to ship as many as two hundred slaves from Seville for sale to the settlers of Hispaniola or for work on the royal properties there.[37] Eventually slaves were shipped directly from Africa to America, though they continued to come to Seville as well.[38] Throughout the century, merchants, sea captains, and others brought slaves to the Sevillian market, located in the heart of the business district. Here slaves were bought and sold amidst the noise and bustle of street vendors hawking their wares and future conquistadors recruiting men for their New World expeditions. Apparently they were not exhibited and sold at the block as was the custom elsewhere. Instead a group of slaves and their owner would go about the streets accompanied by an auctioneer who called out to onlookers offering them for sale. According to Cer-

[37] Clarence H. Haring, *The Spanish Empire in America* (New York, 1947), p. 219; Salvador Brau, *La colonización de Puerto Rico* (San Juan, 1930), p. 87.

[38] Ship captains reported to officials of the Casa de Contratación on their return to Seville instead of on their outward voyage. This permitted direct transport from Africa to America while the captains also complied with the regulation that all slaves had to be registered at the Casa de Contratación (Georges Scelle, *La traité négrière aux Indes de Castille* [Paris, 1906], I, 142; Elena F. Scheuss de Studer, *La trata de negros en el Río de la Plata durante el siglo XVIII* [Buenos Aires, 1958], p. 52).

vantes in *El trato de Argel*, Christian slaves were sold in this same manner in Morocco.[39]

The price range was wide and depended on the age, sex, and physical condition of the slave. An able-bodied slave brought a high market price, the average being slightly lower. Children brought the lowest price because of the element of risk and the expense of rearing them to a profit-bearing age. Some approximate average prices can be estimated on the basis of figures taken from the numerous deeds of purchase and sale among the Sevillian Protocols. During the first decade of the sixteenth century, the average price paid for a slave in Seville was about 20 ducats; in the second and third decades of the century prices fluctuated between 30 and 40 ducats.[40] At mid-century a prospective buyer would have to pay from 80 to 90 ducats for an adult slave, and by the last quarter of the century, 100 ducats or more. Prices of slaves rose steadily during the course of the century, for like other commodities they were caught in the great inflationary wave that overwhelmed all Spain during this period.

Though the branding of slaves was a common practice, this cruel custom was not applied to all, nor was it considered an absolute necessity. There are many examples of unbranded slaves during this period. Some people branded their slaves as a kind of insurance. John Brooks points out that the branding of Carrizales' slaves in Cervantes' *Celoso*

---

[39] Miguel de Cervantes Saavedra, *El trato de Argel*, in *Comedias y entremeses* (Madrid, 1920), V, 229; Morgado, *Historia*, p. 167; Fernández de Oviedo, *Historia general*, CXVIII (Madrid, 1959), 400.

[40] Domínguez Ortiz, "La esclavitud en Castilla," p. 399.

extremeño "may be considered significant of his character and plans." [41] Moreover, branding was specifically used as a punishment for refractory and runaway slaves. Carrizales branded his four "white slaves" but did not apply the same treatment to his two Negro slaves, perhaps because contemporary opinion was that Moorish and Morisco slaves were deceitful and potential runaways, while Negroes were trustworthy and loyal to their masters. Almost all of the Morisco slaves listed in the census of 1580, for example, were branded. Brands were not uniform in shape or location. The most frequent one consisted of an S and a line (*clavo*), standing for *esclavo*, on one cheek and the owner's initial or mark on the other. But several other kinds were also in use. In 1500, for example, there is mention of a slave branded with a fleur-de-lis on one cheek and a star on the other. In another instance, a slave bore the full name of his owner on his face.[42]

Most of the slaves branded and sold in Seville were destined for domestic service in the city's households. Slaves were employed in the kitchen, laundry room, and stable. They served as doorkeepers, as nursemaids for children, as attendants of adults, as valets, porters, and waiters. According to contemporary literature, an especially desirable accomplishment of the female slave was the ability to make

---

[41] John Brooks, "Slavery and the Slave in the Works of Lope de Vega," *Romanic Review*, XIX (1928), 234–235.

[42] Cristóbal Suárez de Figueroa, *Plaza universal de todas ciencias y artes* (Perpignan, 1629), fol. 321v; APS, M. Segura (IV), 29 May 1539, Libro I, fol. 881. For the slave with the fleur-de-lis and the star, see *ibid.*, F. Segura (IV), 5 Sept. 1500, Libro II, fol. Principio del legajo. Both documents are also cited in Gestoso, *Curiosidades*, pp. 86, 89.

fruit preserves and jellies. Since scientific treatises of the day taught that water taken by itself was harmful, orange flower, quince, peach, pear, and cherry preserves were kept on hand and offered to visitors, together with iced water. The master usually took some male slaves with him on his daily activities, perhaps as an escort on foot if he was riding. Merchants like the one portrayed by Cervantes in *El coloquio de los perros* usually went to the Exchange followed by a Negro servant.[43] Slaves also did odd jobs in connection with their master's business. Such was the case of Juan Fernández, a mulatto slave belonging to the inspector of weights and measures in the municipal meat market. When Fernández was called upon to testify in a lawsuit involving his master in 1598, he stated that "he always accompanied his master on his daily round of business, and that on the day in question he had delivered, on his master's orders, a special luncheon to several members of the city council." [44]

Another especially desirable quality in a slave was the ability to sing, play, and dance, as music and dancing were popular pastimes during the period. Negroes showed particular fondness and aptitude for both music and dance and were often in great demand as entertainers at private parties and public celebrations. Loaysa in Cervantes' *Celoso extremeño* noted that three of his Negro pupils, all slaves of wealthy aldermen, played and sang well enough to perform in any dance or tavern. Moreover, Negroes were

[43] A. de Castillo Solórzano, *La niña de los embustes—Teresa de Manzanares* (Madrid, 1929), p. 214; Brooks, "Slavery in Lope de Vega," pp. 235, 240–241; Félix Lope de Vega Carpio, *Servir a señor discreto*, Act I, in *Obras de Lope de Vega*, XV (Madrid, 1913), 573; *La Dorotea*, Act I, scene i (Berkeley, Calif., 1958), p. 124.

[44] Ariño, *Sucesos de Sevilla*, p. 348.

among the most accomplished interpreters of the numerous popular dances of the day, including the two favorites, the zarabanda and the chacona. Several dances—the guineo, ye-ye, and zarambeque or zumbé—had a distinctly African flavor and were probably introduced into Spain by Negro slaves.[45]

In the wealthier homes of the city slaves were considered a necessity—part of the conspicuous consumption of the period that called for long entourages of servants and for coaches, costly wearing apparel, and ornate home decoration. Nevertheless, the ownership of slaves in Seville was not confined to the wealthy classes—nobility and rich merchants—but was widely distributed among all levels of the population. The deeds of purchase and sale among the Sevillian Protocols clearly show that artisans of various occupations, professional people such as physicians, lawyers, clergymen, and even religious orders owned household slaves. Indeed almost every family of some means had two or more of them.

Treatment of domestic slaves varied, depending greatly on the character of the owner, though in general their position did not differ substantially from that of the free servants. There is even some evidence that in Spain slaves received better treatment than free servants.[46] Many slaves

[45] Miguel de Cervantes Saavedra, *El celoso extremeño* in *Novelas ejemplares* (Madrid, 1957), II, 112. For a discussion of these dances, see Emilio Cotarelo y Mori, *Colección de Entremeses, Loas, Bailes, Jácaras y Mojigangas desde fines del siglo XVI a mediados del XVIII*, in *Nueva Biblioteca de Autores Españoles* (Madrid, 1911), XVII, ccxxxiii–cclxxiii.

[46] Jean Bodin, *The Six Bookes of a Commonweale* (Cambridge, Mass., 1962), Book I, 44. He condemned the Spaniards for branding their slaves.

were closely bound to their masters and had their full confidence. Female slaves were particularly close to their mistresses; in the plays of Lope de Vega they are usually portrayed as their confidantes and go-betweens in their love
affairs.[47] The religious life of the slave was of great concern
to the owner. Much care was taken to see that slaves performed their religious duties and that children of domestic
slaves were duly baptized. Godparents, sometimes prestigious ones, were provided for slave children. As members of
the Christian community, slaves were buried in their parish
churches and in some instances in family vaults. It was also
customary to have requiem masses said for them at the expense of their former owners.[48] On the other hand, like free
servants, slaves who committed misdemeanors were often
whipped. More serious offenses could bring a form of punishment known as *pringar* or *lardear*—the dropping of pork
fat, melted by a large taper, or the wax of the taper itself
on the naked skin. Cervantes indicates that this was the
regular punishment for fugitive slaves, but it was also used
on household servants as a means of exacting information
from them. Another more drastic method of dealing with
incorrigible slaves was to "sell them overseas," that is, to
the Spanish colonies, or to donate them to the crown to be
used as galley slaves. There were even some masters who
chose to free rebellious and troublesome slaves; in other
words, they turned them out to starve. Delinquent slaves

[47] Elvira, in Lope de Vega's *Servir a señor discreto;* and
Esperanza, in *Amar, servir y esperar*, in *Obras de Lope de Vega*,
III (Madrid, 1917).

[48] Juan de Mata Carriazo, "Negros, esclavos y extranjeros en
el barrio sevillano de San Bernardo," *Archivo Hispalense*, XX
(1954), 130–132. For the baptismal certificates of slaves belonging
to Sevillian printers, see Hazañas y La Rua, *La Imprenta*.

seem to have been the exception, however, and individual acts of violence committed by slaves against their masters were infrequent.[49]

Although most slaves were well behaved, the existence of a large servile population created security problems for the municipal government. The city fathers feared that the urban slaves, led by the Moriscos, might band together and seize the town, and this official uneasiness found expression in a series of municipal ordinances restricting the movements of slaves. Slaves were prohibited, for example, from carrying arms except in the company of their masters or in the performance of their regular duties. The government also strictly limited the number of slaves permitted to assemble at any given time in public places such as taverns, inns, and cheap restaurants. City officials expressed concern about the gangs of slaves who frequented the Sevillian taverns both day and night and who often became intoxicated and disorderly. A tavern brawl or any disturbance involving slaves was considered especially dangerous to public order. Furthermore, many taverns served as meeting places for members of the city's underworld, who were quick to take advantage of slaves. Unscrupulous tavern owners in league with criminal elements encouraged slaves to steal in order to repay debts and later resold the booty for their own profit.[50]

[49] M. de Cervantes Saavedra, *La Gitanilla* in *Novelas ejemplares* (Madrid, 1952), I, 65. A white servant is given this same treatment in Lope de Vega's *El acero de Madrid,* Act III, scene ix, in *Obras escogidas,* I (Madrid, 1952), 992. See also Domínguez Ortiz, "La esclavitud en Castilla," p. 389.

[50] López Martínez, *Mudéjares y Moriscos,* pp. 54–55; AMS, Ordenanzas, Reales Provisiones, carpeta 24, no. 194; Manuel Chaves, *Cosas nuevas y viejas* (Seville, 1903), p. 37.

Municipal legislation curtailing the actions of slaves may have reassured the city fathers, but these regulations like so many other municipal ordinances were difficult to enforce. Effective policing of a city like Seville was nearly impossible anyway, and the presence of large numbers of slaves must have seriously exacerbated the problem. The municipal authorities had the power to curb the activities of slaves when public security was involved, but they could not interfere in the relationship between masters and slaves or in any way reduce the authority of owners. Slaveholders could be as arbitrary as they pleased with their property, but slaves were subordinate to their masters' will. The owner could free his slaves whenever he was inclined to do so, but he usually did this by inserting a provision in his will.[51] Manumission by will had advantages, for the master retained the services of the slaves as long as he needed them; the prospect of freedom encouraged good conduct on the part of the slave; and the slaveholder could depart this life with a freer conscience. Sometimes wills included trust provisions directing the slaveholder's heir to free a particular slave or slaves at his own death or after a given number of years of service. That such an arrangement could lead to difficulties can be seen in the case of Ana, a mulatto slave belonging to the Sevillian aristocrat Juan de Pineda. When Pineda died in 1526, he willed Ana to his grandson Pedro, with the proviso that she receive her freedom after ten years of service. Two years later Pedro died suddenly. Like

[51] The following conclusions are based on a study of wills and property inventories from the Sevillian Protocols. See also Hazañas y La Rua, *La Imprenta*, for published testaments of Sevillian printers.

his grandfather, he chose not to free Ana, but to include a trust provision for her in his will. Accordingly she was required to spend eight more years of servitude with Pedro's uncle (also named Juan de Pineda). Finally in 1537 Ana received her freedom, and one year later she emigrated to America.[52]

On the other hand, it was not always necessary for slaves to wait until the death of their owner, for they often received their freedom in return for special services, money payments, or both. In 1580, for example, Diego Bello, a Seville resident who had just returned home from a trip to Peru, freed his slave Tomé because of "the services that the said slave had rendered him, especially on the voyage from Peru, in addition to the payment of 100 pesos." The enfranchisement of slave children was a particularly frequent occurrence. Some slaveowners even freed the unborn children of slaves because of special circumstances. The priest Alvaro de Castro did this in 1526 when on the eve of his departure for Cuba he freed the yet unborn child of his slave Catalina as compensation for her separation from her husband Antonio, also a slave of the priest, who had to remain in Seville.[53]

Besides domestic slavery there existed in Seville (as well as in the rest of Andalusia) the systematic exploitation of slave labor for profit. Many Sevillians considered the ownership of slaves an excellent capital investment and a profitable source of income. Some people were totally dependent on the earnings of their slaves; this practice added another

[52] CPI, II, no. 4724, 282, 16 March 1538.
[53] APS, Cívico (VIII), 22 Oct. 1580, Libro IV, fol. Principio del legajo; *ibid.*, Castellanos (V), 13 Jan. 1526, Libro I, fol. 111.

class of laborers to the city's large unskilled working force. They were a common sight on the Seville waterfront, where they worked as stevedores. Many performed menial tasks in the famous soap factories or in the public granary. Others earned a living as porters, street vendors, and bearers of sedan chairs. There is also some evidence that they served as *corchetes* (constables), a rather unpopular calling in sixteenth-century Seville.[54]

Though slaves worked at many occupations, the city's guilds refused to admit them. On the other hand, there were no restrictions against their employment by master craftsmen in their shops. Both slave and free Negroes were employed in many Sevillian printing shops, and other craftsmen purchased slaves for use in their establishments. In 1503, for example, a mulatto slave, Diego de Zamora, was working as a swordmaker in his owner's shop, and in 1514 Juan de Torres, a swordguard maker, had a Negro slave named Francisco as his apprentice.[55] Moreover, the Sevillian Protocols indicate that they were used in the trade between Seville and the New World. Several interesting examples of Negro slaves employed as business agents in America emerge from these documents. As early as 1502, the Sevillian trader Juan de Córdoba sent his Negro slave and two other agents to sell merchandise for him on the

[54] William E. Wilson, "Some Notes on Slavery during the Golden Age," *Hispanic Review*, VII (1939), 173; Domínguez Ortiz, "La esclavitud en Castilla," p. 401; AMS, Escribanías del Cabildo, siglo XVI, tomo 4, no. 45. Regarding slaves in the Sevillian soap factories, see Morgado, *Historia*, p. 156.

[55] Gestoso, III, 191, 219; APS, M. Segura (IV), 23 Jan. 1513, Libro II, fol. carece "Indias"; *ibid.*, 8 Nov. 1525. Regarding slaves in the printing shops, see Hazañas y La Rua, *La Imprenta*.

island of Hispaniola. Seven years later Juan de Zafra, a Negro slave, was commissioned by his master, the well-known Sevillian physician Dr. Alvarez Chanca, to sell goods in the New World. Zafra remained in America for several years, and until his death in 1515 he acted as a commission agent for his master.[56] Most famous of all the Negro traders in America was Pedro Franco, who was freed by his master Franco Leardo, a wealthy and prominent Genoese merchant of Seville, just a few months before he left for America. Leardo gave him 300 ducats and sent him to Panama as his agent, probably under the usual four-year partnership contract (*compañia*). Several other Sevillians besides Leardo entrusted him with merchandise to be sold in the New World. Unfortunately, Pedro Franco was not able to fulfill the terms of his contract with Leardo, for he died within a year after his arrival on the Isthmus. In his last will and testament he left all of his property to his former master.[57]

Slaves who worked at outside jobs to support themselves and their owners usually did not reside in their masters' homes. Although they were scattered throughout the poorer sections of Seville, their traditional quarter was the parish of San Bernardo, located outside the city walls in a swampy region dominated by a foul-smelling stream called the Tagarete. This was a poor parish inhabited by working

[56] APS, M. Segura (IV), 16 April 1509, Libro II, fol. 1060. Material about the Negro slave of Juan de Córdoba is in APS, F. Segura (IV), 8 Jan. 1502, Libro I, fol., Principio del legajo.

[57] Enrique Otte, "Gonzalo Fernández de Oviedo y los genoveses," *Revista de Indias*, XXII (1962), 519; APS, Cazalla (XV), 29 April 1540, Libro único, fol. 994; *ibid.*, M. Segura (IV), 26 April 1515, Libro II, fol. 676v; CPI, I, no. 5, 78, 13 Sept. 1538.

people—gardeners employed in the nearby Alcázar, employees of the municipal slaughterhouse, and bakers who worked in the many baking establishments in the district. It was also a high crime area and was known for its numerous ruffians and bullies, many of whom occasionally worked at odd jobs in the slaughterhouse.[58]

By the last quarter of the century the population of San Bernardo had increased so greatly that church and municipal authorities decided to divide San Bernardo and to create the new parish of San Roque. The chapel of the Hospital of Our Lady of the Angels was chosen to serve as a temporary parish church for San Roque, and, maintained by the Negro religious confraternity, it remained the center of the district's religious life until the completion of the church of San Roque in 1585. Nine years later the confraternity purchased three lots opposite the new church and built a chapel that they occupied in the last years of the century.[59]

In addition to the parishes of San Bernardo and San Roque, several other Sevillian barrios were especially noted for their numerous Negro residents. The parish of San Ildefonso, for example, contained a sizable population of slaves and freedmen. During the second half of the sixteenth century there were enough mulattoes there to justify the creation of a religious confraternity. The confraternity maintained its own chapel in the parish church of San Ildefonso with a private entrance through a back door that opened into a small side street, called appropriately the "Street of Mulattoes." Contemporary literature also tells

[58] Cervantes, *El coloquio de los perros*, pp. 217–218; Mata Carriazo, "Negros," p. 123.
[59] Bermejo y Carballo, *Glorias*, pp. 383, 385.

us that the plaza in front of the church of Santa María la Blanca was a favorite meeting place for Sevillian Negroes.[60] Some of them must have lived in the neighborhood, although no evidence of their residence there has survived.

Among the Negroes who assembled in the Plaza de Santa María la Blanca were many freedmen and women. Although most Sevillian Negroes were slaves, the city also contained a significant free Negro population. Enfranchisement was not a step toward economic and social betterment, however, for Negroes and mulattoes, whether slaves or freedmen, remained on the lowest rungs of the social ladder. Ex-slaves continued to work in unskilled and menial jobs and to reside in the same neighborhoods as before their emancipation. A combination of discrimination and unfavorable economic conditions prevented freedmen from rising in society. The artisans feared Negro competition and jealously excluded them from the few skilled positions which the inadequate Sevillian industry afforded. Even unskilled jobs were at a premium in Seville because of the steady flow of landless peasants from the countryside into the town. Chronic unemployment and severe food shortages were the realities of life for the majority of Sevillians throughout the sixteenth century.[61]

Competition for jobs strained relations between freedmen and the white Sevillian laborers. The whites showed

[60] For the description of such a gathering, see "El entremés de los mirones," in Cotarelo y Mori, *Colección de Entremeses*, p. 162; AGS, Expedientes de hacienda, leg. 170. "The Street of Mulattoes" disappeared with the destruction of the church of San Ildefonso in 1794 (Bermejo y Carballo, *Glorias*, p. 179).

[61] See Chapter III for a discussion of the Sevillian unskilled labor market.

their contempt for Negroes with the customary sidewalk jeer (*estornudo*).[62] On the individual level, however, Negroes and whites mixed freely, and contacts were friendly. Miscegenation and common-law unions were frequent. Many Sevillians, including members of the clergy, maintained illicit relations with female household slaves and in some instances recognized their illegitimate children. Among the servant class miscegenation was common practice, and mixed marriages were not unknown.[63]

Although Negro freedmen and slaves lived on the fringe of Sevillian life socially and economically, they enjoyed full membership in the church. True religious conversion among newly baptized Negroes was unusual, but by the second generation many had become sincere and pious Christians. The very willingness of Negroes to become Christians and to remain faithful to their new religion facilitated their popular acceptance. In addition, their incorporation into the social and ritual activities of the church accelerated the process of their Hispanization. Through their parish churches and their confraternities slaves and freedmen took part in all the city-wide religious celebrations of the period. The Negro and mulatto brotherhoods marched in full regalia in the many religious processions, including those of Holy Week. On one such occasion, the dress and the insignias of the Negro brotherhood were

[62] Lope de Vega referred to this custom in his *Servir a señor discreto*, Act II, scene iii, in *Obras de Lope de Vega*, XV, 587. See also Francisco de Quevedo y Villegas, *Boda de Negros*, in *Obras completas* (Madrid, 1952), p. 379.

[63] Conclusions in this paragraph are based on a study of wills, deeds of purchase and sale, and letters of enfranchisement among the Sevillian Protocols. See also the statements of Negro and mulatto passangers to the New World in CPI, I–III.

so elaborate and costly as to draw censure from the clergy. In another instance, according to the chronicler Ortiz de Zúñiga, a member of the Negro confraternity sold himself as a slave in order to cover the high cost of his group's participation in a religious festival. Negro performers also took part in the *autos* connected with the festival of Corpus Christi. In 1590 the city government paid eight ducats to Leonor Rija, a mulatto, to appear on a float in the Corpus Christi celebration and to sing, dance, and play the guitar, together with four other mulatto women and two men.[64]

If it was difficult for freedmen to improve their status in Seville, they might seize the opportunity to emigrate to the New World. The registers of the Casa de Contratación indicate that many Negro freedmen crossed the ocean to America during the sixteenth century.[65] Most of these emigrants were single men and women, but we can also find instances of women with young children and of family groups. A good example was the Bonilla family—husband, wife, and two children—who signed up at the Casa de Contratación in 1515. Many freedmen accompanied their former masters to the New World as servants. In 1538, for instance, the freedman Bernardo declared that he was traveling to Florida as a valet of his ex-master Captain Pedro Calderón. A year later another freedman by the name of Domingo went to Peru with his former owner, the adven-

[64] José Sánchez Arjona, *Anales del teatro en Sevilla* (Seville, 1898), p. 81. Negro confraternities in religious processions are described in Domínguez Ortiz, "La esclavitud en Castilla," p. 394, and Bermejo y Carballo, *Glorias*, p. 386.

[65] The registers are incomplete and cannot be used for statistical purposes. They do, however, give some idea of types and backgrounds of the Negro and mulatto passengers to America.

turer Lope de Aguirre, whose later exploits in the Amazon region won him the unfortunate epithet of "the tyrant." Many newly freed women came to America as ladies' maids or as members of the large and varied entourages that customarily accompanied wealthy families emigrating to the colonies. Such was the position of Quiteria Gómez, a former slave, who with three other servants—one white male and two white females—traveled with the widow Francisca de Carrera and her seven children to Peru during 1555. Doña Francisca's two sisters made up the rest of the party, fourteen persons in all.[66]

On the other hand, not all the Negroes who crossed the Atlantic went westward. In the second half of the sixteenth century there was a countermigration of Negroes from the New World to Seville. As previously noted, many Spaniards, having enriched themselves in America during the first decades of the sixteenth century, eventually returned home to Seville, where they could maintain their contacts, usually commercial, with the Indies. These returning Spaniards, nicknamed *indianos*, invested their newly found wealth in elegant town houses staffed with Negro slaves from the colonies. Don Alvaro, in Castillo Solórzano's novel *La niña de los embustes, Teresa de Manzanares*, was a typical *indiano* who, with 50,000 ducats obtained in Lima, two white servant boys, and four Negroes, established himself in Seville, spending his days at the Casa de Contratación.[67]

[66] CPI, III, no. 2538, 180, 1555; for the Bonillas, see *ibid.*, I, no. 1997, 141, Aug. 16, 1515; for Bernardo, *ibid.*, II, no. 4481, 267, Feb. 27, 1538; for Domingo, *ibid.*, III, no. 163, March 15, 1539.

[67] Castillo Solórzano, *La niña de los embustes*, p. 124. For more on *indianos* see Chapter II.

Creole slaves, as the Negroes from the colonies were called, also served in the homes of wealthy Sevillian merchants who were engaged in the Indies trade. The witty and attractive creole slave Elvira in Lope de Vega's *Servir a señor discreto* was the maid and confidante of Doña Leonor, the daughter of such a New World trader. The charm and beauty of the creole slave women soon made them a solicited commodity in the Sevillian slave market, as can be seen from the numerous deeds of purchase and sale which appear among the Sevillian Protocols. In 1580, for example, Diego de la Sal, a member of that famous elite family, purchased a "twenty year old creole slave named Isabel de García" from a returning Spaniard.[68] In time many of these creole slaves obtained their freedom either through purchase or the death of their owners, after which they sought to return to America. This accounts for the numerous references to them as passengers to the New World in the Casa registers during the last quarter of the sixteenth century.

Negro slaves and freedmen left many marks on sixteenth-century Sevillian life. Whereas Moors and Moriscos remained on the fringes of society, isolated and disliked by all, Negroes and mulattoes freely accepted Christianity and Spanish culture. When contemporary writers introduced Negro characters into their plays and novels, they only reflected the significant place that freedmen and slaves held in their society. The ethnic variety that characterized sixteenth-century Seville set it apart from other Spanish centers and increased its similarity to the cities of the New

[68] Lope de Vega, *Servir a señor discreto*, in *Obras de Lope de Vega*, XV, 572; APS, Almonacid (IX), 4 Jan. 1580, Libro I, fol. 353v.

World. To this ethnic variety Negroes, Moors, and Moriscos made a unique contribution.

THE UNDERWORLD

Vagabonds, beggars, rogues (*pícaros*), ruffians, prostitutes, and thieves abounded in sixteenth-century Seville, where they represented an organized group with a language of their own (*germanía*) and a large number of well-defined methods and traditions.[69] Such a city, overflowing with wealth, vice, and poverty, presented the most favorable conditions for the shelter and protection of vagrants and lawbreakers of every sort. With a large population and an exceedingly lax and corrupt municipal government, the town was filled with all types of disreputable elements. Disorder and confusion reigned. Criminals could usually escape the law by moving from one district to another or even by fleeing to the Indies. Law officials and criminals often worked together—many police officers were like Cervantes' "constable in charge of vagabonds," who, according to the thieves' chieftain, "was a friend and never came to do us harm." Thieves' jargon was used in common speech throughout the city, and everyone went about armed for protection.[70] Faced with so many disorderly and criminal elements, the city government was hard put to maintain order.

[69] Thieves' cant or *germanía* of the period is discussed by Rafael Salillas, *El delincuente español; El lenguaje* (Madrid, 1896). See also Hesse, ed., *Romancero*.

[70] M. de Cervantes Saavedra, *Rinconete y Cortadillo*, ed. F. Rodríguez Marín (Madrid, 1952), p. 175; Peraza, *Historia*, as quoted in Cervantes Saavedra, *Rinconete y Cortadillo* (1905 ed.), p. 73.

Regardless of their numbers we know very little about the *gente del hampa*, or underworld, for available sources are few and incomplete. Judicial records are practically nonexistent and the notarial deeds, the source of so much information on the social life of Seville, are silent on such marginal and transient beings whose style of life and meager possessions did not require formal recording. What fragmentary information remains comes mainly from literary works and municipal legislation. Literary sources are especially valuable, for Cervantes and other Golden Age writers described in vivid tones those colorful individuals who occupied the lower depths of Sevillian society during this period.

Although contemporary authorities customarily included all undesirables in one comprehensive term—vagabond—and legislated against them as such, the Sevillian *hampa* was not a homogeneous class. Undoubtedly these delinquent elements had much in common; they all shared the same desire to live without working and freely borrowed each other's methods and tricks, but there were important differences. Two main groups can be delineated: the vagabonds and beggars, on the one hand, and the professional criminals (thieves, murderers, and the like), on the other. Vagrants and beggars roamed the city and surrounding countryside begging and stealing in turns. They included both harmful and harmless types and were divided into orders and ranks depending on experience, methods of begging and stealing, and even physical strength. Among the most common were the sham beggars—those who pretended to be blind, lame, mute, mad, or afflicted with some dread disease like palsy. Some excited compassion by means of artificial sores, like the beggar in Quevedo's

Buscón who "had a huge false hernia and used to tie a rope right around his upper arm so that it looked as though his hand was all swollen up as well as paralyzed and inflamed at the same time." [71] Others posed as redeemed captives, false soldiers and sailors, and musicians.

There are no reliable figures for the number of vagrants and beggars in Seville. A few contemporary estimates of the vagabond population at different times are available, but most seem to be mere guesses. The figures most often mentioned date from 1597 when the reforming Asistente, Count of Puñonrostro, decided to reduce their numbers through a system of municipal licensing. He ordered all the city's beggars to present themselves at the Hospital de la Sangre on April 29 of that year to obtain their permits. According to the chronicler Ariño, two thousand men and women appeared; they included the strong and healthy as well as the old and sick, the maimed and deformed. Only the aged and the physically deformed were granted licenses; the sick were sent to the hospital, and the rest were ordered to find work within three days or be flogged and put out of the city by force.[72] Unfortunately, there is no way to determine whether or not these figures are the result of a direct count or are a guess on the part of municipal officials, or even Ariño. Nor do they include part-time beggars—in reality unemployed unskilled workers for whom begging was a temporary resort only.

In addition to vagrants and beggars, Seville harbored a

[71] F. de Quevedo y Villegas, *Historia de la vida del Buscón*, ed. S. Gili Gaya (Zaragoza, 1959), pp. 116–117. A good description of vagabonds, beggars, and criminals is in J. Deleito y Piñuela, *La mala vida en la España de Felipe IV* (Madrid, 1959), and R. Salillas, *El delincuente español: La Hampa* (Madrid, 1898).

[72] Ariño, *Sucesos de Sevilla*, pp. 45–47.

class of professional criminals more numerous than in any other city in Spain during this period. The most typical representatives of this group were the ruffians or bullies (*jácaros, rufos*), who at their lowest level were nothing more than hired thugs and professional assassins. Their principal activities consisted of inflicting punishment for pay—murders, cuts, cudgelings, ink throwings, and the nailing of horns over the doors of cuckolds. The ruffians also acted as procurers (they held the door of the brothel open for customers they had procured) and lived off the earnings of prostitutes. Literary sources further indicate that they often were employed in playing the enraged husband who clamored for reparation from an unlucky victim found with his pretended wife. With sword in hand, threatening murder in revenge for the wrong done to their honor, they forced the culprit to hand over all his money to save his life and reputation. Don Martín, in Agreda y Vargas' *Novelas morales*, had such a trick played on him in Seville.[73]

The Sevillian bullies were especially noted for their valor and arrogance. They had their own code of honor, the first provision of which was to resist all forms of "grilling" rather than reveal the names of accomplices. Torture added prestige to the virtues of *valentía* or "toughness" and even the specter of death at the end of the hangman's noose could not move them. No wonder there was coined the popular expression, "they go to their death as if they were going to their wedding." [74] Cervantes, who had a good knowledge of these Sevillian ruffians, describes them

[73] Frank Chandler, *Romances of Roguery* (New York, 1961), p. 175; Domínguez Ortiz, *Orto y Ocaso*, p. 70.
[74] Cristóbal de Chaves, *La relación de la cárcel de Sevilla*, in

as follows: "Among the latest arrivals were a couple of swaggering young ruffians with large mustaches, broad-brimmed hats, walloon ruffs, colored stockings and large showy garters. Their swords exceeded the length allowed by law, each carried a brace of pistols in place of daggers and their bucklers were suspended from their belts." [75] Among the most notorious of these bullies were those of the San Román parish and the Feria quarter.[76]

Regardless of their notoriety and bravado, ruffians represented only a small group within the ranks of the underworld, for the majority of criminals in Seville were thieves. There were many kinds—a dozen or more categories (all bearing fantastic cant names) were described by Dr. Carlos García in his *Desordinada codicia de los bienes agenos* (1609). Among the most common were the *cortabolsas* (cutpurses), *duendes* (hobgoblins or sneak thieves), and *grumetes* (cat thieves). There were also *capeadores* (cloak-snatchers), *mayordomos* who stole provisions, and even a class of religious thieves called *devotos* who despoiled images.[77] Both thieves and ruffians belonged to so-called thieves' fraternities, one of which, presided over by Monipodio, was so vividly described by Cervantes in *Rinconete y Cortadillo*. These criminal associations were organized

---

Bartolomé José Gallardo, *Ensayo de una biblioteca española de libros raros y curiosos*, I (Madrid, 1863), 1362.

[75] Cervantes Saavedra, *Rinconete y Cortadillo* (1952 ed.), p. 164.

[76] For references to the bullies of San Román and the Feria, see M. de Cervantes Saavedra, *El rufián dichoso*, ed. Edward Nagy (New York, 1968), Jornadas I, III, and Hesse, ed., *Romancero*.

[77] Dr. Carlos García, *La desordinada codicia de los bienes ajenos*, in Angel Valbuena Prat, *La novela picaresca española* (Madrid, 1956), Chapters VII, VIII.

along the lines of medieval guilds with masters and apprentices, rules, and registers. The Sevillian brotherhood, according to Luis Zapata in his *Miscelánea*, "had a prior and consuls (the names being an obvious parody of the Seville Merchants Guild or Consulado) with a depository for stolen goods and a chest with three keys in which the loot is kept." [78] Guild regulations called for an equitable division of streets and territories and their assignment to different thieves who were responsible for whatever was stolen in the district. All booty was divided; the thief shared equally with the chieftain; his accomplices received one-third, and sentinels (*postas*) and scouts (*abispones*), one-fifth. A portion of all thefts was set aside for "benefactors" who, in the words of Monipodio, included "the lawyer who defends us, the constable who tips us off, and the executioner who shows us mercy." [79] A certain percentage was also devoted to pious uses, such as masses for deceased brothers and for the sick and needy of the fraternity.

The thieves and bullies who made up the Sevillian *hampa* lived in a world of their own, one possessing its own heroes and martyrs. These men were the objects of toasts at gang get-togethers, such as the one described in *El Buscón*, and their names and deeds offered inspiration to their brothers.[80] Contemporary chronicles and literary works contain abundant references to the heroes of the underworld, most of whom were also "martyrs" (at least in the eyes of the

[78] Luis Zapata, *Miscelánea*, in *Memorial histórico español* (Madrid, 1859), XI, 49.

[79] Cervantes Saavedra, *Rinconete y Cortadillo* (1952 ed.), p. 168; García, *Desordinada codicia*, Chapter XIII.

[80] Quevedo y Villegas, *El Buscón*, pp. 125–126.

hampa) because they died on the gallows. Among the most
notorious were Pedro Vázquez Escamilla, whose name
served in later years as a rallying cry for ruffians in "battle"
with rival gangs or the police; Gayón, inventor of a special
kind of knife thrust, indispensable for the toughs; and
Gonzalo Genis, known as "king of the ruffians," who was
hanged for murder in 1596, and who during his career had
even dared to fire a pistol at the Asistente of Seville, Count
of Priego. But the most popular and tragic figure of them
all was the poet-ruffian Alonso Alvarez de Soria, over
whom the maudlin bullies wept in *Buscón;* for he was, in
their words, "a fine lad, a fighter with guts—a champion
and a good friend." [81]

Although the ineffectiveness of the Seville police force
allowed the underworld a free run of the city (there was
no quarter in which they did not make an appearance),
they had several chief haunts right in the center of town.
Among their favorite meeting places were two courtyards
of the Cathedral known as the Corral de los Olmos and
the Corral or Patio de los Naranjos. The Corral de los
Olmos was situated at the eastern end of the Cathedral
between the Giralda Tower and the Archbishop's Palace.
In the Middle Ages a mosque had occupied this site, but in
the sixteenth century the area was almost all taken up by a
a mean eating place (*casa de gula*) that catered to the
lowest elements in the city.[82] Here meals were served at

[81] *Ibid.*, p. 126. For more information on these heroes of the
underworld, see A. Domínguez Ortiz, "Delitos y suplicios en la
Sevilla imperial (La crónica negra de un misionero jesuita)," in
Crisis y Decadencia de la España de los Austrias (Barcelona, 1969),
pp. 40–71, and Chaves, *La cárcel de Sevilla,* especially the second
and third *relaciones.*

[82] Caro, *Antigüedades,* pp. 53, 61–62.

all hours of the day and night to the hordes of undesirables in the neighborhood. In contrast to the Corral de los Olmos, the Corral de los Naranjos was the haunt of the "elite" of the underworld—important criminals, notorious rogues, and bullies. Contemporaries thought of it as a kind of "Salamanca" for criminals from which many ruffians like the one described by Salas Barbadillo in *El Sagaz Estacio* had "graduated." [83]

The popularity of the Corral de los Naranjos was in no small part due to the fact that it was within the sanctuary area of the Cathedral. Protected by prevailing ecclesiastical privilege, all churches and religious houses in sixteenth-century Spain offered asylum to persons fleeing from secular jurisdiction. Municipal authorities seldom dared to break the inviolability of church sanctuary since to do so inevitably brought conflict with the church and excommunication of city officials. As a result the sanctuaries often became hideouts for thieves enjoying a *de facto* immunity from the law. Such was the situation in the Seville Cathedral and the adjoining Corral de los Naranjos. The delinquents who took refuge there customarily left the sanctuary at night and went out into the streets, where they committed all kinds of crimes. During the day they received visits from whores, who brought them food and clothing, and gaming went on both day and night. The ecclesiastical authorities repeatedly tried to put an end to the scandals and disorders connected with sanctuary life. In 1586, for example, they limited the right of asylum within a given church to eight

[83] Alonso Jerónimo de Salas Barbadillo, *La Peregrinación sabia y el sagaz Estacio, marido examinado*, ed. F. A. de Icaza (Madrid, 1958), p. 227. Both *corrales* are mentioned continuously in Hesse, ed., *Romancero*.

days and prohibited gambling and the entrance of women into the sanctuaries.[84] Unfortunately, these well-intentioned regulations proved difficult to enforce, and the abuses continued.

Like the sanctuaries, the city jail served as a refuge for criminals and a base for their operations. The Seville jail (Cárcel Real de Sevilla) was famous throughout Spain for its large number of prisoners and the variety of their crimes. There are several estimates of the regular prison population. In 1579, when the city fathers petitioned Philip II for additional financial aid for the jail, they said that it usually held 1,000 prisoners, male and female, but that at times it housed as many as 1,300. Similar figures were given in 1587 by Morgado, who placed the prison population at from 1,000 to 1,500. A third estimate, made in the same period when Morgado was writing, was 1,800.[85] It would be useless to comment on the validity of these figures; those of 1579 were official, but it is not clear whether or not they were the result of a direct count. In any case, a high rate of lawlessness characterized the city during this period.

One of the best descriptions of the prison of Seville is in Cristóbal de Chaves' *Relación de la cárcel de Sevilla*, begun after 1585 and completed in 1597. Chaves, a lawyer

[84] These prohibitions can be found in the Ecclesiastical Reform Ordinances of 1512 (ordinance no. 39); see Cotarelo y Valledor, *Deza*, p. 200. For an excellent description of sanctuary life in the Cathedral, see Quevedo y Villegas, *El Buscón*, pp. 126–127.

[85] Chaves, *La cárcel de Sevilla*, p. 1341; Morgado, *Historia*, p. 192. The figures for 1579 can be found in BM, MS. Add. 28.341, "Carta a Felipe II de los deputados y administradores de la cárcel de Sevilla."

of the Audiencia, had ample opportunities to observe the members of this picturesque community, whom he viewed with both sympathy and humor. He vividly portrays the daily existence of the prisoners in the courtyards and various sections of the jail—vaults, old and new gallery, the chamber of iron, and the women's prison—and describes the duties of the governor and undergovernor, the ruses and tricks of the inmates, and anecdotes of famous criminals. Some of the most interesting details relate to the curious customs of the inmates. Prisoners who resisted torture were acclaimed by fellow inmates—sheets drenched in wine were hung out in their honor, and lutes and tambourines sounded when they entered their cells. Similarly, an execution became a heroic moment in which prisoners in rented mourning garments crowded about a condemned man, shaking his hands and alternately consoling and extolling him. Then, chanting litanies, they accompanied him through the streets to the place of execution.[86] Thus a death march became a triumphant procession, and a convicted criminal was turned into a hero.

Life in jail could be quite tolerable for delinquents and criminals. Prisoners were permitted to receive visits from friends, confederates, and mistresses. From the time the doors were opened early in the morning, until ten at night, a steady procession of visitors brought food and clothing to the inmates. Luxuries of all kinds were available to those who could pay; others lived off charity or on donations from friends and relatives. There were four taverns, a similar number of restaurants, and two shops that catered to the needs of the prisoners. Gaming went on

[86] Chaves, *La cárcel de Sevilla*, pp. 1344, 1362.

from morning to night; fights, knifings, and thefts among the inmates were common. Most prisoners were armed even though weapons were confiscated at regular intervals.

Unlike the criminals, the poor debtors endured great sufferings in this vicious environment. They were protected principally by the Jesuits, who worked tirelessly distributing charity and spiritual comfort. The Jesuits often acted as intermediaries between the debtors and their creditors. In addition, the Confraternity of Nuestra Señora de la Visitación, founded in 1585 by a judge of the Audiencia, Andrés Fernández de Córdoba, helped poor prisoners. Its membership included some of the most prestigious Sevillians —nobles, professionals, and merchants. Every week two members of the brotherhood visited the jail to listen to the complaints and problems of the inmates. Through the combined efforts of this confraternity and the Jesuits, some two to three thousand prisoners were freed each year.[87]

Outside the city proper quite a few places were frequented by the underworld. Among the more important were the outer fortifications of the city (*barbacanas*) and the Campo de Tablada, a favorite spot for gang fights. The whole right bank of the Guadalquivir up to San Juan de Alfarache was popular, and there were several inns on that side of the river where they gathered for merrymaking. One of these, known as the Venta de la Barqueta, was for many years a thieves' den. In 1595 the Count of Priego, upon being informed that the notorious ruffian

---

[87] For information about the Confraternity of Nuestra Señora de la Visitación, see Morgado, *Historia*, pp. 196–201, and Chaves, *La cárcel de Sevilla*, pp. 1342–1343. The activities of the Jesuits are described in Domínguez Ortiz, "Delitos y suplicios."

Damián de Carmona was at the Venta de la Barqueta, took a company of armed men there to arrest him. Carmona was eventually captured, but only after a pitched battle between the municipal force and the criminals inside the inn. As a result of this incident, the Count of Priego ordered the inn razed to the ground.[88] Also on the right bank of the river was the Huerta del Alamillo, often mentioned as a recreation area for the *hampa*. It was here that the ruffians and their girl friends from the brothel enjoyed a rather sumptuous picnic in Cervantes' *Rufián dichoso*.[89]

Notwithstanding these places, the principal stamping ground of the Sevillian underworld was an extramural area on the Seville side of the river known alternately as El Compás, El Compás del Arenal, or simply El Arenal. It covered all the low-lying swampy terrain from the city walls to the river between the Triana and Arenal Gates. The Arenal came close to being an authentic criminal quarter where immunity from arrest was based partly on custom, but mostly on the strength of the criminals and the weakness or indifference of the law. Here, in sight of the incessant movement and turmoil of the port, could be found the inns, taverns, and cheap rooming houses that harbored and serviced the underworld. The Arenal also served as a kind of second-hand market where fraud and cheating were the order of the day.[90]

One of the main centers of activity within the Arenal

[88] Domínguez Ortiz, "Delitos y suplicios," p. 59.

[89] Cervantes Saavedra, *El rufián dichoso*, Jornada I.

[90] Additional information on the Arenal is in José María Asensio y Toledo, "El Compás de Sevilla," in *Cervantes y sus obras* (Barcelona, 1902), pp. 405–424.

district was a collection of small shacks (*boticas*) lying close to the city walls on the left side of the Arenal Gate. This was the site of the notorious Sevillian brothel, El Compás, which had given its name to the entire quarter. Like most urban property in Seville, these miserable dwellings belonged to both the municipality and the several ecclesiastical corporations (Cathedral chapter, hospitals, religious houses) which leased them to private individuals, usually government employees and law officials. Thus at the end of the sixteenth century the city's twenty houses of prostitution were rented to the public executioner, Francisco Vélez. The lessees in turn collected a daily rent of one and a half *reales* from the prostitutes who occupied the shacks and selected persons to serve as brothel keepers. The brothel keepers were almost always men (known as *padres de la mancebía*), but occasionally mention of women keepers can be found. In 1571 the constable Marco Ocaña chose Mari Sánchez de Marquina as *madre* for his eleven shacks. According to Ocaña she was an excellent selection because "she was a mature woman experienced in her trade; she resided in the brothel district and was the mother-in-law of Rafael Rodríguez, also a brothel keeper." [91]

Whether male or female, all appointments to brothel keeper had to be approved by the city. Furthermore, all appointees were required to take an oath before the town clerk to uphold the statutes of the brothel (*Ordenanzas de la mancebía*). The fact that these posts offered ample oppor-

[91] Rodríguez Marín, *El Loaysa*, p. 355; Cervantes Saavedra, *Rinconete y Cortadillo* (1905 ed.), pp. 107, 110; AMS, Varios Antiguos, Mancebías, no. 339, as quoted in *ibid.*, p. 112. This legajo no longer exists in the Municipal Archives.

tunities for gain made them popular and highly prized. The *padres* easily exploited the women through their unscrupulous dealings. They rented clothes to them at a profit and lent money on their future earnings. One of their principal activities was pawnbroking, and they would lend money on all kinds of pledges including the women themselves, who were often "pawned" by their ruffian boy friends for 10 or 20 ducats. Throughout the century the brothel ordinances repeatedly prohibited such abuses, but seemingly to no avail. In the opinion of the Jesuit Juan de Mariana, the *padres* were cruel and avaricious men who tyrannized the unhappy women under their control; they were *padres* in name only.[92]

Surprisingly enough, at the time such positions were not considered demeaning or dishonorable. The brothel keepers, like Padre Carrascosa in *El rufián dichoso*, prided themselves on being honest, respectable men who held "honorable posts in the country." Similarly, the brothel owners held themselves in as high esteem as they did the *padres*. In 1584 Licenciado Francisco Díaz addressed a petition to the city council in which he proudly described himself as the owner of twenty *boticas* and his keeper as a "respectable married man and a good Christian." [93] Moreover, some of the *padres* had overly scrupulous consciences. The Jesuit Pedro de León (who for many years conducted

[92] Juan de Mariana, *Tratado contra los juegos públicos* in *Biblioteca de Autores Españoles*, XXXI (Madrid, 1950), Chapter XIX; BM, MS. Eg. 1873, "Ordenanzas a los Padres de la mancebía (año 1570)," folios 155–156.

[93] Cervantes Saavedra, *El rufián dichoso*, Jornada I, p. 45; AMS, Varios Antiguos, Mancebía, no. 339, as quoted in Cervantes Saavedra, *Rinconete y Cortadillo* (1905 ed.), p. 113.

missions in the brothel) tells of a *padre* who so feared for his salvation that he confessed every eight days.[94]

One of the best sources of information about the Sevillian brothel is the collection of governing ordinances that were enacted by the city government during the sixteenth century. These statutes had two main objectives: to protect the rights of the women and to insure the proper functioning of an evil but accepted institution. To begin with, restrictions were placed on admission to the brothel. Women who wished to enter had to be approved by city officials. They had to prove that they were commoners of more than twelve years of age; had lost their virginity; were orphans, of unknown parents, or had been abandoned by their parents; and were in good health (this required a certificate from the official brothel physician). Municipal officers had the moral obligation to try to dissuade candidates from such a perditious path, but failing this, they were empowered to issue documentation authorizing them to enter the brothel. Strict penalties were provided for those who failed to comply with these regulations. When in 1600 a certain Mariana Martínez was found to be exercising her profession in the brothel without prior municipal examination and authorization, she was forcibly expelled "until such time as she has satisfied the regulations," and the brothel keeper who accepted her was fined 12 *reales*.[95]

[94] Domínguez Ortiz, "Delitos y suplicios," p. 27.

[95] AMS, Colección del Conde del Aguila, tomo 7, Letra A, no. 73, as quoted in "Documentos relativos a la Mancebía," *Archivo Hispalense*, IV (1888), 16; BM, MS. Eg. 1873; Asensio, "El Compás," p. 412.

If the brothel statutes helped to protect women from being forced into a life of prostitution against their will, they also effectively kept down their numbers. There is no way to determine the brothel population because of lack of documentation. One set of figures exists for the sixteenth century, that is, the census of 1561, but it only includes women who were denizens of Seville, a meager fourteen in all. Some comparative statistics for the seventeenth century (especially those of 1620) are no more illuminating because they reflect a period in which church authorities were exercising pressure to close the brothel and had succeeded in placing restrictions on it.[96]

The origins of the brothel inmates remain obscure. All those mentioned in the census of 1561 were *vecinos* of Seville, but apparently a substantial number came from neighboring towns and villages. Some were apparently drawn from the brothels of nearby cities—like La Pintada in Francisco de Lugo y Dávila's novel *De la hermanía*, who left the San Lucar de Barrameda brothel for that of Seville where "more money could be earned." [97] The brothel ordinances of 1570 specifically excluded mulatto women, and similar prohibitions existed for married women and those whose parents resided in Seville, but it is quite clear that all three groups were amply represented. The number of married women is surprising; some of their husbands are listed among the male residents of the brothel district in the

[96] AGS, Expedientes de hacienda, leg. 170, p. 525. Figures for 1620 are in "Documentos relativos a la Mancebía," pp. 16–18. An excerpt from another list dated 1600 has been published by Rodríguez Marín, *El Loaysa*, p. 152.

[97] Francisco de Lugo y Dávila, *Teatro popular (Novelas)*, ed. Emilio Cotarelo y Mori (Madrid, 1906), p. 133.

census of 1561 and on the seventeenth-century lists. Other male inhabitants of this quarter were either relatives or boy friends. Among the latter category were ruffians who acted as procurers for the women and even a number of men who worked as police officers (*criados* or *mozos de la justica*).[98]

The income of the brothel women varied, but age and physical appearance were important factors. Good-looking young prostitutes (*marcas godeñas*) earned from 4 to 5 ducats a day, while older or less attractive women received around 60 *cuartos* (4 maravedís). Typical of the second category was La Pericona, the idol of the ruffian Trampagos in Cervantes' *El rufián viudo*, who was fifty-six years of age, practically toothless, and had taken the sweat cure for syphilis more than eleven times. La Pericona had been in the brothel for fifteen years, and the documents indicate that many prostitutes were there for as many years and even longer. Some women were active for twenty or more years. Age and defects were concealed by heavy makeup and the skillful use of cosmetics and dyes. La Pericona, for example, with dyed hair (her own was white) and false teeth, was able to "pass for thirty-two years of age." Painted faces, rouged lips, and bosoms painted with ceruse were the marks of the prostitute.[99]

To facilitate the task of law officers in enforcing regula-

[98] Rodríguez Marín, *El Loaysa*, p. 152; BM, Eg. 1873, Ordenanza XIII, folios 156v–157; AGS, Expedientes de hacienda, leg. 170, fol. 525.

[99] Cervantes Saavedra, *El rufián viudo*, p. 23. In 1620 two prostitutes, Angela del Castillo and Ana María, were ordered to leave the brothel because of "age, ill health and the many years that they had been there." The names of both these women appear on the list of 1600; a certain Gerónima "la rubia" is also on the 1600 and 1620 lists.

tions concerning prostitutes, these women were subject to certain restrictions in dress. They were not permitted to wear hats, gloves, mantles, or slippers, but only half-mantles (like modern-day mantillas), for which reason they were called the "ladies of the half-mantle" (*damas de medio manto*). Throughout the sixteenth century municipal authorities stipulated that these mantles be yellow, as they had been in the Middle Ages, and it was not until the seventeenth century that they finally approved what had been the garb of prostitutes for many years—the short black mantle. This distinctive dress had to be worn by the women at all times in public, except in church, when they "might wear their mantles long like respectable women."[100]

Finally, the city fathers did not neglect the prostitutes' spiritual life. On Sundays and feast days when the brothel was closed, they were required to attend church, where they were taken as a group by the "constable of the brothel." During Lent especially strong efforts were made to convert them, but most seemed to be like La Pericona, whose "ear had been bent by the droning out of thirty Lenten sermons," but who had resisted them all.[101] The Jesuits in particular carried their message of redemption directly into the brothel, exhorting the inmates to abandon their sinful lives. On these occasions the doors of the brothel were closed, and it was sealed off from the surrounding area. The Jesuits apparently met with little success, although Padre Pedro de León, who spent his life redeeming prostitutes and criminals, reports that he once

[100] AMS, Escribanías del cabildo, siglo XVII, tomo 22, no. 14; BM, Eg. 1873, Ordenanza XI, fol. 156v.
[101] Cervantes Saavedra, *El rufián viudo*, p. 24; AMS, Colección del Conde del Aguila, Letra A, tomo 7, no. 20.

secured the conversion of eleven of the women. This was most unusual. Repentant prostitutes were given refuge in the convent of the Dulcísimo Nombre de Jesús which had been founded for this express purpose.[102]

The brothel represented an officially sanctioned center of promiscuity outside the walls; the intention of city authorities was to draw all coarse and vicious elements into one area that could be watched closely, and in doing so to purge the streets. It is apparent that they failed; undesirables roamed about, and the city was powerless to stop them. Furthermore, stringent municipal policies in regard to the brothel inmates actually increased the number of prostitutes on the streets. Contemporaries constantly complained about their conspicuous presence all over the city, especially in the barrio of La Resolana (between the Golden Tower and the Arenal Gate) and in the extramural districts of San Bernardo and Triana. In 1601 the prebendary Porras de la Cámara estimated that there were some three thousand prostitutes in Seville, and it is quite clear that most of them were out on the streets rather than in the brothel.[103] Undoubtedly, the streetwalkers included women who had been expelled from the brothel because of ill health. At least this is what the brothel physician Licenciado García Arroyal claimed in a petition that he sent to the city council in 1572 urging the municipality to

[102] Domínguez Ortiz, "Delitos y suplicios," pp. 25–29. For more about the convent of the Dulcísimo Nombre de Jesús, see Morgado *Historia*, p. 448.

[103] "Memorial del Licenciado Porras de la Cámara al Arzobispo de Sevilla sobre el mal gobierno y corrupción de costumbres en aquella ciudad," *Revista de Archivos, Bibliotecas y Museos*, 3ª época, IV (1900), 552.

round up these women and send them to the appropriate hospitals. His opinion is confirmed by Padre León, who blamed them for the existence of so much syphilis in the city.[104] In addition to these hapless creatures, another category of streetwalkers was described by Porras de la Cámara. They were usually young and attractive and worked under the direction of a male procurer who often maintained quarters for them in some cheap rooming house. According to the prebendary Porras, their earnings could amount to 4,000 ducats a year, and they usually maintained friendly relations with the police. La Colindres in Cervantes' *Coloquio de los perros* is a good example of this kind of prostitute. She worked the streets under the protection of her lover, a constable. With the cooperation of a notary friend (who also lived with a prostitute) they made a living by trapping and blackmailing men (preferably foreigners with money) who were lured into compromising situations with La Colindres.[105]

Much has been said in the foregoing pages about the ineffectiveness of the Sevillian government in dealing with organized crime, but it is not true that city officials ignored the problem or willingly accepted it. That they constantly legislated against "vagabonds and criminals" can be seen from the large number of laws on the statute books, but graft and corruption prevented this legislation from being carried out. Nevertheless, it is doubtful whether they

[104] Domínguez Ortiz, "Delitos y suplicios," p. 28; AMS, Escribanías del cabildo, siglo XVI, Mancebía, no. 62; *ibid.*, siglo XVII, Mancebía, no. 90.

[105] Cervantes Saavedra, *El coloquio de los perros*, pp. 261–268; "Memorial del Licenciado Porras de la Cámara," p. 552.

could have been more successful even if there had been less corruption and maladministration. What really defeated the efforts of the city fathers was a basic defect in the Spanish system of government during this period: the lack of a clear division of powers among governing authorities. The whole century was characterized by bitter conflicts of jurisdiction between the church and the municipality; between the Asistente and the Audiencia; and between the Audiencia and the city. These constant struggles made strong and effective government impossible.

The administration of the reforming Count of Puñonrostro (1597–1599) amply illustrates the limitations of the system. Upon assuming the position of Asistente, Puñonrostro, a stern disciplinarian, inaugurated a vigorous campaign against misgovernment and corruption in Seville.[106] His program included energetic measures against vagabonds and delinquents. In addition to the establishment of a municipal licensing system for beggars, he ordered the frequent inspection of inns and rooming houses where undesirables gathered, and he personally accompanied the inspectors on many occasions. Several notorious criminals who for many years had operated openly in Seville were seized and executed; others fearing for their lives fled the city. But Puñonrostro's success doomed him, for a strong executive in the person of the Asistente was the last thing

[106] For information about the career of Francisco Arias de Bobadilla, Count of Puñonrostro, see J. Guichot y Parody, *Historia del Excm. Ayuntamiento de la Ciudad de Sevilla* (Seville, 1896), II, 133–136; Ariño, *Sucesos de Sevilla*, pp. 45–99. Reference to his "persecution of criminals" is in M. de Cervantes Saavedra, *La ilustre fregona* in *Novelas ejemplares*, ed. F. Rodríguez Marín, II (Madrid, 1957), 236–238.

in the world desired by the Audiencia. Fearful of a diminution of their powers and prerogatives, the judges opposed and counteracted his efforts to such a degree that he finally gave up in despair. With the departure of the Count of Puñonrostro the normal state of disorder and confusion returned. Maladministration and corruption; fabulous wealth and massive poverty; overpopulation and insecurity—all that was Seville in the sixteenth century—enabled the underworld to survive and prosper and its members to live out their marginal and nonproductive lives.

Underworld elements were just one of the many groups that made up the population of sixteenth-century Seville, but whose presence along with that of other marginal classes—Moriscos, freedmen, and slaves—greatly added to the diversity and cosmopolitanism for which the city was justly famous.

The heterogeneity that characterized the lower ranks of society also prevailed at the top. The usual stereotype of the Spanish nobility as a narrow Old Christian caste obsessed with the idea of racial and religious purity and profoundly anticommercial has no place in Seville. On the contrary, the Sevillian nobility was never a closed or homogeneous class; there had always been incursions into its ranks by nonnobles, especially in the fifteenth century by wealthy merchants of *converso* background, and this movement reached its culmination in the sixteenth century. By the middle of that century the majority of the Sevillian nobility consisted of recently ennobled families of mixed social and racial origins whose commercial orientation and activities reflected their mercantile background. In cooperation with enterprising merchant-commoners of similar *converso* descent to whom they were often related through blood or marriage, they created a powerful elite that by 1550 dominated the transatlantic trade. These same families controlled the church, monopolized the municipal government, and constituted the largest number of titled professionals. With the stigma of their origins carefully hidden under false genealogies and their lives and ideas patterned along the lines of the official ideology of religious orthodoxy and *limpieza de sangre*, these aristocrats and traders directed the destinies of their city, and it is to them that Seville owed its period of greatness and prosperity in the sixteenth century.

Bibliography

PRIMARY SOURCES

Manuscripts

Archivo de Protocolos, Seville, Siglo XVI. Escribanos: Pedro Almonacid, año 1580; Gonzalo Alvarez de Aguilar, años 1504, 1520; Juan Alvarez de Alcalá, año 1508; Alonso de la Barrera, años 1523, 1525, 1536; Cristóbal de la Becerra, año 1536; Francisco de Castellanos, años 1518, 1524–1526, 1528; Alonso de Cazalla, años 1526, 1537–1540, 1543–1546, 1548–1551; Alonso de Cívico, año 1580; Juan de la Cuadra, años 1512, 1516–1517; Mateo de la Cuadra, años 1509–1510, 1512, 1514–1515; Francisco Díaz, año 1577; Pedro Fernández, año 1523; Juan Franco, años 1550–1551; Luis García, año 1508; Baltasar de Godoy, año 1590; Bernal González Vallesillo, años 1508–1510, 1512–1513, 1515–1516; Gaspar de León, año 1595; Diego López, años 1518–1520; Diego de la Palma, año 1570; Hernán Pérez, año 1555; Luis de Porras, año 1574; Melchor de Portes, años 1548, 1550; Bartolomé Quijada, año 1505; Fernán Ruiz, año 1506; Antón Ruiz de Porras, año 1525; Fernán Ruiz de Porras, años 1515, 1520; Francisco Segura, años 1500, 1502, 1504; Manuel Segura, años 1509, 1513–1515, 1518, 1520, 1525; Gaspar de Toledo, año 1580; Pedro Tristán, año 1527.

Archivo General de Simancas, Valladolid. Sección: Expedientes de Hacienda, legajo 170.

Archivo Histórico Nacional, Madrid. Sección: Clero, legajos 6676, 6677, 6678: Ordenes Militares, Pruebas de Calatrava, expediente 71, Pruebas de Santiago, expedientes 1357, 5076.

Archivo Municipal, Seville. Sección: Primera, Archivo de Privilegios, Tumbo, carpetas 1, 5, 8; Reales Provisiones, carpetas 24–26; Sección: Tercera, Escribanías del Cabildo, siglo XVI, 20 vols.; Sección: Quarta, Escribanías del Cabildo, siglo XVII, tomo 20; Sección: Décima, Actas Capitulares, 1570–1598; Libro de Propios, años 1581, 1597–1599, 1600, 1602: Papeles Importantes, siglo XVI, tomos 5, 6, 9; Varios Antiguos, carpetas 125, 144, 335.

Biblioteca de la Real Academia de Historia, Madrid. Sección: Colección Juan Bautista Muñoz, MS. 4859, tomo 74; Colección Salazar, R-2.

Biblioteca Nacional, Madrid. Sección: Manuscritos, 732=D-42, 3207, 3449, 3449=K-165, 5736=Q-38, 9372=Cc-42, 9577, 18225, 18291, 18735.

British Museum, London. Section: Manuscripts, Add. 21.447, 28.257, 28.335, 28.341, 28.349, 28.358, 28.369, Eg. 1873.

Published Documents and Contemporary Writings

Alcázar, Baltasar del. *Poesías.* Ed. Francisco Rodríguez Marín. Madrid: Real Academia Española, 1910.

Alemán, Mateo. *Guzmán de Alfarache.* In Angel Valbuena Prat, *La novela picaresca española.* Madrid: Aguilar, 1956.

Ariño, Francisco de. *Sucesos de Sevilla de 1592 a 1604.* Seville: Impr. de Tarasco y Lassa, 1873.

Benítez de Lugo, A., ed. *Discurso de la Comunidad de Sevilla.* Seville: R. Tarasco y Lassa, 1881.

Bernáldez, Andrés. *Historia de los Reyes Católicos.* 2 vols. Seville: Sociedad de Bibliófilos Andaluces, 1869.

Bleda, Jaime. *Coronica de los moros de España.* Valencia: Felipe Mey, 1618.

Bodin, Jean. *The Six Bookes of a Commonweale.* Ed. Kenneth

Douglas McRae. Cambridge, Mass.: Harvard University Press, 1962.

Braun, Georg. *Civitates orbis terrarum.* Vols. V, VI: 1576–1618. Cologne: Apud Petrum à Brachel, sumptibus auctorum, 1612–1617.

Caro, Rodrigo. *Antigüedades y principado de la Ilustríssima ciudad de Sevilla.* Seville: Andrés Grande, 1634.

Castillo Solórzano, Alonso de. *Aventuras del Bachiller Trapaza.* Madrid: Colección Cisneros, Edición "Atlas," 1944.

——. *La garduña de Sevilla y anzuelo de las bolsas.* Madrid: Clásicos Castellanos, 1942.

——. *La niña de los embustes, Teresa de Manzanares.* Madrid: M. Aguilar, 1929.

Cervantes Saavedra, Miguel de. *El celoso extremeño.* In *Las novelas ejemplares.* Ed. Francisco Rodríguez Marín. Vol. II. Madrid: Clásicos Castellanos, 1957.

——. *El coloquio de los perros.* In *Las novelas ejemplares.* Ed. Francisco Rodríguez Marín. Vol. II. Madrid: Clásicos Castellanos, 1957.

——. *Don Quijote de la Mancha.* Ed. Martín de Riquer. New York: Las Américas, 1966.

——. *La Gitanilla.* In *Las novelas ejemplares.* Ed. Francisco Rodríguez Marín. Vol. I. Madrid: Clásicos Castellanos, 1952.

——. *La ilustre fregona.* In *Novelas ejemplares.* Ed. Francisco Rodríguez Marín. Vol. II. Madrid: Clásicos Castellanos, 1957.

——. *El Licenciado Vidriera.* In *Las novelas ejemplares.* Ed. Francisco Rodríguez Marín. Vol. II. Madrid: Clásicos Castellanos, 1957.

——. *Rinconete y Cortadillo.* Ed. Francisco Rodríguez Marín. Seville: Tipografía de Francisco de P. Díaz, 1905.

——. *Rinconete y Cortadillo.* Ed. Francisco Rodríguez Marín. Madrid: Clásicos Castellanos, 1952.

——. *El rufián dichoso.* Ed. Edward Nagy. New York: Las Américas, 1968.

——. *El trato de Argel*. In *Comedias y entremeses*, Vol. V. Madrid: Gráficas Reunidas, S.A., 1920.

Chaunu, Huguette and Pierre. *Séville et l'Atlantique, 1504 à 1650*. Paris: S.E.V.P.E.N., 1955–1960. Vols. I–IV, VIII.

Chaves, Cristóbal de. *La relación de la cárcel de Sevilla*. In Bartolomé José Gallardo, *Ensayo de una biblioteca española de libros raros y curiosos*, Vol. I. Madrid: Rivadeneyra, 1863.

Colección de documentos inéditos, relativos al descubrimiento, conquista y organización de las antiguas posesiones españolas de América y Oceanía. 42 vols. Madrid: 1864–1884.

Colección de documentos inéditos, relativos al descubrimiento, conquista y organización de las antiguas posesiones españolas de ultramar. 25 vols. Madrid: Sucesores de Rivadeneyra, 1885–1932.

Cotarelo y Mori, Emilio. *Colección de Entremeses, Loas, Bailes, Jácaras y Mojigangas desde fines del siglo XVI a mediados del XVIII*. In *Nueva Biblioteca de Autores Españoles*, Vol. XVII. Madrid: Bailly-Ballière, 1911.

Covarrubias, Sebastián de. *Tesoro de la lengua Castellana o Española*. Ed. Martín de Riquer. Barcelona: S. A. Horta, 1943.

Fernández de Oviedo, Gonzalo. *Historia general y natural de las Indias*. Ed. Juan Pérez de Tudela Bueso. *Biblioteca de Autores Españoles*, Vols. 117–121. Madrid: Ediciones Atlas, 1959.

García, Carlos. *La desordinada codicia de los bienes ajenos*. In Angel Valbuena Prat, *La novela picaresca española*. Madrid: Aguilar, 1956.

García Mercadal, J., ed. *Viajes de extranjeros por España y Portugal*. Vol. I. Madrid: Aguilar, 1952.

Gestoso y Pérez, José. *Ensayo de un diccionario de artífices que florecieron en Sevilla desde el siglo XIII al XVIII in-*

clusive. 3 vols. Seville: En la Oficina de la Andalucía Moderna, 1899–1908.

González, Tomás. *Censo de población de las provincias y partidas de la Corona de Castilla.* Madrid, Imprenta Real, 1829.

Hernández Díaz, J., and A. Muro Orejón. *El testamento de don Hernando Colón.* Seville: La Gavidia, 1941.

Hesse, J., ed. *Romancero de Germanía.* Madrid: Taurus, 1967.

Las Casas, Bartolomé de. *Historia de las Indias.* Ed. Agustín Millares Carlo. 3 vols. Mexico City: Fondo de Cultura Económica, 1951.

Lope de Vega Carpio, Félix. *El acero de Madrid,* in *Obras escogidas.* Vol. I. Madrid: Aguilar, 1952.

——. *Amar, servir y esperar.* In *Obras de Lope de Vega,* Vol. III. Madrid: Tipografía de la Revista De Archivos, Bibliotecas y Museos, 1917.

——. *El arenal de Sevilla.* In *Obras escogidas.* Ed. Federico Carlos Sáinz de Robles. Vol. I. Madrid: Aguilar, 1952.

——. *La Dorotea.* Ed. E. Morby. Berkeley: University of California Press, 1958.

——. *El premio del bien hablar.* In *Obras de Lope de Vega.* Ed. Emilio Cotarelo y Mori. Vol. XIII. Madrid: Real Academia Española, 1930.

——. *Servir a señor discreto.* In *Obras de Lope de Vega,* Vol. XV. Madrid: Tipografía de la Revista De Archivos, Bibliotecas y Museos, 1913.

Lugo y Dávila, Francisco de. *Teatro popular (Novelas).* Ed. Emilio Cotarelo y Mori. Madrid: Librería de la Viuda de Rico, 1906.

Mariana, Juan de. *Tratado contra los juegos públicos.* In *Biblioteca de Autores Españoles,* Vol. XXXI. Madrid: Ediciones Atlas, 1950.

Marineo Sículo, Lucio. *Obra de las cosas memorables de España.* Alcalá de Henares: Juan de Brocar, 1539.

Mexía, Pedro. *Diálogos o Coloquios de Pedro Mejía.* Ed. Margaret L. Mulroney. Iowa City, Iowa: The University of Iowa Press, 1930.

"Memorial del Licenciado Porras de la Cámara al Arzobispo de Sevilla sobre el mal gobierno y corrupción de costumbres en aquella ciudad," *Revista de Archivos, Bibliotecas y Museos.* 3ª época, IV (1900), 550–554.

Mercado, Fray Tomás de. *Summa de tratos y contratos.* Seville: Fernando Días, 1587.

Morgado, Alonso de. *Historia de Sevilla.* Seville: A. Pescioni y I. de León, 1587 (J. M. Ariza, 1887).

Ordenanzas de Sevilla. Seville: I. Varela, 1527.

Ortiz de Zúñiga, Diego. *Anales eclesiásticos y seculares de la muy noble y leal ciudad de Sevilla, metrópoli de la Andalucía.* Vols. III, IV. Madrid: Imprenta Real, 1796.

——. *Discurso geneológico de los Ortizes de Sevilla.* Cadiz: Pedro Ortiz, 1670.

Otte, Enrique, ed. *Cedularios de la Monarquía española relativos a la isla de Cubagua (1523–1550).* 2 vols. Caracas: La Fundación John Bolton y la Fundación Eugenio Mendoza, 1961.

Pacheco, Francisco. *Libro de descripción de verdaderos retratos, de ilustres y memorables varones.* Seville, 1599; Seville: Litografía de Enrique Utrera, 1870.

Quevedo y Villegas, Francisco de. *Boda de Negros.* In *Obras completas (Obras en Verso).* Ed. Luis Astrana Marín. Madrid: Aguilar, 1952.

——. *Historia de la vida del Buscón.* Ed. Samuel Gili Gaya. Zaragoza: Clásicos Ebro, 1959.

Salas Barbadillo, Alonso Jerónimo de. *La Peregrinación sabia y el sagaz Estacio, marido examinado.* Ed. Francisco A. de Icaza. Madrid: Clásicos Castellanos, 1958.

Seville. Archivo de Protocolos. *Catálogo de los fondos americanos del Archivo de Protocolos de Sevilla.* Vol. IV. Madrid: Tipografía de archivos, 1935.

——. *Catálogo de los fondos americanos del Archivo de Protocolos de Sevilla.* Vol. V. Seville: La Gavidia, 1937.

——. *Catálogo de los fondos americanos del Archivo de Protocolos de Sevilla.* Vols. X, XI, XIV: Colección de documentos inéditos para la historia de Hispano-América. Madrid-Buenos Aires: Compañía Ibero-Americano de Publicaciones, 1930–1932.

Simancas. Archivo General. *Registro General del Sello.* Vol. X. Valladolid: C.S.I.C., 1967.

Spain. Archivo general de Indias, Seville. *Catálogo de pasajeros a Indias durante los siglos XVI, XVII y XVIII.* 3 vols. Seville: La Gavidia, 1940–1946.

Suárez de Figueroa, Cristóbal. *El pasagero.* Ed. Francisco Rodríguez Marín. Madrid: Renacimiento, 1913.

——. *Plaza universal de todas ciencias y artes.* Perpignan: Luys Roure, 1629.

Veitia Linaje, Joseph de. *Norte de la Contratación de las Indias occidentales.* Seville: I. F. de Blas, 1672.

Vélez de Guevara, Luis. *El diablo cojuelo.* Ed. Francisco Rodríguez Marín. Madrid: Clásicos Castellanos, 1951.

Zapata, Luis. *Miscelánea.* In *Memorial Histórico Español,* Vol. XI. Madrid: La Real Academia de Historia, 1859.

SECONDARY SOURCES

Books

Astrain, A. *Historia de la Compañía de Jesús en la Asistencia de España.* Vol. V. Madrid: Razón y Fe, 1916.

Aubrun, Charles. *La comedia española, 1600–1680.* Madrid: Taurus, 1968.

Azevedo, J. Lúcio. *Épocas de Portugal económico*. Lisbon: Teixeira, 1929.

Beneyto, Juan. *Historia social de España y de Hispanoamerica*. Madrid: Aguilar, 1961.

Bermejo y Carballo, José. *Glorias religiosas de Sevilla*. Seville: Imprenta y Librería del Salvador, 1882.

Bornat y Barrachina, Pascual. *Los moriscos españoles y su expulsión*. Valencia: Impr. de Francisco Vives y Mora, 1901.

Brau, Salvador. *La colonización de Puerto Rico*. San Juan: Tipografía "Heraldo Español," 1930.

Braudel, Fernand. *La Méditerranée et le monde méditerranéen à l'époque de Philippe II*. Paris: Colin, 1949.

Carande, Ramón. *Carlos V y sus banqueros*. Madrid: Revista de Occidente, 1943.

Caro Baroja, Julio. *Los Judíos en la España moderna y contemporánea*. 3 vols. Madrid: Ediciones Arión, 1962.

Castro, Américo. *Aspectos del vivir hispánico*. Madrid: Alianza Editorial, S.A., 1970.

——. *The Structure of Spanish History*. Trans. Edmund L. King. Princeton: Princeton University Press, 1954.

Chandler, Frank. *Romances of Roguery*. New York: Burt Franklin, 1961.

Chaves, Manuel. *Cosas nuevas y viejas*. Seville, 1903.

Cotarelo y Valledor, Armando. *Fray Diego de Deza*. Madrid: 1922.

Deleito y Piñuela, José. *La mala vida en la España de Felipe IV*. Madrid: Espasa-Calpe, S.A., 1959.

Domínguez Ortiz, Antonio. *Los Judeoconversos en España y América*. Madrid: Ediciones Istmo, 1971.

——. *Orto y Ocaso de Sevilla*. Seville: Imprenta de la Diputación Provincial, 1946.

——. *La sociedad española en el siglo XVII*. 2 vols. Madrid: C.S.I.C., 1963–1970.

Elliott, John. *Imperial Spain, 1469–1716.* New York: St. Martin's Press, 1963.

——. *The Old World and the New—1492–1650.* Cambridge: Cambridge University Press, 1970.

Fernández de Navarrete, Martín. *Vida y Obras de Martín Fernández de Navarrete,* In *Biblioteca de Autores Españoles.* Vols. LXXV–LXXVII. Madrid: Ediciones Atlas, 1954–1955.

Fernández Duro, Cesáreo. *Armada española desde la unión de los reinos de Castilla y León.* Vol. I. Madrid: Sucesores de Rivadeneyra, 1895.

Gestoso y Pérez, José. *Curiosidades antiguas sevillanas, serie segunda.* Seville: En la oficina del periódico El Correo de Andalucía, 1910.

——. *Historia de los Barros vidriados sevillanos.* Seville: La Andalucía Moderna, 1903.

——. *Noticia histórico-descriptiva de la bandera de la hermandad de Nuestra Señora de los Reyes y San Mateo (vulgo de los sastres).* Seville: Gironés y Orduña, 1891.

Giménez Fernández, Manuel. *Bartolomé de las Casas.* 2 vols. Seville: Escuela de Estudios Hispano-Americanos, 1953–1960.

Góngora, Diego Ignacio de. *Historia del Colegio mayor de Santo Tomás.* 2 vols. Seville: Rasco, 1890.

González, Julio. *Repartimiento de Sevilla.* 2 vols. Madrid: Consejo Superior de Investigaciones Científicas, 1951.

González de la Calle, Urbano. *Sebastián Fox Morcillo.* Madrid: Imprenta del Asilo de Huérfanos del Sagrado Corazón de Jesús, 1903.

González de León, Félix. *Noticia artística histórica y curiosa de todos los edificios públicos, sagrados y profanos . . . de Sevilla, y de muchas casas particulares. . . .* 2 vols. Seville: José Hidalgo y Compañía, 1844.

González Moreno, J. *Fernando Enríquez de Ribera, Duque de Alcalá.* Seville: Imprenta Provincial, 1968.

Guerra, Francisco. *Nicolás Bautista Monardes, su vida y su obra.* Mexico City: Compañía Fundidora de Fierro y Acero de Monterrey, 1961.

Guichot y Parody, Joaquín. *Historia de la ciudad de Sevilla y pueblos importantes de su provincia desde los tiempos más remotos hasta nuestros días.* Seville: Imprenta de Gironés y Orduña, 1875–1886. (Especially Vols. III and IV.)

——. *Historia del Excm. Ayuntamiento de la Ciudad de Sevilla.* Vol. II. Seville: Tipografía de la Región, 1896.

Haring, Clarence. *The Spanish Empire in America.* New York: Oxford University Press, 1947.

——. *Trade and Navigation between Spain and the Indies in the Time of the Hapsburgs.* Cambridge, Mass.: Harvard University Press, 1918.

Hazañas y La Rua, Joaquín. *Historia de Sevilla.* Seville: Academia de Estudios Sevillanos, 1933.

——. *La Imprenta en Sevilla.* 2 vols. Seville: Diputación Provincial, 1945–1949.

——. *Maese Rodrigo, 1444–1509.* Seville: Librería e Imp. de Izquierdo y Comp.ª, 1909.

——. *Vázquez de Leca, 1573–1649.* Seville: Imprenta y Librería de Sobrinos de Izquierdo, 1918.

Jordán de Urríes y Azara, José. *Bibliografía y estudio crítico de Jáuregui.* Madrid: Est. Tipográfico Sucesores de Rivadeneyra, 1899.

Kamen, Henry. *The Spanish Inquisition.* New York: New American Library, 1965.

Lapeyre, Henri. *Une famille de marchands, Les Ruiz: Contribution à l'étude du commerce entre la France et l'Espagne au temps de Philippe II.* Paris: S.E.V.P.E.N., 1955.

Lapeyre, Henri. *La Géographie de l'Espagne morisque.* Paris: S.E.V.P.E.N., 1959.

Lea, Charles H. *History of the Inquisition of Spain.* Vol. II. New York: Macmillan Company, 1906.

Lockhart, James. *Spanish Peru, 1532–1560.* Madison: University of Wisconsin Press, 1968.

Lohmann Villena, Guillermo. *Les Espinosa, une famille d'hommes d'affaires en Espagne et aux Indes à l'époque de la colonisation.* Paris: S.E.V.P.E.N., 1968.

López Martínez, Celestino. *Mudéjares y Moriscos sevillanos.* Seville: Tipografía Rodríguez Giménez y Compañía, 1935.

Lynch, John. *Spain under the Habsburgs.* 2 vols. New York: Oxford University Press, 1964–1969.

Maravall, José. *Las Comunidades de Castilla.* Madrid: Revista de Occidente, 1963.

Márquez Villanueva, Francisco. *Investigaciones sobre Juan Alvarez Gato.* Madrid: Anejos del Boletín de la Real Academia Española, 1960.

Mata Carriazo, Juan de. *Los anales de Garci-Sánchez, jurado de Sevilla.* In *Anales de la Universidad Hispalense,* Vol. XVI. Seville: Imprenta de la Gavidia, 1953.

Matute y Gaviria, Justino. *Hijos de Sevilla señalados en santidad, letras, armas, artes o dignidad.* Vol. I. Seville: En la oficina de "El Orden," 1886.

——. *Noticias relativas a la historia de Sevilla que no constan en sus anales.* Seville: Rasco, 1886.

Medina, José Toribio. *La Primitiva Inquisición americana (1493–1569).* Santiago de Chile: Imprenta Elzeviriana, 1914.

Méndez Bejarano, Mario. *Diccionario de escritores, maestros y oradores naturales de Sevilla y su actual provincia.* 3 vols. Seville: Tipografía Gironés, 1922–1925.

Menéndez Pelayo, Marcelino. *Historia de los heterodoxos españoles.* Vol. V. 2nd ed. Madrid: V. Suárez, 1928.

Montoto de Sedas, Santiago. *Las calles de Sevilla.* Seville: Imprenta Hispania, 1940.

——. *Sevilla en el imperio, siglo XVI.* Seville: Nueva Librería Vda. de C. García, 1938.

Pérez de Guzmán y Boza, J. *Discursos leídos ante la Real*

Academia Sevillana el 26 de abril de 1892. Seville: Rasco, 1892.

Pérez y López, Antonio Xavier. *Teatro de la legislación universal de España e Indias.* Vol. XI. Madrid: En la Imprenta de M. González, 1796.

Pike, Ruth. *Enterprise and Adventure: The Genoese in Seville and the Opening of the New World.* Ithaca: Cornell University Press, 1966.

Rodríguez Marín, Francisco. *Cervantes estudió en Sevilla (1564–1565).* Seville: F. de P. Díaz, 1905.

——. *Discursos leídos ante la Real Academia Española.* Seville: Tipografía de F. de P. Díaz, 1907.

——. *Estudios Cervantinos.* Madrid: Ediciones Atlas, 1947.

——. *El Loaysa de "El celoso extremeño": Estudio histórico-literario.* Seville: Francisco de P. Díaz, 1901.

——. *Nuevos datos para las biografías de cien escritores de los siglos XVI y XVII.* Madrid: Revista de Archivos, Bibliotecas y Museos, 1923.

Rumeu de Armas, Antonio. *España en el Africa Atlántica.* 2 vols. Madrid: C.S.I.C., 1956–1957.

——. *Historia de la Previsión social en España.* Madrid: Editorial Revista de Derecho Privado, 1944.

Salillas, Rafael. *El delincuente español: El lenguaje.* Madrid: Librería de Victoriano Suárez, 1896.

——. *El delincuente español: La Hampa.* Madrid: Librería de Victoriano Suárez, 1898.

Sánchez Arjona, José. *Anales del teatro en Sevilla.* Seville: Rasco, 1898.

Scelle, Georges. *La traité négrière aux Indes de Castille.* 2 vols. Paris: L. Larose and L. Tenin, 1906.

Schäfer, Ernst. *Beiträge zur Geschichte des spanischen Protestantismus und der Inquisition im sechzehnten Jahrhundert.* 3 vols. Gutersloh: C. Bertelsmann, 1902.

——. *El consejo real y supremo de las Indias.* 2 vols. Seville: M. Carmona, 1935.

Scheuss de Studer, Elena F. *La trata de negros en el Río de la Plata durante el siglo XVIII.* Buenos Aires: Universidad de Buenos Aires, 1958.

Velázquez y Sánchez, José. *Anales epidémicos.* Seville: Imprenta y Litografía, Librería de D. José María, 1866.

Verlinden, Charles. *L'esclavage dans l'Europe médiévale. I: Péninsule Iberique—France.* Bruges: De Tempel, 1955.

Vicens Vives, Jaime. *Historia social y económica de España y América.* Vols. II, III. Barcelona: Editorial Teide, 1957.

——. *Manuel de historia económica.* Barcelona: Editorial Teide, 1959.

Villa, Antonio Martín. *Reseña histórica de la Universidad de Sevilla.* Seville: E. Rasco, 1886.

Articles

Asensio y Toledo, José María. "El Compás de Sevilla." In *Cervantes y sus obras.* Barcelona: F. Seix, 1902. Pp. 405–424.

Brooks, John. "Slavery and the Slave in the Works of Lope de Vega," *Romanic Review,* XIX (1928), 232–243.

Carande, Ramón. "Sevilla, fortaleza y mercado," *Anuario de historia de derecho español,* II (1925), 233–401.

Caro Baroja, Julio. "Honor y vergüenza, examen histórico de varios conflictos." In J. G. Peristiany, *El concepto del honor en la sociedad mediterránea.* Barcelona: Nueva Colección Labor, 1968. Pp. 77–126

"Documentos relativos a la Mancebía," *Archivo Hispalense,* IV (1888), 16–18.

Domínguez Ortiz, Antonio. "Los conversos de origen judío después de la expulsión," *Estudios de historia social de España,* ed. C. Viñas Mey, III (1955), 226–431.

——. "Delitos y suplicios en la Sevilla imperial (La crónica

negra de un misionero jesuita)." In *Crisis y Decadencia de la España de los Austrias*. Barcelona: Ediciones Ariel, 1969. Pp. 13–71.

———. "La esclavitud en Castilla durante la Edad Moderna," *Estudios de historia social de España*, II (1952), 369–428.

———. "Notas para una sociología de los Moriscos españoles," *Miscelánea de estudios árabes y hebráicos* (1962), 39–54.

———. "La población de Sevilla en la Baja Edad Media y en los tiempos modernos," *Boletín de la Sociedad Geográfica Nacional*, LXXVII (1941), 595–608.

Fita, Fidel. "La Inquisición Toledana: Relación contemporánea de los autos y autillos que celebró desde el año 1485 hasta el de 1501," *Boletín de la Real Academia de Historia*, XI (1887), 289–322.

———. "Los judaizantes españoles en los cinco primeros años (1516–1520) del reinado de Carlos I," *Boletín de la Real Academia de Historia*, XXXIII (1898), 307–348.

Giménez Fernández, Manuel. "El alzamiento de Fernando Cortés según las cuentas de la Casa de la Contratación," *Revista de historia de América*, XXXI (1951), 1–58.

Guillén, Claudio. "La disposición temporal del Lazarillo de Tormes," *Hispanic Review*, XXV (1957), 264–279.

———. "Un Padrón de conversos sevillanos (1510)," *Bulletin Hispanique*, LXV (1963), 49–89.

Hauben, Paul. "Reform and Counter-Reform: The Case of the Spanish Heretics." In Theodore Rabb and Jerrold Siegel, *Action and Conviction in Early Modern Europe*. Princeton: Princeton University Press, 1969. Pp. 154–168.

Helleiner, Karl. "The Population of Europe from the Black Death to the Eve of the Vital Revolution," *The Cambridge Economic History*, IV (1967), 1–95.

Konetzke, Richard. "Entrepreneurial Activities of Spanish and

Portuguese Noblemen in Medieval Times," *Explorations in Entrepreneurial History*, VI (1953–1954), 115–120.

Ladero Quesada, Miguel Angel. "La esclavitud por guerra a fines del siglo XV: El caso de Málaga," *Hispania*, XXVII (1967), 63–88.

Le Flem, Claude and Jean-Paul. "Un censo de Moriscos en Segovia en 1594," *Estudios Segovianos*, XVI (1964), 433–464.

Márquez Villanueva, F. "Conversos y cargos concejiles en el siglo XVI," *Revista de Archivos, Bibliotecas y Museos*, LXIII (1957), 503–540.

Mata Carriazo, Juan de. "Negros, esclavos y extranjeros en el barrio sevillano de San Bernardo," *Archivo Hispalense*, XX (1954), 121–133.

Otte, Enrique. "La Flota de Diego Colón—Españoles y Genoveses en el comercio transatlántico de 1509," *Revista de Indias*, XCVII–XCVIII (1964), 478–503.

Pike, Ruth. "The *Converso* Family of Baltasar del Alcázar," *Kentucky Romance Quarterly*, XIV (1967), 349–365.

———. "The *Converso* Origin of Sebastián Fox Morcillo," *Hispania*, LI (Dec. 1968), 877–882.

Rodríguez Marín, Francisco. "El divino Herrera y la Condesa de Gelves." In *Miscelánea de Andalucía*. Madrid: Biblioteca Giralda, 1927. Pp. 155–202.

Ruiz Almansa, Javier. "La población de España en el siglo XVI," *Revista internacional de sociología*, I (1943), 115–136.

Sancho, Hipólito. "Los conversos y la Inquisición primitiva en Jerez de la Frontera," *Archivo Ibero-Americano*, IV (1944), 595–610.

Serrano y Sanz, Manuel. "Nuevos datos sobre la expulsión de los moriscos andaluces," *Revista contemporánea*, XC (1893), 113–127.

Steggink, Otto. "Beaterios y monasterios carmelitas españoles en los siglos XV y XVI," *Carmelus*, II (1963), 149–205.

Utterström, G. "Climatic Fluctuations and Population Problems in Early Modern History," *Scandinavian Economic History Review*, III (1955), 3–46.

Wilson, William E. "Some Notes on Slavery during the Golden Age," *Hispanic Review*, VII (1939), 171–174.

Index

Library of Congress Cataloging in Publication Data
(For library cataloging purposes only)

Pike, Ruth, date.
  Aristocrats and traders.

  Bibliography: p.
    1. Social classes—Seville—History. 2. Seville
—Social conditions. I. Title.
HN590.S4P54   309.1'46'86   76-37756
ISBN 0-8014-0699-4